VIETNAM

First Edition
1995

TABLE OF CONTENTS

MAP LIST

VIETNAM
© Nelles Verlag GmbH, 80935 München
  All rights reserved

First Edition 1995
ISBN 3-88618-410-2
Printed in Slovenia

Publisher: Günter Nelles
Project Editor: Annaliese Wulf
English Editor: Anne Midgette
Translations: Sue Bollans, Ginger
          Henry-Künzel, Robert Rowley

Photo Editor: K. Bärmann-Thümmel

Cartography: Nelles Verlag GmbH
Lithos: Schimann, Karlskron
Printed by: Gorenjski Tisk

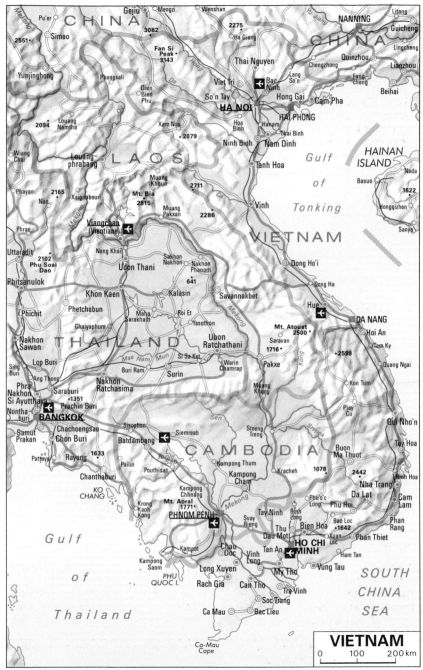

VIETNAM

0   100   200 km

THE VIETNAMESE
AND THEIR HISTORY

A PEOPLE BETWEEN
MOUNTAINS AND WATER

Kinh, plains-dwellers: thus the Vietnamese term themselves. Ethnically, they are a Melano-Indonesian people, also called Austro-Malayan, who came from southern Siberia to Yunnan (southern China) during the Neolithic period, following the great rivers and settling in the mainland areas of Southeast Asia and the islands. Until into the modern age, they were followed by Mongolian and Sinitic groups, who came as far as northern Vietnam. Chinese immigrants, however, live as a separate minority, Hoa. On their way south, the Vietnamese came into contact with the Cham and Khmer tribes. Today, they are an ethnic mix; and the general appearance and character of the population differ in the northern and southern regions of the country. Over the last decades, migrations and shifts in the population have rendered these differences less discernible, especially in the cities. Among the more sedentary rural population in northern Vietnam, you can make out a stronger Mongolian influence; one encounters people with high, strong cheekbones; dark, sloping eyes; pale skin with a yellowish cast; black hair; and a reserved, taciturn, but reliable manner. In the south, people's faces appear softer and rounder, their eyes bigger; sometimes there's a reddish tinge to their black hair; and they seem generally more open and cheerful.

Preceding pages: Land between mountains and water. You can carry a lot on a rickshaw. Vegetable harvest. A crowd of boisterous children. Left: Imperial dragon as roof ornament on the Imperial Palace of Hue.

Distinguishing the Vietnamese people from the Chinese is their Melano-Indonesian heritage. Other distinctive customs include body tattoos, filing and blackening the teeth, chewing betel nuts, cooking in bamboo pipes; also characteristic are totemism, clothing, hairstyles, architecture, sleeping and eating habits, and religious ceremonies. Many traditions were crowded out by Chinese customs centuries ago or have been lost with the dawn of the modern age, but others have survived to the present day.

Vietnamese society, dominated by agricultural and Confucian influences, is a homogeneous community with a distinct inclination toward isolation. This is due to geographic circumstances, the richness of rural peasant tradition, and the two-thousand-year struggle for political and cultural independence. Since 1901, the population has grown from 13 to about 73 million. The growth rate from 1975 to 1979 was 2.6%, and since 1980 it has been 2.3%. About half the population is under 20 years old. This means the state is faced with virtually insoluble problems in the areas of education, employment and construction of housing.

The Sons of Au Co, the Primal Mother

The Kinh ascribe their origins to the primal mother Au Co, a mountain fairy, and the primal father Lac Long Quan, the dragon king. The oldest of their hundred sons is said to have been the first Hung king of the legendary Hong Bang dynasty. Vietnamese historians, like the historians of Japan and Korea, set their first dynasty in the third or second millennium before Christ: at the same time, that is, as the dawn of Chinese history.

Every Vietnamese knows the legends of Mother Au Co, who laid one hundred eggs and hatched one hundred sons, and Father Lac Long Quan, who left the mountain goddess because he came from

the sea and their natures proved too different. Au Co returned to the mountains with 50 sons, and Lac Long took 50 sons with him to resume his battle with water in the lowlands. Legends indicate an animist and matriarchal society which worshipped the gods of nature and accorded Vietnamese woman a respect and status uncommon in Southeast Asia. With the Hung emperors, however, the Viet, too, went over to a patriarchal society. The story of sons hatched from eggs indicate a link with mountain tribes such as the Muong, whose totem is a bird. The Kinh totem is a dragon, which protects them from the dangers of water. Until 1293, Vietnamese kings had a dragon tattooed on their upper thighs; and the dragon remained a symbol of the ruler until 1945.

The wealth of Vietnamese tales and legends tell of *ha-son*, water and mountain. Water and mountain are the two typical features of the Vietnamese landscape; and *ha-son* also means homeland, fatherland. The Viet came down from the hills into the alluvial plains of the delta, created by the Red River; in a hard struggle with nature, they emerged victorious, transforming them into fertile rice paddies and into the cradle of Vietnamese culture.

Early Chinese dynastic writings reporting on the *Bach Yue*, the hundred Viet tribes, are the earliest documents about the country. When the Han Chinese armies left the overpopulated regions along the Yellow River in search of land and moved south across the Changjiang in the 3rd and 2nd centuries BC, they either destroyed or assimilated the Yue. Only the Lac and Au tribes in the hill country along the Red River were able to resist. They are the ancestors of the Vietnamese.

THE 54 MINORITIES

The minorities, according to legend, descend from the 50 sons of Au Co who

The Vietnamese have lived on rice for more than 2,000 years. Above: Preparing a field. Right: Putting out the young rice shoots.

went with her to the mountains. Since the 1989 census, they've increased by one million to 8.3 million, or about 8% of the total population. They are spread across 65% of Vietnamese territory, mostly in the mountainous and hill regions, where they also straddle the borders with China, Cambodia and Laos.

The mountain tribes are representatives of different civilizations and cultures. The tribes in the plains and in the mountain valleys lived under more favorable conditions. They adapted the handicrafts and techniques of the Kinh and gradually conformed to them in their architecture, clothing and education. Researchers assume that the Viet are related to the Tay and Thai and only split off from the Muong when they left the hills and made the Red River Delta arable. There are linguistic and religious similarities between the Kinh and the Muong. Both peoples have *dinh*, huts for men with temples for guardian spirits, which the other minorities do not have, as well as similar funeral rites. A general study of

the mountain tribes has yet to be done; until now, scientists have only investigated individual ethnic groups.

The mountain dwellers often live in small groups. They clear land by slashing and burning (*ray*), grow dry rice, raise cattle and utilize the products of the mountains. In some cases they still live in matriarchal societies, worship mother goddesses and practice fertility cults.

The mountain tribes and the inhabitants of the plains need each other. The mountain tribes cannot live without salt, which is derived from the sea, and they need the technical products from the flatlands. In the past, these were metal products; today, they tend to be plastic goods, watches and radios. For the people of the plains, ivory and rhinoceros horn, medicinal herbs, rare wood, gold and precious metals, resin and fruit were either essential items or luxury and trade goods.

Under the Chinese and Vietnamese dynasties, the minorities enjoyed such freedoms that the chieftains were often in-

duced to rebel and try to throw off the yoke altogether. Others fought on the side of the Viet for independence.

Of the 54 mountain tribes, 32 live in the southern highlands. The French and Americans mobilized and trained them to fight against Vietnam. Similar attempts have continued to the present day; this has led to considerable unrest over the last few years.

The minorities can be divided into three large linguistical families. More than a million Chinese, called Hoa in Vietnam, belong to the Sino-Tibetan linguistic family. In the north, they are for the most part fishermen and mountain peoples, in the cities they are retailers, small businessmen, or restauranteurs. In Socialist Vietnam, many of them lost their chances for employment. After 1975, they constituted a majority of the boat people in the south; in the north, many fled to China. Of the 5.6 million in

the Austro-Asian linguistic family, 900,300 are Muong, 2.9 million Tay and Thai, 1.4 million Mon-Khmer, and 383,000 Meo-Zao. The third linguistic family, the Austronesians, numbers 465,000. There are also groups and subgroups of about 100-300 people, which often differ only through their dialects. Many of these adhere strictly to their customs and rituals; others are prepared to give them up in exchange for a more comfortable life.

BASIC PROBLEMS IN VIETNAM

Since the very beginning, Vietnam has been faced with problems caused by its geography, climate, need for security, or sociopolitical questions.

Natural Catastrophes

The constant threat of floods or droughts, insect plagues or typhoons, require precautions, an active assistance program, and organized community

Above: Women of the Thai minority near Hoa Binh, northwest mountain country.

work directed by a strong central government.

Securing the Borders

The need for military defense against China in the north required the build-up and maintenance of an army and navy on active duty, the construction of defensive walls, fortifications and strategic roads. From the beginnings of its history up to the punitive campaign in 1979, Vietnam had to be armed against a Chinese invasion (with the exception of a short interruption during the Second Indochina War, when China supported Communist North Vietnam). Vietnam has never invaded Chinese territory; but a Vietnamese ruler's authority was called into question whenever Vietnamese territory was lost. Between 111 BC and 938 AD, China ruled Vietnam, and it tried time and again to reconquer it in the years afterwards.

The Dinh dynasty could buy its freedom with tributes; the Early Le dynasty had to use tributes to seal its victory. Between 1075 and 1079, the Le dynasty, led by the royal prince Ly Thuong Kiet, fought a bitter battle. In the 13th century, the Tran dynasty had to fight three times against the Mongolians and the Chinese Yuan dynasty of Kublai Khan, grandson of Genghis Khan. From 1407-1427, Vietnam was again completely controlled by China's Ming dynasty. During these 20 years, temples and palaces were destroyed, and works of literature and art taken to China. The people had to adopt Chinese clothing, hairstyles and habits.

Le Loi, founder of the Le dynasty, succeeded in liberating the country after a 10-year battle (1418-1427). A new, serious threat brought about the downfall of the restored Le dynasty. Nguyen Hue defeated the Chinese in 1788 and founded the Tay Son dynasty. The Ho and Mac dynasties lost the support of their court and the general population, and the official recognition of historians, because they had lost Vietnamese territory to China.

The Move Southwards

In the 10th century, the independent Dai Viet empire began a fight for its very survival when the Cham crossed over its southern borders. The battles brought about *nam tien*, a trend of southward migration; Viet from the overpopulated Red River Delta took over land all along the coast, down to the Mekong Delta.

The Danger of Division

As the country extended to the south along a strip of coast between the ocean and the mountains which at its narrowest point measures only 32 miles (52 km), there was a danger that the north could become separated from the south. From 1673 to 1788, the country was indeed divided into two separate states after a 50-year civil war. During French colonial rule, the land was divided into three parts: the south became the colony of Cochin China, central Vietnam became the An Nam Protectorate, and the north the Tonkin Protectorate.

In 1954, the Geneva Conference established a provisional division of North and South Vietnam along the 17th parallel. Reunification followed in 1976.

Agriculture

Vietnam was and is an agrarian land; over 70% of its population is rural. Agricultural productivity has always been an existential issue for Vietnam. Into the 20th century, the only people who had to pay property or income taxes, in the form of money or natural products, were male farmers between 18 and 60 years of age. Only farmers were conscripted as soldiers, and had to provide compulsory labor on dikes and irrigation systems,

military and street construction, as well as performing services for the upkeep of the court. The aristocracy, large plantation owners, mandarins and monasteries were exempt from taxes, compulsory labor or military service.

Originally, the emperors owned the land and repaid the loyalty of their families and the aristocracy with appanages and gifts of land. Monasteries and mandarins also received land and estates.

During the Tran dynasty, the land barons could force people without land or property to work as slaves to make fallow lands arable and thus add new land to their own property. Farmers who owned or leased land became dependents; tax debtors became slaves and serfs. The feudal system was a serious problem. Villages grew poor, and unrest, revolts and peasant uprisings led Dai Viet more than

Above: Building in Lao Cai, northwest Vietnam, near the Chinese border. Right: Temple of Literature, Hanoi – stelae for those who have passed the literature tests.

once to the brink of ruin. The rulers' attempts to provide relief through land and tax reforms failed. There were laws stipulating the rights of the farmers, but feudal lords and government officials found ways and means to get around them.

Plantations were created during the colonial period, but they exported their products, and the farmers and their families still suffered from poverty. Even the Socialist economy, which broke up the large plantations and introduced collectivism, didn't bring much change. The Vietnamese farmers, who are considered to be among the most industrious in Asia, gave up. Vietnam, once the breadbasket of Asia, had to import grain.

After 1989, farmers were once again allowed to lease land, work it and sell their products themselves. By the second harvest, they had already produced surpluses and exports. Vietnam is now the second-largest rice exporter in the world. The villages were engulfed in a construction boom. Private homes, temples and *dinh* are being restored or rebuilt.

THE COURSE OF HISTORY

When Dai Viet appeared on the historic scene, the East Asian states of Korea and Japan were already well-established. The Southeast Asian regimes of Burma, Angkor and Champa had reached their zenith; Malaya, Laos and Thailand did not yet exist. The Vietnamese in the Red River Delta, however, had all the qualifications to take over a leading role in the region. For 1,000 years they had been part of China's development, and were not far behind the Empire of the Sun in matters of administration, military science, agriculture, science, literature or philosophy. Vietnam was already a unified, structured state with parallel historical and economic developments. In spite of the dominance of the Chinese model, agricultural Vietnam retained its own identity, its own traditions, religions, and language. Even the Vietnamese emperors came from the working classes of farmers or fishermen.

The Vietnamese kingdom was based on the Chinese model; the Vietnamese emperors, too, viewed themselves as sons of Heaven. But they were not infallible rulers graced by God. They only had the mandate from heaven for as long as they could successfully defend the regime against invaders and increase domestic prosperity. If they failed, they could be deposed. Each new ruler had to prove himself through his achievements and success. Whenever a new ruler or dynasty took over, therefore, there was often a period of civil unrest.

The Vietnamese emperors, as pious Buddhists, chose their advisers from the ranks of educated monks. To counterbalance the growing power of the aristocracy and the landowners, they created a civil service, the mandarins. As graduates of the Confucian academy, the civil and military mandarins, organized into a hierarchy of nine ranks, had to pass tests in classical literature. With the decline of monastery education and morals, the power of the Confucians increased. Dur-

HISTORY TABLE

Legendary and Early Kingdoms

Legendary: 2879 BC-258 BC: Van Lang, Hong Bang Dynasties
Historic: 690 BC-258 BC

258-208 BC: Au Lac, Thuc Dynasty
Capital city Co Loa

208-111 BC: Nam Viet, Trieu Dynasty, capital city Quangzhou (Canton)

China's 1,000-year Rule
111 BC-938 AD
111 BC-622 AD: Giao Chi Colony

40-43 AD: Trung Dynasty

187-226 AD: Giao Chau Province

248 AD: The Trieu Au Rebellion

544-603 AD: Early Ly Dynasty

622-679 AD: Governor-generalship

679 AD on: General Protectorate An Nam

722 AD: Revolt led by Muong chieftain Mai Thuc Loan

Until 938 AD: General Protectorate Tinh Hai

Independent Vietnam
939-965: Ngo Dynasty, capital city Co Loa

968-979: Dinh Dynasty, capital city Hoa Lu (Ninh Binh Province)

980-1009: Early Le Dynasty, capital city Hoa Lu

1009-1225: Late Ly Dynasty, capital city Thang Long (Hanoi)

1225-1400: Tran Dynasty, capital city Thang Long (Hanoi)

1400-1407: Ho Dynasty, capital city Tay Do (Thanh Hoa Province)

1407-1427: Chinese Ming Dynasty

1428-1527: Late Le Dynasty (1788), capital city Thang Long

1527-1592: Mac Dynasty (1592), capital city Thang Long

1532-1788: Restored Le Dynasty, capital city Thang Long

1627-1673: Civil War

1673: Division of the country
North: Trinh lords, seat in Thang Long
South: Nguyen lords, seat in Phu Xuan

1788-1802: Tay Son Dynasty, capital city Phu Xuan (Hue)

1802-1945: Nguyen Dynasty, capital city Hue

1863-1945: French Colonial Period
Cochin China Colony, An Nam and Tonkin Protectorates, capital Saigon

1945: Declaration of Independence

1946-1954: First Indochina War

1954: Division of North and South Vietnam at the 17th parallel

1964-1975: Second Indochina War (Vietnam War)

1975: Reunification

1979-1989: Third Indochina War in Cambodia

From 1989 on: New Politics (*Doi Moi*)

ing the Le dynasty, a dogmatic form of Neo-Confucianism from China gained influence over the state, society and family.

The legal code of the Ly dynasty prescribed some harsh punishments, but reflected the Vietnamese sense of justice. The Tran dynasty expanded criminal law and created the basis for civil law. The codex of the Le kings from 1481, a legal volume of no fewer than 271 articles, also laid down the rights of women and farmers. In the late 19th century, the Nguyen dynasty turned back to medieval Chinese law; but this did not conform to the legal sense of the Vietnamese.

The **Ly dynasty** (1009-1225) created a strong central power with a powerful army and a productive agricultural system. It laid the cornerstone for the Vietnamese empire, its culture and art.

The **Tran dynasty** (1225-1400) distinguished itself by reforms. In order to se-

Above: Memorial temple and statue of Confucius, Temple of Literature, Hanoi.

cure the succession, the king's successors were initiated into office while the emperor was still alive; the emperor, however, retained the right of final decision, even after he stepped down. In order to lessen the powers of individual government officials, high administrative positions were occupied both by a military and a higher-ranking civilian mandarin. An oath of office ensured the loyalty of these civil servants.

The Le dynasty (1428-1788) led Dai Viet through ups and downs during its 360 years of rule. It gave the country its first important rulers and ended, as every other dynasty, in power struggles between incompetent heirs to the throne. An ambitious court official usurped the throne and founded the short-lived Mac dynasty. Two powerful, rival aristocratic families, the Trinh and the Nguyen, returned the throne to the restored Le dynasty. In Thang Long, the Trinh lords turned the Le emperors into puppet rulers. From 1599 on, the Nguyen lords established their own center of power in

the south. The civil war between the two factions led to the country's division in 1673, as well as a division of responsibilities. The Trinh lords saw to securing the borders in the north; the Nguyen lords in Phu Xuan, later known as Hue, continued to fight against the Champa and to expand farther south. By cleverly intervening in the struggle for the Cambodian throne, they were able slowly to gain control of the Mekong Delta. The Nguyen came into contact with European missionaries and traders before the people in the north; they also had the first skirmishes with the French.

Three rebellious brothers from Tay Son near Quy Nhon, Nhac, Lu and Hue of the Nguyen family, usually called the Tay Son Brothers, were blessed with luck. When the Trinh lord was victorious over a weak Nguyen ruler but was unable to take advantage of the victory, they

Above: Cannon, bronze casting from early 19th century, in the citadel of Hue. Right: Colonial-period theater in Hanoi.

conquered the territory of the Nguyen lords. The youngest and most talented, Nguyen Hue, was able to drive the Chinese Qing dynasty out of Thang Long and remove the Trinh lords and the last, unworthy Le emperor from power. In 1788, he had already founded the Tay Son dynasty, but he died four years later before he could carry out his planned social reforms. His son could not prevent the victory of the rightful Nguyen successor, Nguyen An. Nguyen An conquered the region from the Mekong Delta up to the Red River during a 20-year struggle and founded the last Vietnamese Nguyen dynasty (1802-1945). He called the land Vietnam, and transferred his capital city from Thang Long to Phu Xuan (Hue) in 1804.

The Nguyen were strict Confucians and defended their concept of state, the Buddhist religion, and absolute monarchy against the ideals of the French Revolution and the encroachment of democracy and Christianity with the arrival of European settlers.

The Colonial Regime 1863-1945

Among the early seafaring traders along the East Coast of Indochina were the Spanish and Portuguese, who called the country Cochin China. They were followed by the Dutch, the English and the French. When they arrived in the harbor of Hai Pho (Hoi An), the port already had Chinese and Japanese colonies. Thrown out of Japan by the shoguns, missionaries came to Hoi An and went as far as the Red River Delta. But Dai Viet was a poor country, its markets of little importance, and its emperors had a monopoly on international trade. Only the French stayed, because their mission flourished.

19th-century Europe was searching throughout the world for raw materials and export markets for its industries, and it turned its gaze to the heavily populated country of China.

Great Britain violently forced its way into the Chinese markets with the Opium War, 1840-1842. The French tried to move into southern China along the Mekong River, and later along the Red River. The rivers proved to be bad for shipping because of their rapids and variable water levels. France, however, recognized Indochina's potential as a source of raw materials, but the country was too poor to become an export market for industrial goods.

The colonial era began in 1847 with the shelling of the Bay of Da Nang. This was meant to force the Nguyen kings in Hue, 62 miles (100 km) away, to open their land to missionaries and merchants. When that did not succeed, the French turned to the Mekong Delta and captured the Giah Dinh fortress, which later became Saigon. By 1863 they had conquered the entire Mekong Delta.

In 1872, a French merchant with a small troop of soldiers forced his way up the Red River, conquering Hanoi in 1873. After heavy fighting in the Red

River Delta, the Nguyen dynasty had to recognize Cochin China (the Mekong Delta) as a French colony in the Treaty of Hanoi of 1875. In 1884, the Protectorate Treaty of Hue declared northern Vietnam as the Tonkin Protectorate and central Vietnam as the An Nam Protectorate. The colonial regime of Indochina developed in 1887 when the Vietnamese colony and protectorates merged with the protectorate of Cambodia; in 1893, Laos was added. Saigon became the seat of government.

At first, the conquests in Asia aroused little interest in France. After the French Revolution, the republic was deemed indivisible: its colonies had equal status, and their citizens the same rights as citizens of the mother country. The colonial possessions were supposed to be assimilated. Such theories, however, were put into practice in various ways around the globe. There were considerable differences in constitutional law for the colonies and protectorates. The Vietnamese did not have any civil rights or freedoms.

The conditions which a Vietnamese had to fulfill to become a French citizen were impossible to meet, even had one wanted to do so. Applicants for French citizenship could not practice a non-Christian religion and had to give up their traditions and customs; they had to be able to speak French and prove a certain level of education. Only 6% of the Vietnamese population, however, was Christian, and only a few city dwellers had a school education. At the end of the colonial period, more than 80% of the population was illiterate, and only 600 people had graduated from universities or institutions of higher education. The Vietnamese were denied access to science and research.

The colonial possessions served the motherland as a source of raw materials, as an export market, and as an investment as well as a source for soldiers to defend

Above: Vietnamese prisoners under the colonial regime. Right: Ho Chi Minh; rug from a carpet factory near Hanoi.

the mother country. The colonial ministry was not founded until 1894; before that, the colonies were under the jurisdiction of the Ministry of the Navy. After 1907, the center of power was the National Assembly in Paris, and the situation in the Indochinese colony changed for the better. There was a basic difference between the French idea of colonialism and the practices of colonists in the colony itself, who were often extremely poor executors of their country's ideals.

Many historians reproach the Nguyen kings for not defending the country and for betraying it to the Europeans. Others complain about their resistance to progress and new ideas which forced Vietnam into a state of isolation from which it is still suffering today. But in fact it took another century before the colonial mindset had broken enough to enable Europe to recognize how valuable these foreign, ancient Asiatic cultures are. It was even harder for the institution of the church and many Christians to tolerate the rest of the world's religions.

Sporadic uprisings occurred throughout Vietnam, and escalated towards the end of the colonial period. Rebellions broke out in every part of the country, and every class of society took part. For decades, however, there was a lack of coordination and a central leadership.

While in France, Ho Chi Minh noted the colonial government's lack of understanding, but also the support he got from the French Communist party, of which he was a founding member. He returned to Vietnam by way of Moscow, and founded the Indochinese Communist Party, the ICP, in 1930. This group's activities led to the founding of the League for the Independence of Vietnam, the Viet Minh, in 1941. As in other Asian colonies, the last phase of the Vietnamese fight for independence was organized and coordinated by Communist leaders.

From 1940-1945, Vietnam was occupied by Japan, although the French colonial administration was retained. Not until March 1945, did the Japanese terminate this relationship and disarm the French colonial army. The last Emperor of the Nguyen dynasty, Bao Dai, declared Vietnam's independence in March, 1945, at the behest of the Japanese. In August, 1945, Japan was forced to surrender unconditionally. Two days later the National Committee for the Liberation of Vietnam, an organization of the Viet Minh, took over the provisional government with Ho Chi Minh as its leader. Emperor Bao Dai was forced to abdicate ten days later. On September 2, 1945, Ho Chi Minh declared independence and proclaimed the Democratic Republic of Vietnam (DRV).

The First Indochina War 1946-1954

After World War II ended, France returned to Indochina. On March 6, 1946, it recognized the DRV as a state with its own government, army, and treasury

within the Union Française. The DRV demanded step-by-step withdrawal of French troops within five years. Free elections were to take place in Cochin China. On March 9, 1946, French troops landed in Tonkin; in June, the High Commissioner for Indochina proclaimed the Republic of Cochin China. The DRV saw this as a violation of the agreement, and tension grew between the Hanoi government and France. In November, French warships shelled the harbor of Hai Phong. Negotiations were unsuccessful, and Viet Minh troops attacked French garrisons. In 1948, France gave the ex-emperor, Bao Dai, the leadership over a provisional centralized Vietnamese state, which was recognized by the U.S. and Great Britain. In 1950, it became part of the Union Française; both China and the U.S.S.R. recognized the DRV and offered their support. In 1951, the Indochinese Communist Party was dissolved, and national Communist parties formed in Vietnam, Laos, and Cambodia. The three countries of the former Indochina

went on to form an alliance, and this was followed by a trade agreement between the U.S. and the Bao Dai government.

In Vietnam, there were heavy battles between the French Foreign Legion and the Viet Minh. They ended on May 7, 1954, with the defeat of the French at Dien Bien Phu.

On April 26, 1954, the Indochina Conference began in Geneva. In June, Ngo Dinh Diem, a Catholic, formed a government in Saigon. The closing declaration of the Geneva cease-fire agreement on July 21, 1954, guaranteed the sovereignty, independence and unity of the states of Cambodia, Laos and Vietnam. The French agreed to withdraw their troops. The conference established a temporary division of the country of Vietnam along the 17th parallel; country-wide elections were to determine the future of Vietnam. Both parts of the country were

advised to negotiate with each other. They were not, however, to enter into any alliances and not to allow any foreign countries to establish military bases on their territory; however, they were to permit international control commissions into their country. The governments of the U.S. and South Vietnam did not sign the Geneva accords. In a supplementary agreement, the U.S. promised to respect the Geneva accords and to refrain from intervening in Indochina with armed force.

The Second Indochina War (Vietnam War) 1964-1975

As early as 1954, President Eisenhower offered military support to Diem's South Vietnamese government, and this commenced in 1955. American advisors arrived in Saigon when the French troops withdrew. In 1955 and 1956, Diem refused to hold elections. Emperor Bao Dai was dethroned by a referendum; Diem proclaimed a republic, and became its

Above: Rice grows again on the battlefield of Dien Bien Phu (1954). Right: American soldiers drag a Viet Cong to prison (1966).

first president. South Vietnam responded with resistance fighting. From 1960 on, there were several putsch attempts against the Diem government, and the National Liberation Front for South Vietnam (NLF) was founded.

In the north, rigorous collectivization of agricultural areas led to unrest. Ho Chi Minh took over as the general secretary of the Workers' Party and initiated more gentle reforms. In 1961, the Revolutionary People's Party of Vietnam was founded.

U.S. military support for South Vietnam escalated under the Kennedy administration. The number of military advisors swelled to 5,000. After the fall of the Diem government, which occurred with the Americans' blessing, 25,000 U.S. troops landed in South Vietnam in 1964. In March, 1968, their numbers had reached 500,000. The so-called Tonkin Incident, when North Vietnam supposedly attacked an American battleship, was used as an excuse to bomb North Vietnam, and thus marked the beginning of the Vietnam War. The U.S.S.R. and China began to provide weapons for North Vietnam.

On January 30, 1968, the Tet Offensive (New Year), an attack by North Vietnamese troops on Saigon, Hue and other fronts, introduced a new phase in a war which the U.S. had no hope of winning. In the ensuing period, peace negotiations in Paris, in which the NLF also took part, alternated with new battles and bombings of North Vietnam. In 1969, President Nixon continued the Vietnamization of the war and the disengagement of the U.S., announcing the withdrawal of American troops.

Ho Chi Minh died in 1969. The war moved into Cambodia in 1970. As the electronic McNamara line, 56 miles (90 km) north of Hue, was an impenetrable barrier for the North Vietnamese, supplies for the Viet Cong resistance in the South had to move along the so-called

Ho Chi Minh Trail, which led in places across the border through Laotian and Cambodian territory. After 1972, regular North Vietnamese troops fought in South Vietnam. The withdrawal of U.S. troops, however, continued as the anti-war movement in the U.S. grew. In 1973, a treaty to end the war was signed by the U.S., the governments of South and North Vietnam, and the NLF; this provided for a cease-fire and the complete withdrawal of American troops from South Vietnam.

The withdrawal was completed in April, 1973; the war, however, was not over. In 1974 the relationship between North Vietnam and China worsened after China occupied the Paracel Islands. In 1975 Vietnam landed on the Spratley Islands, which were claimed by China. There was supposed to be oil in the region of the archipelago, or it had already been found. The U.S. reduced its military support for South Vietnam.

April 30, 1975, saw the culmination of the North Vietnamese offensive which

had begun on January 1 when Saigon fell without bloodshed. In 1976, North and South Vietnam were reunited. The Communist revolutionary armies were also victorious in Laos and Cambodia.

The Third Indochina War 1979-1989

It began with the confrontation between Vietnam, which had become a part of the East Bloc, and the Khmer Rouge in Cambodia, who were dependent on China. In 1978, China suspended its support of Vietnam. When Vietnam marched into Cambodia at the beginning of 1979, drove Pol Pot's murderous regime out of Phnom Penh and eastern Cambodia, and set up a government friendly to Vietnam, its army numbered more than one million soldiers, the fifth-largest in the world. From February 12 to March 19, 1979, the

Above: The Chinese punitive expedition (1979) left destruction in its wake; here, Sa Pa. Right: Relics of the Vietnam War.

Chinese led a punitive campaign against Vietnam.

The first Vietnamese offensives in Cambodia, during the dry season, were successful. But then problems with supplies began to make themselves felt, a result of the gradual collapse of the East Bloc countries and the U.S. embargo. In addition, the international community's condemnation of the invasion of Cambodia had its effect. Another factor was the military support from China, Thailand and the U.S. for the three-way coalition of the Khmer Rouge, Prince Sihanouk and the former minister president Sann Son.

Responding to international pressure, Vietnam withdrew from Cambodia in the autumn of 1989.

New Politics (Doi Moi)

Since 1954, North and South Vietnam had gone their separate ways, politically, economically and in terms of their world view. Reunification in 1976 brought tremendous difficulties in its wake. The attempt to convert South Vietnam to a socialist economic structure was largely unsuccessful. There was a general exodus from Vietnam, most evident in the flight of the boat people – who were, for the most part, Chinese merchants – which put Vietnam once again in a bad light. After 1986, you could start to see signs of a change in course. The 1989 collapse of the East Bloc, Vietnam's allies, led to Vietnam's opening up to the West. The constitution was renewed in 1992, and Western investments and trade were suddenly sought after. The U.S. embargo was still having an extremely negative effect on the Vietnamese economy, but Asian states were adhering to it less strictly than European ones. Japan was in the lead, but Taiwan, Singapore, Thailand, India, Malaysia and Indonesia were also able to establish themselves in the Vietnamese markets. They utilized the country's industrious, cheap work force, intelligence, and desire, as a nation of 73 million people, to catch up to the rest of the world. Europe was less decisive. The Federal Republic of Germany took steps to solve the problem of Vietnamese in the former East Germany with the Vietnamese government. The U.S. embargo was lifted in February, 1994, and in January, 1995, diplomatic relationships were established between the two countries. Vietnam is scheduled to join ASEAN in 1995.

The Vietnamese economy is starting to chalk up successes. In 1994, Vietnam ceased to be a rice-importing country and became instead he world's second-largest rice exporter. Workshops, industries, shops, restaurants and hotels are opening up in both rural and urban areas. The North-South road and rail networks, harbors and power plants require improvement. The country can not come up with the costs on its own. It needs investments, know-how in the fields of banking, technology and science. The country's future

depends on industrialization, which will also give it a chance to make use of its natural resources, water power, and oil.

There is no organized opposition. The Confucian tradition is still proving the strongest force. The desire for civil freedoms does not automatically lead to a demand for Western-style democracy, which is basically foreign to the Asian way of thinking. Party and government are extremely flexible in handling economic questions. Two factors play a decisive role: the younger generation, many of whom studied in East Bloc countries and can speak foreign languages; and the Vietnamese who are returning to their country from exile in every corner of the world. There seem to be efforts to replace the provisional dollar currency with the Vietnamese dong. Inflation will have to be reduced still further, however, before this can be achieved.

Vietnam is a country on the move. It's also in transition, and the rules that apply today may have lost all significance by tomorrow.

RELIGIONS

ANIMISM AND ANCESTOR WORSHIP

Vietnamese farmers are just as dependent upon nature today as they were 2,000 years ago. The northern and central regions of Bac Bo and Trung Bo, in particular, are in the path of destructive typhoons. Every year these storms destroy houses and harvests over vast areas and claim many lives. The northern delta is subject to flooding of the Red River and its tributaries, but is also prone to droughts. Farmers see the powers of nature as very powerful gods, and they are at their mercy. The gods can provide surplus or famine. Farmers try to pacify them or win them over with sacrifices, cults, and worship.

More powerful than all the nature gods are the primal mother Au Co, the mountain goddess, and the primal father Lac Long, the dragon lord, as well as the mountain spirit Than Nui and the water spirit Than Thuy. Nature and all things have either good or bad spirits. Imperishable rocks are divine spirits; the mortal trees which surround and protect the villages also have spirits living in them. Even the springs, earthen walls and bamboo groves surrounding the villages are occupied by guardian spirits, all of whom have to receive the proper offerings at the proper time. To neglect or make a mistake in the sacrificial cult can bring misfortune upon an individual and the whole village. The pottery shards which you see lying by trees as if carelessly tossed away are the remains of household objects which had their own spirits, and have now been entrusted to the protection of tree spirits.

Left: Monks are happy to explain the confusing medley of the Vietnamese pantheon.

Every village has a guardian spirit, housed in the temple in the *dinh*, the communal house for men. They are often nature gods, *than*. There are twice as many *thanh*, heroes and demigods, kings, generals, clan elders and founders of villages. Women, children or animals can also become guardian spirits.

During the Le dynasty in the 15th and 16th centuries, the villages became autonomous. "The power of the king stops at the village gate," ran one saying of the period. The guardian spirits became so powerful in the 15th century that the Ministry of Rites made a list of them and issued them with certificates of investiture. They were presented with diplomas and could rise to three official ranks, like civil servants, but could also be demoted for subordination. The Communist administration forbade the cult of guardian spirits. Many of the *dinh* fell into ruin, but since 1989 they have been being restored. Even *dinh* festivals, in which the guardian spirit is borne through the village, are being reinstated.

The Vietnamese believe that a person has two groups of souls. The *phach*, usually called *via*, accompany the body from birth until death. They stay close to the body after death and are summoned back by a relative or respected male of the village by beating on wood and calling out loudly. If a dead person does not receive an honorable burial, his souls wander about as *ma* or *quy*, evil spirits, trying to kill someone and steal his souls in order that they can receive proper burial honors in their place. *Ma* are souls of people who have died unknown and far from their families, because no family would ever deny a deceased person a proper burial, however bad he may have been in life. Death extinguishes all guilt. Anyone who passes an unknown grave places a small offering on it. Everyone who dies has to be worshipped by his or her children; childless couples often adopt a son.

The second group of souls, the three *hon*, is the spiritual substance which leaves the body at the hour of death. The dead are worshiped by three generations at ancestor altars within the home. Thus they are always present and take part in family life. During festivals of the dead, they are treated as if they were there in person. They enter into a new life, similar to the one on earth, but more luxurious. During festivals of the dead, the living make sacrifices of food and money, and burn cardboard depictions of such objects as houses and cars, to be used in the afterlife.

ADAPTED RELIGIONS

Taoism

The philosophical, metaphysical roots of Taoism go back to Lao Tu (old mas-

Above: Every Vietnamese house has an ancestor altar. Right: A bus driver honors the ma, or restless spirits, at Cloud Pass.

ter), known in the West as Lao-tse. This honorary title is said to have been for Li Erh (*po yang*), a wise man from the state of Zhou in China, who was periodically the state archivist in the capital city of Luo Yang. Some claim that he lived from 604-517 BC; other sources place his dates at 480-300 BC; and some doubt whether he ever actually existed at all, attributing his teachings to several philosophers.

Tao means the path, origin, nature or the original principle. The term comes from the Chinese Imperial religion, called universalism, which is the basic idea underlying the Chinese way of thinking. The term already appears in the I Ching, or Book of Changes, in the second millennium BC. This book of oracles represents the tao with eight diagrams, each with three solid, strong lines and three broken, weak lines. This yields 64 combinations which help one to connect with extrasensory powers. Taoists relate the diagrams to the *dai chi*, an octagon with a circle in the middle containing the bright, masculine *yang* and the dark, feminine *yin*, representing the dualisms in the microcosm and the macrocosm. A dark point in the bright *yang* and a bright point in the dark *yin* illustrate that these antithetical principles are not absolute. *Yin* and *yang* stand for the opposites in the cosmos: heaven and earth, night and day, warmth and cold, sun and moon, fire and water, etc.

Taoists live as hermits. They teach that individual happiness matures through inactivity and contemplative rest. A person's fate is predetermined by heaven and cannot be influenced by his or her actions. Later sects sought to become one with primal matter through mediation, asceticism and various exercises, some of a sexual nature. *Tho* (a long life), happiness, wealth and health are a preliminary stage to Tao. Tho is depicted as an old man. Later on, magicians and sorcerers told fortunes, exorcised spirits and healed the sick, often with the help of a medium. The philosophical teachings developed into popular, or folk, Taoism.

In the second millennium, trained Taoists as well as magicians and sorcerers came from China to Giao Chi province. The Vietnamese saw folk Taoism as supplementing and enriching their ancestor and spirit cults. From the rich Taoist pantheon they adopted the *Supreme Triad*, the *Eight Immortals* and the *chu vi*, or Many Spirits. Most venerated member of the Supreme Triad is the Jade Emperor; *pan yu*, symbol of the primal beginning, is not well-known; but the deified *Lao Tu*, riding a black ox, is frequently depicted. In Vietnam, the *Eight Immortals*, seven men and one woman who drank the elixir of immortality, became 27 Immortals, thirteen men and fourteen women. The number of *chu vi*, the Many Spirits, is virtually endless; among them are the *tu phu,* or Venerated Mothers – Mother Heaven, Mother Earth, Mother Water and Mother Forest – who are worshipped in their own temples

(*dien*). These four mothers rule the four points of the compass, protect the rice fields and help the people. Mother Heaven sits in a red robe on a throne in their middle, with Mother Water, dressed in white, and Mother Earth, dressed in blue, on either side of her. On a throne in front of the three guardians of the living is Mother Forest in a green robe. She takes on the deceased, and is invoked by mourners. She often has her own altar or her portrait in a grotto.

The *tu phu* have many male and female helpers, of whom five kings and four goddesses belong to the pantheon. The Jade Emperor and General Tran Hung Dao, both protectors of women, also have a place in the temple of the mothers. Figures of children on the altars serve as a reminder that people are reborn as happy children after death. Under the altar of the mothers, in a grotto, are tigers, symbols of the five directions. The black tiger stands for the north, the red one for the south, the green one, west, the white one, east. The yellow tiger, which rules

over the middle of Earth, is often depicted alone, representing all five.

Confucianism

K'ung-fu-tse, Master Kung, Khong Tu in Vietnamese, whom the Jesuits dubbed Confucius, was born in 551 BC to a poor but educated family in Qufu, in northern China. His ancestors can supposedly be traced to the 11th century BC; and his descendants are also documented down to the present day.

After the early death of his father, Khong Tu was able to study thanks to the financial help of a patron. He acquired knowledge of ancient Chinese customs and rituals. He married at the age of 19 and had a son. When the Zhou kingdom fell on hard times, Khong Tu saw the problem as resulting from the loss of the Five Virtues, loyalty, justice, wisdom,

Above: In the Temple of Literature, Van Mieu, Hanoi. Right: Village elders in My Duc, Ha Tay Province.

morality and sincerity. For the rulers, he became an uncomfortable critic. When he found that his advice fell on deaf ears in the Zhou kingdom, he left his family, gathered disciples around him, and traveled throughout the country as a wise man. Now and then, he took a position at the courts of princes, but these didn't satisfy him because his theories weren't sufficiently regarded. He died, disappointed, in 479 BC.

Only after his death did he gain widespread recognition and respect. His philosophy has remained the basis of East Asian customs and political thinking all the way into the 20th century. No other person has ever enjoyed such a position of honor. In the year 739 he was named a king (*wang*, in Vietnamese *vuong*); in 1008 he was given the title *hsien*, in Vietnamese *hien*, Perfect Wise Man. Shortly before the end of the Chinese Empire in 1911, he was accorded the rank of *Supreme God*. Emperors built temples in his home town of Qufu; and he was worshipped at similar temples in every capi-

tal and provincial city throughout China and East Asia. Sacrifices to him had to be performed by the country's ruler or a high state official, and were on the same level as those performed at the Altar of Heaven.

His teachings are described as a state philosophy, but have characteristics of a religion. Confucius was driven by his sense of a mission, to which he sacrificed his own personal happiness. He demanded that people worship and perform sacrifices to their ancestors and the gods. The teachings of Khong Tu go back to the earliest Chinese philosophy, universalism, from which the concept of Tao also derives.

Confucius saw the concept of empire as having eternal validity. He was not trying to found a new religion or revive one; rather, he sought to preserve the status quo. His teachings are based on metaphysics. The task of every person, in his eyes, was to perfect his virtues and knowledge, and thereby to determine his own fate.

The Five Classics and the Four Analects are the foundation of his teachings, and have remained the basis for a classical Vietnamese education into the 20th century.

The **Five Classics** are: the *I Ching*, the Book of Changes, 2nd century BC; *Shih Ching*, the Book of Songs, 305 poems from the 6th-9th centuries BC; *Shu Ching*, the Book of History, probably from the 9th-7th centuries BC; *Chun Chiu*, Spring and Autumn Annals, poems from 722-481 BC; and *Li Ching*, the Book of Rites, compiled in the 1st century BC.

The **Four Analects** are: *Lan Yu*, conversations between Khong Tu and his pupils; *Tai Hsich*, the Great Teachings, a moral treatise; *Quang Yung*, the Middle Path; and the *Notes of the Philosopher Men Zi*, in Vietnamese Meng Tu, in Latin Mencius (372-298 BC), Khong Tu's most important successor.

For every Confucian, the basis for state affairs, society and the family are the **Five Fellowships**:

- the benevolence of the ruler – the loyalty of the subjects
- the father's love – the son's piety
- the benevolence of the elder – the reverence of the younger
- the man's justice – the woman's obedience
- the faithfulness of the friend – the faithfulness of the friend

A later disciple of Confucius, Chu Hsi (1130-1200), developed a dogmatic, rigid form of Neo-Confucianism which influenced East Asian society and family life. Unlike the Chinese Communisits, the Vietnamese never questioned these teachings, which continue to determine people's relationships with each other.

Buddhism

It was in northern India, today's South Nepal, that the teachings of Buddha

Above: Young monk of the Thien Mu Pagoda, Hue. Right: Buddhist monks gather for prayer.

(560-480 BC) developed. Its early form is **Hinayana Buddhism**, the pure teachings. From this developed **Mahayana Buddhism**, which helps people to free themselves from the endless cycle of re-birth with the help of a bodhisattva. In Gaio Chi, which was then occupied by China, Mahayana Buddhism became important in the 2nd century AD. Gaio Chi lay on one of the main pilgrimage roads between India and China; in the monasteries, linguistically gifted monks acted as translators. Mahayana Buddhism came to China from Central Asia and spread from there to Korea, Japan and Vietnam. At first, the only Vietnamese familiar with it were scholars and monks. Religious bigwigs and founders of sects from China taught various different theories; Vietnam didn't develop any teachings of its own. Emperors and commoners practiced Zen Buddhism.

In the period between the 10th and the 13th centuries, emperors, the aristocracy and the court promoted the teachings of Buddha and built a number of monasteries and *chua*, Buddhist temples, called pagodas in Vietnam. They donated statues, religious objects, and countless bells. Educated monks lived in the monasteries, which had become wealthy from the many gifts. Many emperors were educated in these monasteries and were Buddhist scholars and authors of Buddhist literature.

The strain of popular Buddhism which developed among the common people was marked by the adoption of animistic and Taoist spirits and gods. The educated preachers of the pure teachings turned into magicians and faith healers. These miracle-working monks were much in demand; women, in particular, visited the pagodas. The worship of guardian spirits in the *dinh* remained a man's job. In the 15th century, scholarship and morals in the monasteries degenerated, and Confucians moved into key positions at court and in politics.

It wasn't until the success of Christianity in the 19th and 20th centuries that Buddhism was reorganized. Beginning in 1951, centers of study for Buddhism and charitable institutions were set up in Saigon, Hue and Hanoi. During the Second Indochina War, Buddhist monks protested against the Catholic government of Diem by burning themselves in Saigon. After the Communists' victory in 1975, the practice of any religion became much more difficult. Since the end of 1989, restrictions have been more or less lifted, and the monasteries are filling with increasing numbers of monks and nuns.

THE SYNCRETIC RELIGIONS

Caodaism

At the beginning of the 20th century in Vietnam, the decline of Vietnamese and adapted religions created something of a spiritual vacuum. To fill this, sects began to develop, especially in the South. To this day, Caodaism has remained the most successful. It goes back to Ngo Van Chieu, a Vietnamese who worked in the colonial administration; one day, he had a vision of an all-seeing eye in a triangle, the *Cao Dai* (literally: great palace). This became the symbol of the Caodaists and is depicted above every portal and altar in their churches.

When Le Van Trung, an opium smoker and man-about-town from the Chinese city of Cholon, changed his life under the influence of Cao Dai and became the leader, or pope, of the sect, the religion saw a big surge in popularity. It was officially founded in November, 1927, in Tay Ninh, the capital city of the province of the same name, some 62 miles (100 km) northwest of Saigon. A pilgrimage center soon developed in this city, containing the Holy Chair, the seat of the pope.

Caodaists believe in the immortality of the soul and in brotherhood. Its members belonged to a society that was without precedent in Vietnam. The sects became powerful enough to maintain a private

army, which after 1945 became actively involved in the political struggles. The teachings are based on four religions: Buddhism, Taoism, Confucianism and Christianity. Its members worship saints and generals, poets and other important people of every race, from every era. The colorful ceremony of worship is based on the Catholic Mass; but there are also spiritual seances which derive from the magical rites and conjurings of Taoism. Women, as well as men, can hold spiritual office. There are large communities of Caodaists in the Mekong Delta, but members of the sect are found throughout the country.

Hoa Hao

At times a militant sect, the Hoa Hao go back to Huynh Phu So, who experi-

Above: Priests at the Caodaist pilgrimage center by Tay Ninh, Mekong Delta. Right: Catholics on the way to mass in Buon Ma Thuot, southern highlands.

enced a miracle healing in 1930 and received a spiritual mission at the same time. Initially, he enjoyed an enormous following; but the Hoa Hao became involved in political struggles and changed sides more than once. They base their religious practices on Buddhism, and teach the virtues of a simple life. The center of the sect is in Tan Chau (An Giang Province in the Mekong Delta).

Their simpler churches are similar to those of the Caodaists. Adherents of this religion now keep out of politics altogether and tend to stick to their own kind, secluded in their villages.

FOREIGN RELIGIONS

Christianity

An unfamiliar situation was created in tolerant Asia when Christian missionaries started to spread their doctrines at the beginning of the 16th century. Christianity claimed absolute sovereignty. The missionaries demanded that Christians

obey only the Holy Trinity and its earthly representatives, the priests. This requirement brought them into conflict with the state order and the rights of the rulers. Their followers, therefore, were driven into isolation, and found themselves cut off from family, society and tradition. This isolation created small Christian communities which gathered closely around their priests.

Rulers in the Far East had been shocked by the ravages of the Inquisition in Europe. The Opium War in China, the occupation of Singapore and Japan's reaction to the missionaries showed them that they were dealing with people prepared to use brute force to achieve entry to their own domains.

In 1615, the first Catholic mission was established in Hoi An. The French missionaries were especially successful. Alexandre de Rhodes (1624-1646) baptized 6,700 people within a short time, including members of the emperor's court and the family of the Trinh lords. The rulers grew even more alarmed at this outcome, and banished the missionaries from their country. Risking their lives, these missionaries tried secretly to return to the communities they had abandoned, as was their Christian duty. Persecution followed; the absolute rulers could not tolerate disobedience of themselves and their state. When it became known that the French bishop in Vietnam planned to set up a religious state to facilitate the conversion of Asia, the position of the missions became precarious.

Today, the Christian portion of the population is estimated at 6-8%. There are Christian – mostly Catholic – communities in urban and rural areas. Their large churches with their towering spires don't, however, reflect the actual number of believers.

Since 1989, Christianity has been able to freely develop once again in Vietnam; like other religions, it was restricted under the Communists. Today, before Christmas, Ho Chi Minh City again hosts its Christmas market around the city cathedral.

ART AND CULTURE

PREHISTORIC ART

The Stone Age in Vietnam is dated later than in Europe, from about 6000-500 BC. In remote areas of the Southeast Asian mountain ranges, there are still peoples living in the last phases of the Stone Age. French researchers found simple work tools made from stone, bone and wood from the beginning of this period; these were later refined, polished and decorated. The most important archaeological sites are in the Red River Delta, in Hoa Binh and in Thanh Hoa province. Ceramics and jewelry appear towards the end of the epoch. Money in the form of mother-of-pearl discs has been found, while glass beads from India indicate that there was overseas trade.

The Sa Huynh culture in Central Vietnam was a well-organized agricultural society. According to some theories, the Cham people could have descended from this culture. In the necropolises, urns have been found containing burial offerings of ceramic and metal.

Since 1968, Vietnamese archaeologists have been able to establish the existence and extent of prehistoric empires from excavations in the Red River Delta.

In the 1920s, French scientists found burial grounds with a wealth of artifacts near the village of Dong Son in Thanh Hoa province; it's for these sites, accordingly, that the Bronze Age in Southeast Asia (5th-1st centuries BC) is named (Dong Son Culture). Among the finds were richly decorated weapons, axes, various containers, jewelry, and rare statues. There were also a number of utensils, particularly spoons, bells and

Left: Tay Phuong Pagoda, Red River Delta. One of the 18 Lo Han, masterful woodcarvings from the 18th century.

weights. The most important finds, large bronze drums, have kept researchers and collectors busy for more than 300 years.

Stone graves with precious burial items made of ceramic and terra-cotta, fired in kilns in the Red River Delta, are from the period of the Han Viet culture (1st-10th centuries), that is, when the Chinese ruled over northern Vietnam.

EPOCHS OF ART HISTORY

Han Viet Culture (1st-10th century AD): During the era of Chinese control over Northern Vietnam, stone graves were constructed filled with a wealth of burial objects of ceramic and terra-cotta, fired in the kilns of the Red River Delta.

Dai La art (8th-early 9th century): The French named this art after the fortress wall of what was then the capital city of a province ruled by China. Countless objects made of stone and fired clay as well as glazed bricks were found close by. The typical Dai La motifs, volutes, small spirals and floral patterns, are scattered over the clothes and hair of the statues; there are also leaves, twigs, tendrils and rosettes, dragons and phoenixes. The oldest surviving construction is Thap Binh Son, 62 miles (100 km) northeast of Hanoi. It is a narrow tower built with alternating square and round floors, tapering off at the top.

Courtly Art (939-1945)

Like most of the art in East Asia, royal art from this period in Vietnam patterned itself on that of the Chinese Imperial court. The country of Dai Viet and its imperial courts, however, were poorer, and their art more modest. It also bore the stamp of the peasant tradition.

Palace grounds and the court ceremonies of Dai Viet are described in Chinese and Vietnamese dynastic documents, as well as by Chinese and, later, European travelers. Not much of it sur-

vived. Most of what did withstand the moist, aggressive climate was destroyed in wars, revolts, palace revolutions and peasant uprisings. When the court moved from Thang Long to Hue in 1804, the old capital city lost its last spark. During the colonial period, living quarters and barracks were built on the former grounds of the emperor's palace, and French business and administrative quarters were erected on the sites of large temples and palaces. Most of the art of the Nguyen period (1802-1945) was also destroyed in the wars with the French and Americans. More artifacts have been preserved in museums around the world, especially in Paris, than have survived in Vietnam.

Peasant Art

In the villages of the Red River Delta, peasant tradition and culture managed to

Above: Woodcarving in the roof-beams of a dinh, or community house. Right: Ceramic vase in the Imperial Palace, Hue.

survive a millennium of Chinese dominance. After the country had gained its independence from China, the villages started to specialize in various artisan skills. The artisans formed guilds and hired themselves out throughout the region. Carpenters built houses and temples; woodcarvers decorated them with figurative and decorative ornamentation. Painters created images on silk and lacquer. Ceramics were fired in the village kilns; metal tools and cult objects were forged in the smelting furnaces. Theater, dance and songs also have their origins in the villages.

The most beautiful works of the peasant artists were woodcarvings; but the most original of these remained unknown for a long time. Even the French scientists overlooked them. In 1972, an exhibit in Hanoi came as a surprise even to Vietnamese art historians. Nguyen Do Cung, a painter and the director of the Research Institute for Vietnamese Art, founded in 1965, had started as early as 1962 systematically to research the extant *dinh* from the 15th and 16th centuries. Aided by young researchers, photographers, draughtsmen and painters, he clambered up bamboo ladders into the roof frameworks of the *dinh*, armed with flashlights and candles.

Tracings, drawings and photographs were made of the woodcarvings on the columns, beams, struts, wainscots and pediments, and were put on exhibit ten years later. In a natural, lifelike manner, without any kind of artificial convention, the artists had portrayed daily life in the villages. Their works display an excellent eye for observation, fantasy, narrative and humor, which resulted in an original style. Sowing and harvesting, hunting scenes, chess players, women picking flowers, girls bathing, children playing and lovers are surrounded by decorative frames of animals and vines.

The emperors, who themselves had been farmers and fishermen, were dependent on the peasant craftsmen and artists, and summoned them to their capital. Village art developed further in the capital, but never became, as it did in Europe, a city culture. Not until the colonial period did Vietnam see the rise of a bourgeoisie in the European sense. Export and regional trade were imperial privileges; the common people were only allowed to work as retailers. The wealthy merchant class which could have established a city culture was, therefore, lacking. In terms of social prestige, farmers followed the aristocracy, and craftsmen came after them. Merchants had an even lower social position; only fishermen and comedians were below them. However, there was not actually a caste system as such.

ARTISAN CRAFTS

Ceramics: Simple pottery with woven or scratched-in designs has been found from as early as the Neolithic period. At the end of the Bronze Age, ceramics improved in form and quality due to the in-

troduction of the potter's wheel, better clay, and higher kiln temperatures. Villages and rural centers specialized in household items, tools, jewelry or clay figures. There is a definite correlation between the decoration of bronze and ceramic. While motifs and ornamentation of ceramics has changed, form has been determined by function until the present day.

In the 11th century, works of great beauty were created in Dai Viet. Characteristics of particularly fine pottery were elegant form, accomplished decoration, and a high-quality glaze. Emperors, mandarins and members of the aristocracy became patrons of the large kilns in the Red River Delta and in Thanh Hoa province. Buddhism provided new impetuses for ceramics, as well: there was a growing demand for statues and religious objects with the symbols and images of the new teachings. In the 12th century, faiences were produced with whitish, ivory-colored and jade-green glazes; they started to be more richly ornamented in

the 15th and 16th centuries. Around this time, Vietnam adopted the color cobalt blue from China. Blue-white ceramics, faiences and porcelain with special patterns were produced in the village of Bat Trang (Hanoi) from the 16th century on, and in the royal workshops in Hue in the 19th century. Through the centuries, ceramics were put to a variety of uses, such as decoration on buildings, bricks and roof tiles, and as figurative roof ornamentation on religious and secular structures.

Woodcarving: The craft that developed into the artisan skill most typical of Vietnam made use of ironwood and ebony, reddish mahogany and red-brown rosewood, called yak wood. The warm colors of natural wood, as well as red and multi-colored lacquers or gilding, give statues and temple interiors a certain festive atmosphere. In the flowing, rounded

forms of Vietnamese carving, you can see the artist's link with nature. Even in small, remote villages, you can find works with an extremely high level of technical proficiency and artistic excellence.

Stonecarving is more common in the Indian regions than in the Chinese sphere of influence. This art came to Dai Viet by way of China. Stonecutters worked on the pedestals of columns and statues, balustrades, steps and railings, terraces and stone bridges.

Painting has less of a tradition in Vietnam than in China and Japan. Only a few works remain; the earliest are from the late 18th century. Painters did use handmade paper, but preferred – and still use – native silk and lacquer.

At first, paper was imported from China, but later it was produced in Vietnamese villages. Images used for religious purposes were given a coating of gold, silver, bronze and pewter powder, or varnished with a layer of ground-up pearls, until the surface gleamed with a

Above: Enamel work from a lacquer factory in Saigon. Right: "Bamboo," 1958: enamel painting by Nguyen van Binh.

subtle, matte shimmer. Paper that was to be used for royal edicts was adorned with an imperial dragon.

The **woodcut** came from China, but became a native art in Dai Viet and is therefore counted a traditional art. This medium allows the large, rounded images favored by artists to achieve maximum effect. The most frequent applications are book illustrations and *Thanh Tet*, traditional New Year's pictures. Modern poster art has been influenced by woodcuts.

Lacquer, or **enamel**, has been used as a protective coating on wood in China since 5000 BC; it's not clear when the technique arrived in Vietnam. Lacquer was probably used for secular and religious items as early the 10th century. Statues coated in dark red or black lacquer have been dated to the 12th century. To make enamel in East Asia, latex is used from the sap of native trees. It dries quickly when exposed to air, becomes water-resistant, solid, and resistant to scratches, and takes on a dark color.

The art of enamel painting was revived in Vietnam in the mid-15th century, and it is still practiced today. Wood is used as a surface, with an application of lacquer putty to smooth over any unevenness. In the old days, the best-quality lacquer works had more than 200 layers; today, a good piece should have at least 12 layers. Each layer has to dry for several days, and then has to be carefully smoothed out and polished.

In Vietnam, the painting is usually executed under the layers of lacquer; each color receives its own layer. Gold and silver dust under the veneer can produce surprising effects. Traditional lacquer paintings are executed in black and dark red; nowadays, other colors are occasionally used as well.

Inlays: Since the mid-18th century, mother-of-pearl inlays were created depicting animal and plant patterns as well as for calligraphy. Such inlays are used on religious objects, furniture, and folding screens. Vietnamese artists also make inlays from pieces of eggshells.

MUSIC, SONG, AND DANCE

Musicians and comedians did not have much social prestige, but their art was always very popular. Traditional music was influenced by the quick, pentatonic rhythms of China; and it was considerably enriched by the melodic, heptatonic music of the Cham. Asian musical instruments are made of stone, bamboo or wood. There are percussion and wind instruments, as well as stringed instruments that are bowed or plucked. Each musician has to master five instruments for instrumental music and accompaniments: the 16-string zither, the 2-string, 3-string and 4-string violin, and the moon guitar. The *dan bau* is a single-stringed zither found only in Vietnam. The string runs from a bamboo body, which lies flat, to an upright neck; a good player can entice from it melodic, vibrating tones. Viet-namese musicians can also use these instruments to give European and South American music a unique timbre. In addition, they use drums, gongs, flutes and lutes with anywhere from 5 to 25 strings. Lithophones were used as early as the Neolithic period. The first ones were made of stone; later, they were made of bamboo. The earth zither is an instrument which comes from the region's Indonesian-Melanesian past, and is still used in North Vietnam.

Song can be divided into three groups. There are Vietnamese songs with lyrics from classical dramas, and there are the old songs which the minority groups have kept alive. The largest group, however, are *hat*, songs from daily life. These include marching and military songs, improvised singing (*ho hat*) between alternating groups of men and women, and choral songs. Included in this group are songs sung at temple festivals or in the marketplace; harvest songs; lullabies and children's songs; the songs of artisans; and love songs.

Above: Classical Vietnamese opera is alive and well. Right: It takes talent to apply one of the traditional character make-ups.

Dance has more of a tradition among the minorities than among the Kinh. Ritual dances in the courtyards of the *dinh* or during Buddhist temple festivals have measured rhythms. Except for the sword dances and the boatmen's dances, they are danced by women.

THEATER AND OPERA

Vietnamese folk opera, *cheo*, consists of folk songs with pantomime, instrumental music and dances, combined with instructive or interpretive sketches dealing with stories from legends, poetry, history or even daily life. Also brought into play are acrobatic scenes and magic.

The costumes, makeup, gestures and language create typical characters familiar to every member of the audience. The props are simple. *Cheo* was forbidden from time to time, as the actors often worked criticism of the authorities into the pieces.

Court opera, *tuong*, came to Vietnam from China in the 13th century and was forbidden, for the same reason as *cheo*, in the 15th century. It was able to survive underground, finally to be revived at the Nguyen court, when the texts were written down. In this form of drama, too, there's a core group of stock characters. Because these characters never change, Far Eastern theater lacks the element of character development in the course of a play which is so essential to Western drama. Since the beginning of the 20th century, a new form of music theater has been evolving in southern Vietnam; called *cai luong*, it's resulted from the advent of European theater mingling with a revival of folk opera.

RELIGIOUS AND SECULAR ARCHITECTURE

Forms and techniques: All of Vietnamese architecture proceeds from the basic form of the Vietnamese house. An exception is the village community house (*dinh*). The house is built on the ground, as in China; the floor consists of packed

earth, or is tiled over. In its most basic form, the structure consists of four posts, columns or pillars which support a simple roof. The walls can be made of bast fiber mats, bamboo, wood or even bricks, but they don't actually function as support. This is as true of the teahouses at the roadside as it is for large temple halls. In larger and more complex buildings, more exterior supports are used, and more rows of supporting columns are added to the interior. In the case of temples and palaces, these supports bear the weight of heavy, elaborately sweeping roofs. The roof framework is reinforced with rafters and collar beams. These wooden constructions, even the supporting frameworks and the roof, are put together without nails, joined by means of shafts, dowels, or wooden pegs. This technique makes for extreme flexibility within the structure. Because of

Above: Strong pillars support the temple roof; support beams and rafters are ornately carved. Right: Altar in a memorial temple.

their great weight, the heavy roofs have a stabilizing effect. From an engineering standpoint, therefore, the only necessary components are the supporting framework and the roof.

Citadels and palaces: Graves dating from prehistoric times contain burial offerings in the form of small, well-fortified houses made of fired clay. At first, fortifications consisted of earthen walls; these were later reinforced with ceramic tiles, and finally replaced altogether with walls of brick. This method of construction was retained up until the 20th century. Sole exception is the citadel of the Ho dynasty in Thanh Hoa province, which is built of blocks of sandstone. Remains of the fortress of the Au Lac Empire (258-208 BC) in Co Loa (Hanoi) and a fortress in Ha Bac province are the oldest known fortress complexes in the country.

These citadels also enclosed the emperor's palace, as evidenced by the fortress Thang Long (Hanoi). The individual buildings stand amidst garden complexes with ponds, bridges, pavilions and temples. They were modeled on the Chinese imperial courtyards. The royal buildings had red-lacquered wooden columns with gold and silver decorations, such as dragons and phoenixes, which were exclusively for the ruler. Even the roof tiles were plated with gold or silver enamel, or were colored Imperial yellow. The royal family and the concubines lived in the inner areas of the palace, the Forbidden City. Citadels and palaces lay on rivers or canals which could be used for defense and supply routes. For the palaces of lords or high-ranking mandarins, there were directives which established the permissible size and application of ornamentation and decor.

Imperial graves: The emperors often had their burial complexes, complete with temples and places of worship, built in their native villages. Only the Tran Dynasty chose to use a holy mountain, and the Nguyen Dynasty emperors built their graves by their capital in Hue. For the graves of aristocrats and mandarins, exact regulations specified permissible size and decoration.

Den, nghe, mieu: Places of worship for national, regional and local ancestors, heroes and village fathers are simple buildings. They are built close to the burial sites and are sometimes also called graves (*lang*). Rarely are there statues on the altars; you more often see symbols, swords, pieces of clothing, crowns, etc. The worship of ancestors and hero cults at private house altars and temples has survived through the Communist era.

Dinh: Between the 10th and the 14th centuries, *dinh*, community houses, are mentioned as places of rest. The *thanh hoang*, guardian spirits, date back as early as the 12th century. Stelae from the early 15th century report the construction of *dinh* as cult sites for the guardian spirits of villages. Today, the oldest extant *dinh* date from the end of the 15th century. Every Vietnamese village had a

dinh by the end of the 17th century. As the country expanded to the south, the Vietnamese took their guardian spirits into the Mekong Delta and built places of worship for them there.

The *dinh* stands in the middle of the village, preferably at a slight elevation, and consists of a complex of several buildings surrounded by a wall. The rectangular main building has a high roof with eaves extending far down over the walls, corners flared upwards, covered in monochrome tiles. This building, Vietnamese architecture's most impressive construction, probably derives from the country's Malayo-Indonesian heritage. It stands on piles, and the main entrance is on the broadest side. Inside, mighty columns rise up to the ceiling. Woodcarvings in the country's *dinh* are the most beautiful examples of peasant art.

Until the 18th century, the temple for the guardian spirit (*hau cung*) was a separate shrine within the *dinh*, located in the middle of the wall across from the main entrance. In the 18th century, an

annex was appended to the building at this spot, and at the end of the century a *tien te*, a smaller, separate *dinh*, was placed in front of the main building. This was used to prepare for temple festivals and for sacrifices. On the guardian spirit's throne in the *hau cung*, you can see its symbols, or, in rare cases, a statue. The size of the *dinh* and the number of adjoining buildings depends on how well-off the village is.

Nghe: Smaller temples for guardian spirits in villages or hamlets, without meeting places.

Taoist temples are called *quan* and *dien*. *Quan* are meeting-places for Taoist scholars. *Dien* (house, temple) are simple constructions for the *chu vi*, the Many Spirits. They are usually found within Buddhist temple complexes. Until 1989, they were shut down, and the cults were forbidden. Many of the statues were lost

Above: Dinh, village assembly-room and cult site. Right: Roofs in tam quan style. Tay Phuong Pagoda, Red River Delta.

in this period, so that today, the pantheon is often incomplete.

The Buddhist temple (*chua*) is called pagoda in Vietnam, and is part of a monastery. The multistory memorial or burial stupas in the courtyards are called *thap*, tower.

During the Chinese occupation in the 5th and 6th centuries, statues of the Buddha were protected by a simple roof on four posts; this later evolved into a small building. From the 11th to the 13th centuries, hundreds of *chua* were built. They became wealthy thanks to land donations, and their tall *thap* were visible far and wide. Later architects, however, abandoned the *thap*. In the Ly dynasty, emperors founded large temples and presented them with entire domains of land. Many of these were on hills or rivers outside the cities. They contained rooms for the emperor and his entourage to be used during temple festivals. Even more numerous were pagodas founded by the aristocracy, landowners, or mandarins, and enriched by their donations.

Farmers built *phat dien*, Buddha houses, in every village. After experiencing a decline in the 15th century, Buddhism saw a renewed upswing in the 16th and 17th centuries. The pantheon became bigger. Dating from this period are the three groups of three Buddhas each which sit on the main altar.

In the Red River Delta, the *noi cung - ngoai quan* style of construction developed. The ground plan of these pagodas resembled an "H" laid on its side (*cung*). It consisted of three parts: a rectangular vestibule, an almost square house for incense offerings, and another rectangular main temple. The whole thing was surrounded by a rectangular wall (*ngoai*). Within the complex, galleries were ranged along the inner side of this wall; on its other side was the *hau duong*, the house for the monks or nuns, which also served as a guest house as well as a display space for statues of benefactors, abbots and Taoist spirits. A triple gate (*tam quan*) leads into these temple complexes; the bell and drum tower stands in the courtyard. Many of the temples lost portions of their landholdings during the land reform of 1954.

Temples in the form of a "T" standing on its head are older and, because they take up less space, are often found in cities. In the 17th century, temples were constructed in the *tam quan* style, with three rooms one after the other and three roofs placed one over the other, their upturned corners ending in small dragons. In small *chua*, the tripartite division is sometimes effected by having three altars in one room, instead of three separate buildings. Pagodas are often built on a hill, so that the main temple with the main altar is somewhat higher than the rest of the complex. In the flatlands, the altar has to be raised artificially.

High up in the roof framework of the main altar are three rows of Buddhas. In the upper row are the Buddhas of the Three Generations, the Buddha of the Present, the Past and the Future. The Buddhas in the second row personify the teachings of Buddha (*dharma*), Buddha and the community of monks (*sangha*). The third row depicts the mystic body of Buddha. The thousand-armed goddess of mercy, Quan Am, the Chinese version of Bodhisattva Avalokiteshvara, has her place in the next row. No *chua* is without an image of the fat-bellied, merry monk Di Lac, one embodiment of the Buddha of the Future. In the lower section, at the viewer's eye level, are the Jade Emperor, the Lord of Paradise, and their companions from the Taoist pantheon. The Child Buddha, *Tich Ca Cuu Long*, is only found in pagodas in the Red River Delta. The representation of this child, surrounded by nine dragons and clouds, goes back to an Indian legend. Two demons are said to have poured water over Buddha after his birth. In Vietnam, it was nine dragons which poured water from rain clouds over the child. On side altars, there are statues of gods, spirits and demigods from different religions.

BAC BO
The North

NORTHWEST

NORTH

NORTHEAST

RED RIVER DELTA

HANOI, THE CAPITAL

DELTA PROVINCES

Bac Bo – country and people

In Europe, the north of Vietnam is known as Tonkin, its colonial name. Called Bac Bo in Vietnam, this region includes the mountains in the northwest, north and northeast and the Red River Delta with the capital Hanoi. Although it comprises only 20% of Vietnam's total area, it is the most densely populated part of the country, with 40% of the population. While vast areas of the mountains are deserted, in the hills and on the Delta plain there are 500 inhabitants per square kilometer, and up to 1,600 in population centers. To the north, Vietnam borders on China, to the west and southwest on Laos and Cambodia, and to the east on the Gulf of Bac Bo (Gulf of Tonkin), part of the South China Sea, which the Vietnamese call the East Sea.

The mountains were formed over a period of 400 million years. The folds in the south of Vietnam are less pronounced than in the north, where limestone mountains are a typical feature of the landscape. They acquired their present form

Preceding pages: Near Hoa Lu, Ninh Binh Province. Hanoi: objects are made and sold in the hang, the alleyways of the Old Town. Left: The mountains of Bac Bo are home to many peoples.

in the Triassic period, and are characterized by deep gorges cut by the rivers. Minerals, precious woods and medicinal herbs are abundant. It is harder here than it is in the plains to provide the population with electricity and drinking water.

Over the centuries, the ethnic minorities of the north often came into conflict with the Kinh. Tribal chieftains struggled to gain autonomy. The population was burdened with heavy taxes, particularly the salt tax, and cheated by government officials. While the Vietnamese rulers punished rebellions severely, they also tried to make recompense by granting privileges and by marrying the daughters of tribal princes. In the war for independence, the tribes fought alongside the Kinh. Today, members of ethnic minorities often occupy high positions in government. The North's mountain tribes are faring better as the country's general economic situation improves.

THE NORTHWEST

The mountains (*son*) are in Hoa Binh, Yen Bai, Lao Cai, Lai Chau and Son La Provinces. Vietnam's highest mountain, Fan Si Pan, (10,248 feet/3,134 m) rises above the Tay Nguyen plateau in Lai Chau Province. The Red River (Song Hong) and its large tributaries, the Black

57

River (Song Da) and the Clear River (Song Lo), irrigate the northern part of the Delta, while the Song Ma waters the province of Thanh Hoa. With their rapids and falls, the rivers are only suitable for local traffic. The roads are only paved with crushed stone; near the border, they are also of strategic importance. Typical of the region are plateaus dotted with bizarre, fissured limestone peaks and ringed by high mountains. The scenery is like many other mountain landscapes, except that none of the peaks is snow-capped year-round, and even the highest summits are forested right to the top.

Spa and mountain fort of Sa Pa

The border town of Lao Cai, capital of the province of the same name, was taken briefly by the Chinese during the punitive campaign of 1979 and badly damaged. Road and railway run from Hanoi to Lao Cai through the Red River valley. The 14-mile (23 km) road from Lao Cai to Sa Pa is steep and winding. Sa Pa was built in 1922 as a French border post, but quickly developed into a popular summer resort. Temperatures range from 63-73°F (17-23°C); in winter, they drop to freezing point, and it snows. Best time to visit is in summer, from April on. On a hill above Sa Pa is the ruin of a fort, which commands a good view of the valley. Sa Pa itself is situated at a height of 5,232 feet (1,600 m) at the foot of Fan Si Pan, and is famous for its plums, peaches and medicinal herbs. Nearby are the **Thrac Bac**, the Silver Falls, and **Cau May**, Cloud Bridge, over the river Muong Hoa.

Old French villas have been turned into guesthouses, some of which are closed in winter. The mountains are the home of ethnic minorities: the Hmong (Meo) are recognizable by their dark-blue embroidered garments. Their villages of straw-thatched houses are set amidst rice fields. From Sa Pa, you can also reach Dao and Thai settlements.

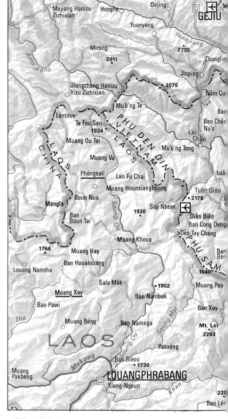

Hoa Binh and the mountain villages

Highway 6 runs from Hanoi to Hoa Binh (50 miles/80 km). The Black River valley, 25 miles/40 km from Hanoi, has weathered limestone cliffs with bizarre vegetation. 6 miles (10 km) outside Hoa Binh on the Black River is a dam and what is still the largest power station in the north, built with Russian assistance. Boats cross the lake to the caves where relics of prehistoric **Hoa Binh Culture** have been found; you can enter one of these, **Thu Do** cave. On the shores of the lake, which is ringed by mountains, are the pile houses of the Muong, an ethnic minority related to the Vietnamese. Visitors to their villages are offered *ruou can*,

an alcoholic drink made of *ruou*, a kind of rice, drunk from *can*, bamboo stalks.

The provincial capital **Hoa Binh** lies 968 feet (296 m) above sea level on the Song Da. Its ruined fortifications date from the colonial period. The rice plain is surrounded by mountains, and the hill tribes come down to sell their products in the city's marketplace. Some Muong dwell in the mountain gorges, and the Muong villages **Ban Dam** (5 miles/8 km) and **Giang** (3 miles/5 km) are accessible from Hoa Binh. While the men work in the rice fields, women, children and old people stay in the pile houses in the villages. In these large, high-roofed clan houses on stilts, each family has its own hearth. The women of this ethnic group wear long skirts; they were exempted from having to adopt the wide black Chinese trousers and diagonally-buttoned white blouses which became compulsory attire for everyone else during the rule of the Ming Dynasty at the beginning of the 15th century.

After a further 22 miles (35 km) on Highway 6, a fairly poor road branches off south at Soui Rut, and 15.5 miles (25 km) further on, reaches **Mai Chau**. Set in a valley between irrigated rice fields, this village with its pile houses is home to around 50 large families of the Thai minority. A profitable sideline of the Thai people is extracting gold from the sand of the riverbeds by panning, a laborious task which the people perform in seasons

when there's nothing to do in the fields.

From Hoa Binh, trekking tours can be organized to Hmong (Meo), Thai and Muong villages. The bus goes as far as Bo Bau, and the first day's tour brings you to **Xa Linh** (10.5 miles/17 km), a Hmong village. On the second day you hike from Xa Linh to the Hmong village **Hang Kia** (9 miles/15 km), and on the third day from Hang Kia to the Muong village **Cuu Pheo** and the Thai village **Sam Kheo** (9 miles/15 km), which is also a bus station. From here it's 9 miles (15 km) to the Muong living in **Van Mai**. Accommodation in the villages is basic.

Through the Northwest
to Dien Bien Phu

A tour of five days will lead you the approximately 600 miles (1,000 km)

Above: Woman from a Thai tribe in the northwest mountain country near Sa Pa.
Right: The tradition of silk-making goes back a thousand years.

from Hanoi via Hoa Binh and Son La to Dien Bien Phu. The gravel roads from Hoa Binh to Dien Bien Phu are best traveled by jeep, even in the dry season. The route leads through ever-changing mountain scenery, over passes and plateaus with sparse pine forests and savannahs. Since the rains of the summer monsoon seep quickly away into the karstic limestone, the region suffers from a shortage of water.

The mountain ranges of Hoang Lien Son have a maximum height of 6,540 feet (2,000 m) in the south. In winter, they protect the region from the rain and cold of the northeast monsoon, so that temperatures do not drop below 52°F (11°C), while in the summer the warm winds from Laos bring temperatures of up to 80°F (27°C). Cultivating such crops as cotton, vegetables and flax is only profitable with intensive irrigation; tea, on the other hand, thrives well in the damp mountain mists, both on plantations and in the wild. There is a plentiful supply of water for irrigation and generating electricity. Up to now, real economic development has been prevented by the lack of good roads that can be used year-round, communications, and infrastructure; but this is already changing, in particular along Highway 6, which leads up onto the plateau on the other side of Hoa Binh over the **Deo Pha Ly** (Pha Ly Pass).

Moc Chau, capital of a district in Son La province, lies at the foot of Phu Dong Tinh (4,856 feet/1,485 m). It is the center of the tea and silk industry. To date, 12,500 acres (5,000 ha) of mulberry trees have been planted in the province, and the production of silk cocoons has been extraordinarily successful. Now, inhabitants of other villages along Highway 6 between Moc Chau and Son La are being encouraged to plant mulberry trees and to give up the production of opium and the unprofitable cultivation of rice.

Son La, the provincial capital and the first day's destination (186 miles/300 km), has liberated itself from its grim past. Only the fort and the prison from colonial times are visible reminders of the violent suppression of the rebellion of the hill tribes. There are plans to improve, with some help from Japan, the city's water and electricity supply. The province is planning to develop three economic zones, with coffee and mulberry trees along Highway 6, agriculture in the Da valley, and forestry and stock breeding in the highlands. The results of a Cuban experimental station have shown that in addition to meat production, there's also a market for milk. In Vietnam, as in all the other East Asian countries, there has hitherto been no demand for milk and milk products; the annual consumption was around 3 American pints (1.4 liters) per person per year. This is now to be increased to around 8.5 American pints (4 l). The Moc Chau - Son La area is already a leading region for domestic stock breeding.

The high mountain regions of the province are home to the Hmong (Meo), who

cultivate corn and flax and breed pigs, oxen and horses. A little lower down are the Man, and below them, on the more humid plateaus, the Thai, who cultivate rice and cotton and breed buffaloes. Steep, eroded mountain paths lead to the high villages; but you can also encounter people from the tribes who live here selling goods at the markets of the villages along the road.

From Son La, it's 136 miles (220 km) along a rough road to Dien Bien Phu. On the other side of **Deo Pha Din** (3,172 feet/970 m), the road crosses into Vietnam's second-largest, sparsely populated province, **Lai Chau**. At a junction, surrounded by rice fields, is **Tuan Giao**, an important trading center for the region; from here, Highway 6 leads north to the provincial capital, Lai Chau. After Dien Bien Phu, the road continues past Muong Phan to the Muong Thanh plateau, following an old trade route which was also used by Buddhist pilgrims on their way from China via Laos to Burma (Myanmar) and India.

Since 1992, the **Dien Bien Phu** region (1,443 square miles/3,700 sq. km) has become the most prosperous region in the northwest. Dien Bien Phu lies in a narrow valley with mild winters and warm summers. 10,000 acres (4,000 hectares) are given over to rice cultivation, and the climate is also ideal for sugar cane, coffee, cotton and flax. 140,000 people, mostly members of ethnic minorities, live in this region. Forty years after the victory in Dien Bien Phu, the number of foreign tourists suddenly shot up and the city experienced a building boom, resulting in a horrendous rise in property prices.

Dien Bien Phu – the end of the colonial era

When it took over the protectorate of Tonkin, France found the northwest of Vietnam and the northern part of the kingdom of Luang Prabang (Laos) in an uproar. Siamese (Thai) troops were attempting to gain control over the kingdom of Laos, and in the process advanced into the northwest of Vietnam, which was already being terrorized by militant Chinese bands known as the Black, Red and Yellow Flags, according to their war colors. The French army established bases and garrisons in the northwest.

In 1946, when the French returned to Vietnam, there were outbreaks of resistance to the colonial power all over the country. In 1953, France tried to force matters to a conclusion; the U.S.A. had already gotten involved, and financed the undertaking. The French general Henri Navarre drew up a plan to defeat the Viet Minh once and for all at the impregnable fort of Dien Bien Phu. However, General Vo Nguyen Giap, who had joined forces with Ho Chi Minh, was an ingenious strategist. He conceived a plan, based on the old mountain path strategy, of attacking

Right: The falls of Song Quy Xuan, 100 feet (30 m) high, northwest of Cao Bang.

Dien Bien Phu. The complex consisted of 3 strong forts, 49 outposts, and 2 landing strips. In November, 1953, he attacked the provincial capital Lai Chau while preparations for the Dien Bien Phu attack were in full swing. His plan could never have worked without the hill tribes: men, women and children hauled heavy weapons, ammunition and supplies to mountain positions above the fort. On November 20, the French flew in elite battalions and parachute troops. They were expecting an infantry attack, but not heavy artillery fire from the mountains. The decisive battle began on March 31 and ended with the defeat of the French on May 7, 1954. The Vietnamese took prisoner the surviving officers and French troops. In January, 1954, the major powers had already invited China, as well, to participate in a conference in Geneva on April 21. On July 21, 1954, the Geneva Accords put an end to the colonial era in Indochina. Vietnam was provisionally divided along the 17th parallel, and the U.S.A. stepped into the shoes of France, supporting the country's non-Communist south.

From the hill known as A1, on which a monument has been erected, there is a good view of the ruins of the fortress. The museum contains ground plans and relics of the battle; you can also visit the underground headquarters of General de Castries. 18 miles (30 km) away in Muong Phang is the dugout of General Giap; a bombed road leads to this hideaway, 294 feet (90 m) long, 5.5 feet (1.70 m) high and 4 feet (1,20 m) wide, concealed inside a wooded mountain.

THE NORTH

The mountainous north consists of the provinces of Ha Giang, Tuyen Quang, Bac Thai and Cao Bang. Here, the mountains reach heights of between 3,270 and 4,900 feet (1,000 to 1,500 m); they are made of slate stone with fissured gorges

and caves. The region is forested and has many lakes and waterfalls. In the northern mountains, the winters are colder than in the northwest and there is snow, while the summers are not as hot. Only 7.8% of the region consists of cultivated land, where rice and corn are grown. The mountains yield precious woods and medicinal herbs, as well as many rare animals and plants. The rivers are used for hydroelectric power.

Highway 2 leads from Hanoi to **Ha Giang**, capital of the province of the same name, and on to China. **Dong Van** is the northernmost town in Vietnam.

Cao Bang, capital of the neighboring province of the same name, is on Highway 3, 196 miles (317 km) from Hanoi. Also located on the Chinese border, Cao Bang was badly damaged in the 1979 border war. With its rich mineral resources of gold, silver, brown coal, tin, tungsten, phosphate and magnesium, it has been the object of Chinese invasions for centuries. For a long time there was no established border, as many areas were claimed by both states. The present one is 195 miles (314 km) long, and border trade was only re-established in 1989.

In addition to Vietnamese, 41% of the population consists of Tay and other ethnic minorities, including Nung, Dao, Hoa and Meo. Ho Chi Minh, who spent 30 years of his life outside his own country, lived at **Truong Hoa**, 37 miles (60 km) from Cao Bang, from 1945 to 1954; today, there is a memorial to him here.

Lake Ba Be, surrounded by wooded mountains, is situated between the provinces of Cao Ba and Bac Thai. It is fed by mountain streams, and reaches a depth of 33 feet (10 m). There are boat trips to the **Pang Grotto** and the **Dau Dang Falls**. Large numbers of water birds populate the two large islands and the shores.

Thai Nguyen (50 miles/80 km from Hanoi, on Highway 3) is the capital of the province of Bac Thai. There is a rail connection between Hanoi and Thai Nguyen and the line continues from there to Hong Gai. Thai Nguyen is an important, expanding and densely populated town, which

produces steel, cement and machinery.

65% of Bac Thai Province is covered with mountains and forests, and the region has a rich supply of precious woods and mineral resources; it also produces black and green tea and silk. In addition to the Vietnamese population, Bac Thai is home to ethnic minorities who continue to practice their old traditions, the best-known of which are the legends and the folk songs of the Tay, *sli, luon* and *die then*, the texts of which are composed by the singers themselves and accompanied on traditional instruments. Their festivals are of religious character and take place when the crops are sown and harvested.

Nui Coc, a lake 10 square miles (25 sq. km) in area surrounded by mountains, is 9 miles (15 km) from Thai Nguyen. Within it are approximately 50 islands, large and small; these and the lake shores are being developed as a holiday area.

In the district of **Na Nang**, in Tuyen

Above: Highway 1 by Lang Son, the Chinese border.

Quang Province, 180 miles (290 km) north of Hanoi, at an altitude of 980-3,920 feet (300-1,200 m) and extending over an area of 30,000 acres (12,000 ha), is a jungle containing rare animals and plants, and many species of bird, including peacocks. The area has been made a nature reserve.

THE NORTHEAST

The northeastern mountain and hill country includes the provinces of Lang Son and Quang Ninh. 80% of this area consists of forested mountains, home to tigers, panthers, bears and scaly anteaters. In addition to the Kinh, the ethnic minorities of this region are the Tay, Nung, Zao, Ngai, Hmong and Hoa. The same crops are cultivated as in the neighboring provinces. Tobacco from Lan Son is popular for its taste and yellow color.

The rail connection between Hanoi and Lang Son is part of the international railway line to China. The border town of **Dong Dang** (accessed by train and Highway 1) is 8.7 miles (14 km) from the provincial capital of Lang Son. The border is also to be opened again to foreigners; this means that it will once again be possible to travel by rail from Saigon to North Korea or China, and through Manchuria or Mongolia on to Russia and Western Europe.

When, at the beginning of 1979, Vietnam drove the Khmer Rouge, who were supported by China, out of eastern Cambodia and Phnom Penh, the Chinese "taught the Vietnamese a lesson" by invading the northern provinces, and Lang Son also suffered heavy damage. Many Hoa (ethnic Chinese), a people who had lived in northern Vietnam for centuries, fled to China. The railway line was stopped 12.4 miles (20 km) before the border. Border traffic and trade were not resumed until 1989.

The invaders crossed the passes in the northeast, and came through the **Chi Lang Gate**, 68 miles (110 km) from Hanoi and 37 miles (60 km) from the Chinese border, into the Red River Delta. In 981, 1285 and 1427 the Chinese had already suffered severe defeats at the hands of the Vietnamese in this area.

The ethnic minorities, in particular the Nung and Ray, sell their products at the market in **Ky Lua**. The market is also known for performances of antiphonal singing (*sli* and *luon*) by members of the Tay ethnic minority.

The **Tam Thanh Grotto** near Lang Son consists of three caves, Nhat Thanh, Tam Thanh and Nhi Thanh. A legend is attached to the rock of **To Thi**, also called Vong Phu (the spouse): a fisherman's wife, holding her child, stood on the cliff looking out for her husband's boat, which never returned, until in her sorrow she turned to stone.

From Lang Son, one road leads over the mountains to Cao Bang, and another to **Quang Ninh Province** on the Gulf of Bac Bo. The latter is, however, easier to get to from Hanoi or Haiphong.

Note: The numbers after a village's name (...) are its telephone area code.

NORTHWEST
Accommodations
LAO CAI, PHO LU, YEN BAI: *BUDGET:* train station hotels. **SA PA: Guest houses** in old French hotels and villas, some closed in winter. **HOA BINH** (8 43 45): *MODERATE:* **Hoa Binh Hotel** in the style of Muong pile houses. 6 km outside the city on Highway 6 toward Son La. Muong food and dances can be ordered (for American dollars). *BUDGET (outside the city):* **Guesthouse of the Union** (Khach Sam Cong Doan); **Hoa Binh Hotel**, 5 km on Highway 6 toward Son La; *(in the city):* **Da Giang Hotel**, near the marketplace;
SON LA: Guesthouse (Nha Khach Tinh Uy).
DIEN BIEN PHU: two guesthouses
Getting There / Transportation
From Hoa Binh, the best vehicle for Highway 6 is a jeep. There are also buses. Hanoi – Dien Bien Phu flights with ATR 72, Tuesday and Friday. Reserve at Vietnam Airlines in Hanoi, tel. 25 08 88. **Trekking tours** from Hoa Binh are organized by Vinatours, 54, Nguyen Du, Hanoi, tel. 25 29 86.

THE NORTH
Accommodations
CAO BANG (84 26): *BUDGET:* **Nha Khach Giao Te**, tel. 5 22 41, in the city.
NGUYEN THAI (8428), Bac Thai Province: (in the city): **Chuyen Giai Hotel**, tel. 55360.
BA BE LAKE: simple accommodations.
Tourist Information
Bac Thai-Tourist, Thai Nguyen, Phuong Trong Vuang, tel. 5 56 89
Getting There
Highway 2 Hanoi – Bac Giang (348 km). From Viet Tri, you should only try this in the dry season. Highway 3 Hanoi – Thai Nguyen (55 km) – Cao Bang (288 km). From Nguyen Thai, only try this in the dry season, preferably with a jeep.

NORTHEAST
Accommodations
LANG SON: New **tourist hotel**; guesthouse **Nha Khach** (very simple).
Getting There / Transportation
Railway Hanoi – Lang Son 148 km, about 7 hours, two trains a day.
Note: In the northern mountains, accommodations are given first to members of the Party, government, or army. Ask at a tourist office in Hanoi before embarking. It's a good idea to take along a guide to avoid language difficulties.

THU DO HANOI
Capital and city-state

History and topography

On the lower reaches of the Red River, around 62 miles (100 km) from the sea as the crow flies, archaeologists have found evidence of fishermen's settlements dating from the Neolithic period. From 607 on there was a Chinese administrative center, Tong Binh, on the site of the present capital, which was surrounded by the citadel La Thanh. In 866 the protective rampart Dai La, of which fragments have remained, was built around the citadel. In the year 1009 Emperor Ly Thai To, the founder of the Late Ly Dynasty, was elected in the old capital Hoa Lu in the province of Ninh Binh; a year later, he embarked on a search for a new capital in his home province of Ha Bac. According to legend, he saw a golden dragon rising above the citadel of La Thanh, and recognized the favorable position of this site between *ha* and *son*, water and mountains, surrounded by rice fields and protected against flooding by dikes: there were numerous lakes around the citadel. On its northern edge he built ten hills, atop which he erected temples for guardian and ancestor spirits: on Nung Hill there is still a temple for the guardian spirit of the river To Lich.

The Emperor called his capital Thang Long, City of the Soaring Dragon. In the 15th century it was renamed Dong Kinh, which the Europeans corrupted into their name for northern Vietnam, Tonkin. Foreign traders called the city Khe Cho, market, but to its inhabitants it remained Thang Long until the emperor's seat was moved to Hue in 1804. After this it was Thanh Tich, then Bac Thanh, and, since 1931, Hanoi, "between the rivers." The French ruled their colonial territory from

Left: Ba Dinh Square with the Ho Chi Minh Mausoleum, Hanoi.

Saigon. In 1945, Ho Chi Minh declared Vietnamese independence in Hanoi; in 1954, after the division of the country at the Geneva conference, Hanoi became the capital of North Vietnam, and in 1976 capital of reunified Vietnam.

The topography of the first city map, which dates from 1490, is still identifiable in spite of all the changes. The Red River bordered the city to the east. West Lake, an old river bed, formed its northern boundary, and To Lich, a river with several branches, flowed through the city and, together with the Nhue, surrounded it on its west and south sides. On the Red River and the To Lich, ocean-going junks and fishermen's boats from the Delta weighed anchor. Peasants tilled their fields and tended their orchards on the riverbanks, while markets were held outside the city gates. Spanning the To Lich were four bridges made of bamboo and coconut wood and one made of stone. Than Long was one of the liveliest cities in Southeast Asia. Up until 1804 it consisted of the citadel with the royal palace, and, at its gates, the homes of members of the court, military and mandarins. This administrative center was surrounded by Thanh Kinh, the city of peasants, craftsmen and traders.

The modern capital

Today, the capital city of Hanoi covers an area of 356 square miles (913 sq. km). It consists of Noi Thanh, the inner city (15.6 square miles/40 sq. km) with four city districts (*quan*) – Quan Hoang Kiem with the Old Town, Quan Hai Ba Trung, Quan Dong Da and Quan Ba Dinh – six suburbs (*huyen*), and many villages (*ngo*) within city limits and also in the Delta.

In 1902 the French built the old **Long Bien Bridge** (5,500 feet/1,682 m) over the Red River. It had a traffic lane and a pavement on either side of the railway line from Hanoi to the Red River Delta. Of its 21 supports, 11 were destroyed in the heavy bombing by the Americans in the Vietnam War and patched together again in a makeshift fashion. Since 1984, therefore, its use has been restricted to cyclists and pedestrians. Much later on, the **Thang Long Bridge** was built 6.2 miles (10 km) to the north. It was designed by the Chinese, who discontinued building in 1974, and completed by the Russians in 1984/85. 3.4 miles (5.5 km) long, it spans the flood plain of the Red River and has two levels for use by rail and road traffic. The **Chuong Duong Bridge** (1.7 miles/2.8 km) crosses the Red River to the south of the old Long Bien Bridge, and was opened in 1985, also with the assistance of the Russians. It is the shortest route from Hanoi to the international airport Noi Bai (18.6 miles/30 km), as well as to the port of Haiphong (65 miles/105 km).

Hanoi is a green city. Wide, tree-lined boulevards (*duong*) run through the inner city, and the lakes surrounded by old trees, parks, and a botanical and zoological garden help give the capital its own special atmosphere. The streets (*pho*) feature villas and business premises in the French colonial style, and there are as yet no high-rise buildings. Only in the suburbs are there monotonous, prefabricated residential tower blocks, and, more recently, also modern hotels. There is a serious shortage of housing; often, several generations live crammed into very small spaces. Living space is expensive. The public transportation system cannot cope with the commuter traffic, and workers, salaried employees and officials have to travel long distances from the suburbs and villages in the Delta on bicycles, mopeds and motorbikes to get to work. During rush hour, these vehicles cause frightful traffic tie-ups. But the number of cars and trucks is steadily increasing, as well. In 1990, traffic police were introduced, as the march of motorization led to a rapid increase in the number of serious traffic accidents. By 1995,

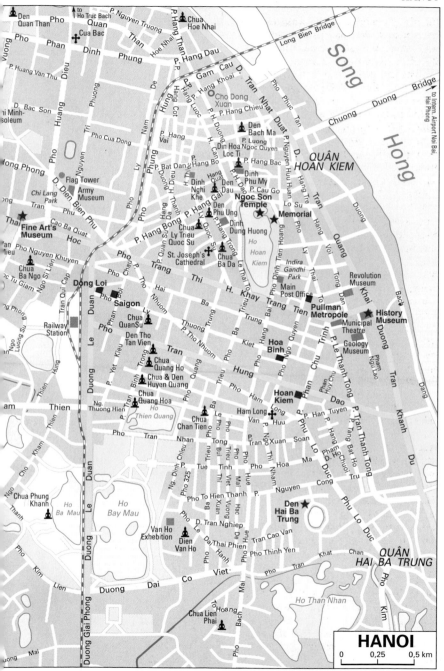

HANOI

0   0,25   0,5 km

151 traffic lights are to be installed on the main roads of the inner city and the arterial roads in the suburbs, and a central traffic control system set up for the whole city. In addition, 90% (37 miles/60 km) of the through roads are scheduled for repair and asphalting, and 130 miles (209 km) of road lighting is being installed. Garbage disposal is also being replanned; and Finland is to help improve the water supply, with three new waterworks.

In the city, neither side of the Red River has a promenade. The river lies unseen behind the dikes which run through and around the city and are supposed to protect it from high water. Still, every year during the heavy monsoon and typhoon rains, the river comes over the top. Water fills the streets, floods the houses, brings traffic to a standstill, and sometimes washes fish over the dikes so that

Above: Hanoi's Long Bien Bridge was often bombed during the Vietnam War. Right: The The Hue Bridge leads to Den Ngoc Son in Hoan Kim Lake, Hanoi.

they can be caught in the streets of the city. Installing drainage at certain critical points is supposed to reduce flooding; and since 1993, 32 of 63 stretches of road that were always flooded are no longer under water, even after heavy rain.

Sights in Hanoi

In the city-state of Hanoi there are more than 300 sacred and secular buildings of interest. Some of them go back to the 11th century when the capital was founded, and many of them have their origins in events that are the subject of legends and sagas. Their names and sometimes even their locations have changed several times. Since they are known by various Vietnamese or Chinese names, the most common ones will be given here. Many pagodas had to relinquish land for the building of houses and roads in the land reforms after 1954, and are now hidden between rows of houses. In the last five years, more has been done to maintain and preserve them than in the previous 45 years, when many *chua* and *dinh* fell into disrepair, were pulled down or pillaged for their art treasures.

Quan Hoan Kiem and the Old Town

Hoan Kiem Lake, also called Central Lake, on the southern edge of the Old Town, is the center of the business district. On its eastern shore are the main post office, department stores, banks and office buildings, and in the side roads are hotels, restaurants and shops. Up until the 17th century, the lake was considerably larger and connected with the Red River, and fleet maneuvers were practiced on it. In the 18th century, the Trinh lords had no fewer than 52 palaces on its shores, none of which have survived. Today, the lake has an area of 30 acres (12 ha). Its name Ho Guom (Sword Lake) or Ho Hoan Kiem (Lake of the Restored

Sword) is derived from a legend: Le Loi, who later became Emperor Le Thai To, fought the Ming Dynasty for ten years at the beginning of the 15th century. Not until a golden turtle appeared from the lake and brought him a sword was he able to repel the invaders. During the fleet's victory parade the turtle appeared again and demanded the sword back, and the Emperor recognized it as a divine spirit. On the lake today there is a small temple dedicated to the golden turtle, which was the guardian spirit and totem of several Vietnamese emperors. The temple is a hallmark of the city of Hanoi.

On the eastern shore, on a small stone mound to the left of the gate to the island of **Ngoc Son** (Jade Mountain), is a monument to the literati in the form of a *But Thap*, or calligraphy brush. The three Chinese symbols at the center of the monument mean "written on the blue sky." A red-painted, arched wooden bridge, **The Hue** (Bridge of the Rising Sun) leads across to the island. The **Ngoc Son** memorial temple, dating from the 19th century, was built on the site of a pagoda. The anteroom is used for preparing sacrifices. The main room is dedicated to the patron of literati, Khuong Muong, and that of healers, La To. A second room is dedicated to General Tran Hung Dao, who defeated the Mongols in the 13th century. A huge stuffed turtle, almost 7 feet (2.10 m) long and weighing 555 pounds (250 kg), which was found in the lake in 1968 and is said to date back to the time of Le Loi, is exhibited in an annex. Water puppet plays are performed on the lake in front of the temple.

The **Chua Ba Da** (Cha Linh Quang Tu) for an honorable lady (*ba*) of stone (*da*) is located west of the lake at Pho Nha Tho 3, and was founded around 1010. According to legend, when the citadel was built a stone statue of a woman was found, for which a memorial temple (*den*) was erected. The statue has not survived, and has been replaced by a stone Shakyamuni Buddha as the object of worship; the temple has become a pagoda. An inconspicuous entrance be-

tween the houses leads into a small court-yard paved with stones which, together with the small stupa also found here, may date from the 11th century, since both paving and building stones demonstrate a format typical of this period.

Chua Quan Su (Pagoda of the Foreign Ambassadors), at Pho Quan Su 73, was built in the 17th century next to the guest-house for ambassadors from Buddhist countries. Since 1934, this *chua* has been the seat of the Buddhist organization in Vietnam, with a seminary for monks and nuns. The present building was put up be-tween 1936 and 1942.

Chua Ly Trieu Quoc Su, at Pho Ly Quoc Su 50, is dedicated to the high priest of the Ly Dynasty, Khong Lo. He attained perfect enlightenment and is de-picted as Buddha on the altar under the Buddhas of the present, past and future; to one side, he is shown as a monk.

Above: Bamboo, an important building material, is sold in the Old Town. Right: Shopping street at the edge of the Old Town.

Den Phu Ung at Pho Ly Quoc Su 25 is a memorial temple for General Pham Ngu Lao, who fought alongside General Tran Hung Dao in the 13th century against the Mongols. He came from a poor family, and after a lengthy contest, Tran Hung Dao made him his comrade-in-arms. In the temple, you can see Pham Ngu Lao below the statue of General Tran Hung Dao. The female figures are Tran Hung Do's daughters, and on the right is Pham Ngu Lao's wife. The *den* is looked after by the family of the hero.

St. Joseph's Cathedral, one of the first churches in the north, was built in 1886 in the grounds of a pagoda in Pho Nha Chung. The high building towers above the surrounding houses.

"The soul of the city has withdrawn into the Old Town, the streets of the bourgeois and the craftsmen," wrote Thanh Quan, a 19th-century poetess. On the city map, the Old Town is laid out like a chessboard between Hoan Kiem Lake and the Red River. It was built in the 11th century under the Ly Dynasty. The emperors were dependent on artisan guilds and artists in the villages; they summoned them to their royal workshops and settled them in their capital and the surrounding villages. In their new homes, these people continued to live in village communities, built their temples to their ancestors and guardian spirits and their *dinh*, and remained in close contact with their native villages. In Hanoi's Old Town, you can still make out the original pattern of settlement. The craftsmen of a village lived in *phuong*, square city dis-tricts. In times of unrest, these phuong were protected by ramparts, hedges and guarded gates. Several *phuong* were under the jurisdiction of two mandarins, who were responsible for administration, fire protection, cleanliness, and collect-ing taxes. The 36 streets of the Old Town were known as *hang*, which means goods. The craftsmen, who specialized in particular products, displayed them for

sale here, and the streets were named accordingly as Silk St., Drum St., Silver St., Paper St., etc. Many *hang* change names at every street corner. One of the best-known is **Hang Dao**; it used to have a tram from the colonial era rattling through it, which has been preserved as an object of curiosity. The focal point of the Old Town is the **Cho Dong Xuan**, the large market with roofed halls. In Hang Dao are the **Dinh Hoa Loc Ti** and the **Dinh Phu My**; in Hang Thieu the **Dinh Nghi Khe**, and in Hang Quat the **Den Dau** (Den Thuan My) for the 18 legendary Hung emperors. The guardian spirit of the **Dinh Dung Huong** at Hang Trong 62 is a young girl. Worth seeing for its carvings is the **Den Bach Ma**, the memorial temple for a white horse, founded in the Ly Dynasty. At the end of Hang Chieu is one of the original **city gates**.

In 1655, a foreign visitor penned the following description: "The city is 6,000 feet long and 6,000 feet wide and its streets are so wide that 10 to 12 riders can pass down them side by side. Twice a month at full moon and new moon there are so many people about that one is constantly being pushed." The reason for the crowds was that the Vietnamese visited the temples on the 1st and 15th day of the lunar month.

The oldest remaining houses of the Old Town date from the 19th century. In the meantime, there's been so much building activity that not an inch of ground has remained unused. The damp climate causes black algae and green moss to grow on the house walls, and unpleasant smells blend with the aromas of the cookshacks and restaurants.

For foreigners, the Old Town's smells and sounds can be confusing. Craftsmen hammer and forge, file and sew their products on the sidewalks in front of their houses, while cars with horns blaring and noisy motorbikes roar through the narrow streets. During the monsoon rains and the drizzles of February and March, dirty water collects in the holes in the road. There's a lot of talk about redeveloping and cleaning up Hanoi, but its

citizens love their old city as it is. Land prices correspond equivalent to those in European capitals.

The soul of the city described by the poetess in the nineteenth century has, in the twentieth century, taken refuge in the temples and *dinh*, which are often hidden away in the courtyards of buildings and can only be reached through narrow passages. The community houses, or *dinh*, still bear the names of the villages whose inhabitants came to the city and settled here centuries ago. Now that most of the old quarters of the Southeast Asian metropolises have been pulled down or redeveloped, a walk through Hanoi's Old Town has become an almost unique experience.

The **History Museum** (Bao Tang Lich Su) is located southeast of Hoan Kiem Lake, near the Red River dike at Pho Pham Ngu Lao 1.

Above: Youngsters look on from the cradle.
Right: In the street of blacksmiths in Hanoi's Old Town.

Following on the large entry hall hung with wall maps are eight sections of exhibits on two floors.

Section I: Prehistory and early history.

Section II: The legendary Van Lang kingdom; findings dating from the Neolithic period to the Dong Son Culture from the Red River Delta, Thanh Hoa and Dong Nai; the Sa Huynh Culture in Trung Bo.

Section III: The Chinese occupation. Drums from the Dong Son Culture, artifacts from the Cham and Oc-Eo Cultures.

Section IV: The first independent dynasties after the victory at Bach Dang River. Findings from the Phat Thich pagoda (a copy of the Buddha) and the Pho Minh Pagoda. Stelae, ceramics, and woodcarvings.

Section V: The struggle against the Ming Dynasty. Ceramics from Bat Trang, Tho Ha and Phu Lang, where the best pottery of the 15th and 16th centuries was produced. A copy of the Quan Am from the But Thap Pagoda.

Section VI: The Tay Son uprising.

Section VII: The struggle against the colonial power.

Section VIII: The battle for independence.

Not far from the museum is the theater from the colonial era.

Quan Hai Ba Trung

This district is named after the first national heroines of Vietnam, known as the Trung sisters (Hai Ba Trung), who led an uprising against the Chinese in 40-43 AD and founded a short-lived kingdom.

The **Den Hai Ba Trun** in Pho Dong Nhan is on the shore of a lake. It was founded in 1143 and is one of the most beautiful sacred buildings in the inner city. The complex consists of the *den*, a pagoda, and a *dien* for the Taoist mothers. The memorial temple has beautiful carvings and a collection of weapons, and also commemorates the twelve female generals of the national heroines. The altar with stone statues of the heroic sisters, depicted on their knees with raised arms about to throw themselves into the river after losing a battle, is only opened on the occasion of the temple festival on the fifth day of the second lunar month.

In the courtyard of **Chua Van Ho**, at Pho Le Dai Hanh 40, is the Dien Van Ho, a temple to the Taoist mothers with a rich, almost fully complete pantheon, the likes of which is seldom found today.

Chua Chan Thien, at Pho Ba Trieu 151, was founded in the 12th century, destroyed several times and rebuilt at different locations. In this pagoda, Le Loi secured a commitment from the Chinese Ming Dynasty after his victory in 1427 that they would never return. In 1888, the French built a prison in place of the pagoda. The Vietnamese rebuilt the *chua* in its present location.

The **Chua Lien Phai**, in Pho Bach Mai, is just over 150 yards (150 m) from the road. The extensive grounds have

been taken over by people who have returned from the New Economic Zones. A beautiful 11-floor stupa has remained.

Chua Ba Ngo (Chua Ngo Ho, Clear Lake), in Pho Nguyen Khuyen, was founded during the Ly Dynasty and renovated by the wife of a mandarin, Lady Ngo, in the 15th century. It has a *dien* with a statue of General Tran Hung Dao.

At Pho Cat Linh 11 there's a grotto. The **Chua Pho Giac** (1774) behind it originally stood in the grounds of the main post office. It was pulled down by the French in 1886 and rebuilt by the faithful on its present site.

Chua Phuong Khanh (Chua Phong Thanh) is a memorial temple for a princess of the Ly Dynasty. It was situated by a lake on which the princess's boat capsized in a typhoon. Since her body was never found, she was believed to be a goddess, and a temple was built to her. Further sacred complexes are the **Dinh**, **Dien** and **Chua Hoa Mai** in Pho Phung Khac Khoan, a pagoda and a mother temple with a statue of the first mother

Au Co. The *dinh* is used as a school. The **Chua** and **Den Huyen Quang**, at Pho Tran Binh Trong 106, are located in a business district. The *den* is dedicated to General Tran Hung Dao. The **Chua Quang Ho**, on the same street, has a small altar behind the main altar dedicated to the Taoist mothers. At number 23, perched on an artificial hill, is the memorial temple **Den Tho Tan Vien** to the mountain spirit Than Nui. In its grounds there is also a *dien*. The **Chua Quang Hoa** (Pagoda of the Shimmering Flower) is on the north shore of Lake Thien Quang. The main altar is flanked by the statues of the ten kings of Hell, who are also called judges. On the left-hand side of the altar is the statue of the mother goddess Mau; on the right-hand side, the statue of a local god.

The village of **Hong Mai** (Yellow Peach Blossom) is located south of Quan

Above: Van Mieu, Temple of Literature, Hanoi. Right: Chess game with living pieces, Tet festival in Van Mieu, Hanoi.

Hai Ba Trung, 4.3 miles (7 km) from the city center. A footpath leads from Pho Truong Dinh 102 to the **Chua** and **Dinh Hoang Mai** (1 mile/1.5 km). The **Chua Hung Ky** is at Pho Minh Khai 4.

Quan Dong Da

This district is named after the hill **Dong Da**, on which Nguyen Hue, later Emperor Quang Trung of the Tay Son Dynasty, defeated the troops of the Chinese Qing Dynasty and liberated the capital Thang Long on the 5th day of the Tet festival in 1789. A memorial was built on this spot in 1989. The hill commands a good view of the surrounding area. The Dong Ga festival, celebrated with reenactments of the battles, is held on the fifth day of the first lunar month.

Along the wide **Pho Tay Son** are various *den*, *dinh* and *chua*: the **Chua Dong Quang** and **Den Quang Trung** (opposite the hill), the **Chua Phuc Khanh** (No. 43), and the **Dinh Nam Dong** (No. 73).

Chua Boc (Sung Phu Tu) in the village of Khuong Thuong, in the southern part of the Quang Dong Da district, was originally located in beautiful wooded surroundings. After being destroyed and rebuilt several times, it became a Buddhist school until 1945. Chua Boc is visited by childless women who pray to the mother goddess Mau, to the left of the main altar. On her right is the statue of the Emperor Quang Trung (Nguyen Hue). It is the only statue of the Emperor in a *chua*: he is usually to be found in memorial temples. In the courtyard of the pagoda is an **incense tree** (*cay huong*). The high, roofless stone altar is connected with the cult of the Taoist mothers (*tu phu*); *ba dong*, shamanistic priestesses, were ordained at this altar. They walked around the altar bearing on their heads the dish containing incense in order to summon the spirits of prophecy. Today, many visitors to the temple put incense sticks into the dish. The temple festival takes place on the fifth day of the first lunar month.

Van Mieu, the temple of literature, is situated in the northern part of this district in Pho Quoc Tu Gian. It was built in the year 1070 by the Ly Dynasty as a memorial to Confucius and his successors and students, and was modeled on the Confucius temple in Qufu (China) where the master was born. At Van Mieu, the state sacrifices to Confucius were conducted by the emperor or highly-placed state officials. In the year 1076, a national academy for princes and aristocrats, *Quoc Tu Giam*, was built next to the temple, which later became a national education center, *Thai Hoc Vien*. The academy was not, however, a university in the European sense: Confucian education and the examination system were based solely on a knowledge of classical Confucian literature. In the year 1807, the educational institution was moved to Hue, where examinations were held until 1918. In 1946, during the struggle for independence, part of Van Mieu was destroyed; it was rebuilt and finally turned into a memorial in 1954.

The complex, surrounded by a brick wall, occupies more than 7.5 acres (3 ha), and is sheltered by old trees. The trapezoidal grounds are 1,144 feet (350 m) long, 245 feet (75 m) wide in the north and 196 feet (60 m) wide in the south. The main entrance on Pho Quoc Tu Giam originally had a lake in front of it, but this has now almost completely dried up and is used for the cultivation of vegetables.

Behind the triple gate are four courtyards, separated from one another by walls and gates. A wooden pavilion with a round window dedicated to the guardian spirit of the literati was built in 1802 atop the Khue Van Cac Mon, the triple gate to the third courtyard; and scholars sat inside and read from their works. In the third courtyard by a lake are 82 stelae from between 1484 and 1779, bearing the names of 1,295 scholars who passed the literature examinations. There were orig-

Above: Ho Chi Minh's residence after 1958, Hanoi. Right: One Pillar Pagoda, Chua Mot Cot, on Ba Dinh Square, Hanoi.

inally thirty more stelae, but none of these has survived. The fourth courtyard was originally lined with temples containing altars for the scholars of Confucius, which were destroyed in 1946. At the end of the courtyard, two temples in the traditional style of the Confucius cult have remained. The curved roofs rest on heavy wooden pillars, and the roof ridges are decorated with dragons and a moon. Two stone pillars dating from 1760 and two stone slabs with clouds and dragons, a wooden statue and four large inkwells dating from 1762 are the only surviving features from the original buildings. In the last building was a memorial for Confucius, which has recently been restored. Until 1807, the academy was located in the open space behind the fourth courtyard. A temple put up in its place was destroyed in 1946, and this open space, located on Pho Nguyen Thai Hoc, is today the site of the annual New Year's market.

Not far from Van Mieu is the **Fine Arts Museum** (Bao Tang My Thuat), at Pho Nguyen Thai Hoc 66. It has exhibits

from the time of the Vietnamese emperors; garments, equipment and jewelry of the ethnic minorities; and a collection of 20th-century paintings. In the corridor on the first floor are copies of the 18 La Han from the Tay Phuong pagoda.

Quan Ba Dinh

This district bears the name of a fort in the province of Thanh Hoa where the Vietnamese fiercely resisted the French in the year 1886. On the spacious Ba Dinh Square, which covers an area of 376,000 square feet (35,000 sq. m), Ho Chi Minh declared the independence of the Democratic Republic of Vietnam on September 2, 1945; his mausoleum, built in 1973-1975, is now located here. On the east side of the square are the Ministry of Foreign Affairs, the National Assembly Building, and the Party house, and to the northwest, surrounded by a park, is the palace of the French Governor-General, built in 1909 and today used for government functions.

From the mausoleum, there is an exit to the park and **Ho Chi Minh's** residence, where he lived from 1958 on. The two-roomed pile house is made of precious woods and resembles those built by the ethnic minorities of the northern mountains. The **Ho Chi Minh Museum**, a three-story concrete building in Pho Son Tay, was completed with the help of the Russians for Ho Chi Minh's 100th birthday in May, 1990.

The **One Pillar Pagoda** (Chua Mot Cot), also called the Chua Dien Huu, is situated between the mausoleum and the Ho Chi Minh museum. It was built in 1049 by Emperor Ly Thai Tong on a single stout wooden pillar in the style of the old nature and ancestor temples. According to legend, the goddess of mercy, Quan Am, appeared to the childless emperor in a dream, sitting on a lotus flower, and held out a boy to him. Soon afterwards, a peasant girl whom he had chosen as his favorite and had crowned empress gave birth to the heir to the throne. Out of gratitude to the goddess, the emperor built the pagoda in a pond shaped like a lotus flower. This was the central sanctuary of a large complex consisting of temples, gardens, pavilions and ponds, which has not survived. The pagoda, too, was destroyed in 1954, but rebuilt in 1955. The pillar, now made of concrete, is 13 feet high (4 m) and 4 feet (1.25 m) in diameter; the temple with the statue of Quan Am is 13 feet by 13 feet (4 x 4 m). Opposite the One Pillar Pagoda is an old *chua* with an extremely beautiful pantheon.

The suburb of Tu Liem and West Lake

Duong Dien Bien Phu leads to the northern part of the city. The French built barracks on the grounds of the old citadel and the emperor's palace, and these were later used by the Vietnamese. This complex contained the prison of Hoa Lo, built by the French in 1904. After the Vietnam War, American pilots who had been shot down were imprisoned here, and nicknamed this grim place the Hanoi Hilton. In March, 1994, the prison was transferred to the suburb of Tu Liem, and a 20-story luxury hotel has been put up in its place.

Duong Hung Vuong, which crosses Ba Dinh Square, is the direct route to West Lake. Shortly before the lake an unknown, rather rural-looking part of the city is worth closer investigation. The second road to the left, Duong Thuy Khue, leads first to a filled-in section of the To Lich and then along the river. After a sharp bend to the left, the Duong Buoi continues to follow the To Lich; and one section of the **Dai La**, the original 9th-century city ramparts, has survived. The road continues on to Den Voi Phuc. From Duong Hung Vuong, Duong Hoang Hoa Tham leads back to Duong Dien Bien Phu. The days of this un-

Right: A new era has dawned for West Lake.

spoiled area are numbered! In the suburb of Tu Liem, to which West Lake also belongs, 21st-century Hanoi is developing on the edge of the 1000-year old city with a skyline resembling those of Bangkok and Singapore. The city of the future is only 30 minutes' drive from the airport of Noi Bai. Roads connecting it with the inner city and arterial roads to the north and south are being built, and a national sports center is planned as the focal point of the new buildings on West Lake. On the south bank of the lake, construction of an international trade and service center has already commenced, with the help of Japan.

The largest of Hanoi's lakes, **West Lake** (Ho Tay) today covers an area of 1,345 acres (538 ha). It has a circumference of 7.7 miles (12.5 km) and is approximately 5 feet (1.5 m) deep. Together with the neighboring **Ho Truc Bach** (White Silk Lake), this was an old, western bed of the Red River. In the 17th century, palaces and temples were built on the lake shores, and white silk was produced in the villages on Truc Bach. In 1620, the Trinh lords built the Co Ngu dike between the two lakes; today the Duong Thanh Nien (Street of Youth) runs along the top, with flame trees on either side.

West Lake is also called Lake of Mist or Golden Calf Lake. According to one of the many legends, the peasants built a temple for their guardian spirit which had a golden bell. This was so loud it could be heard even across the border in China, where there lived a buffalo cow and her calf, both made of gold. One day the calf was looking for its mother and followed what it thought was her voice; but this proved, instead, to be the sound of the bell in distant Dai Viet. For days, the calf circled the temple from which the sound came, and the land it trampled in its desperation became West Lake.

Tran Vu, general in the reign of Emperor Duong An of Co Loa, who defeated

the nine-tailed monster fox, became the guardian spirit of the city of Thang Long. The hero's temple, the **Den Quan Thanh** (Den Vu) is located at the beginning of the Co Ngu dike on the right-hand side, and is said to have been built in 1010. The statue of General Tran Vu, 13 feet (3.96 m) high and weighing 4 tons, is the largest bronze statue in Vietnam. In the relevant literature, this guardian spirit is often referred to as Buddha. On the right is a statue of the master who cast this work. At the Tet festival, a market is held in the castle courtyard, with a singing competition in which the competitors are nightingales.

Chua Tran Quoc is the oldest pagoda in Hanoi. It is said to have been founded in the 6th century and to have been transferred to Goldfish Island in West Lake, left of the dam, in 1600 or 1618. It has 14 stelae dating from the year 1639 and many old statues.

Chua Kim Lien (Golden Lotus) is situated near the Thang Loi Hotel on the Yen Phu dike, and belongs to the village of Nghi Tam. It was built during the Tran Dynasty in the 13th century and was restored in 1988. You enter the pagoda is through a triple gate, a beautiful wooden structure in the style of a royal palace gate with bas-relief flower and dragon patterns and pillars decorated with carving. The *chua*, restored during the Tay Son Dynasty in the *tam quam* style, consists of three buildings one behind the other with high roofs curving upwards at the corners, built in the same style as the Tay Phuong pagoda. The pillars of the main room and the roof beams are richly decorated with carving. The main altar has a large pantheon, and the side altars are dedicated to the Taoist mothers.

A narrow dam 547 yards (500 m) long leads to the village of **Nghi Tam**, on a peninsula in the lake. It is famous for its bonzai plants, tiny apricot and orange trees, with which every North Vietnamese house is decorated during the Tet festival. The wealthy peasants who live here also breed ornamental and fighting fish. Their imposing houses are furnished

with carved furniture, old porcelain and bronze statues. West Lake is the setting of the stories, recorded in verse, of the 15th-century strategist, statesman and poet Nguyen Trai and the talented mat-weaver Nguyen Thi Lo. In the 18th century, the poetess Ho Xuan Hoang, who championed the cause of women's rights, lived on West Lake. 1.2 miles (2 km) away is the **Chua Tay Ho** (Chua Pho Linh), on a peninsula, and the **Den Phu Tay Ho** for the primal mother Au Co, her daughters, and the 18 Hung emperors of the legendary Hong Bang Dynasty. The villages behind the Yen Phu dike have *dinh*, *chua* and *den*. Between these, hotels are being constructed; the lake shores are a popular building site, and their appearance is constantly changing.

The **Den Voi Phuc** (Temple of the Kneeling Elephants), also called Den Linh Lang, is located southwest of the inner city, to the right of Highway 2A, in

Above: La Han in the court of Chua Lang, Hanoi.

the Botanical and Zoological Gardens of Thu Le. In the 15th century, Emperor Le Thanh Tong built an earth hill in Thu Le, Khan Son, on which a memorial temple was erected after his death. It was surrounded by villages and a market. In 1890 the French laid out botanical gardens on this site, and a zoo was added in the 20th century.

Two stone elephants kneel at the gate to Den Voi Phuc, and an avenue lined with 100-year-old trees leads to the temple, which was founded in the 11th century. One of the many legends concerning its hero Linh Lang tells of an emperor of the Ly Dynasty who spent a night with a beautiful peasant girl. The girl then returned to her village. One day, when she was washing herself in West Lake, a snake entwined itself around her. Twelve months later she gave birth to a son, whom the people said was fathered by the snake spirit. The boy grew up to be strong and clever, went into battle as the emperor's general, and returned home victorious. The emperor wanted to keep him at court, but he rode on his elephant back to his mother's house, which stood on the spot where the temple is now. The elephant knelt down before the house; Linh Lang dismounted and lay down on the ground with his head resting on a stone; and the people saw a snake rising to heaven. When the emperor heard of this, he had a temple built for Linh Lang with a statue of the hero and his mother. In front of the altar, you can see a stone marked with the imprint of a head.

The village of **Lang** is part of the suburb of Tu Liem. It is 1.2 miles (2 km) from the Den Voi Phuc (4.3 miles/7 km from the city center), and was once a village of paper-makers. After the **Cau Giay**, the Paper Bridge, a road branches off to the left, and after some 2,000 feet (600 m), a track on the left leads across the fields to the **Chua Nen**, which also has a *den* for the parents of the abbot of the Thay Pagoda. In its courtyard are two incense trees. A few hundred yards further on, another path branches off to the left into the fields. This area borders the university grounds. Outside a cemetery is a plain, almost square brick building, the **Mieu Ba** for the mother of the abbot.

The 12th-century **Chua Lang** (Chua Chien Thien), surrounded by a wall and shaded by tall trees, is one of the most beautiful pagodas in the Red River Delta. This pagoda stands on the site of the house of the parents of the abbot, who was reborn as Emperor Ly Than Tong. The Chua Lang, like the Thay Pagoda, is dedicated to Buddha, the abbot, and the emperor. A large triple gate leads into the first courtyard. The water jug on the gate is the symbol of Quan Am Bo That, who is worshipped in this pagoda. The courtyard is paved with stones from the village of Bat Trang, and statues are set up on the stone pedestals during festivals. In the second courtyard is an octagonal pavilion from the 19th century, which is also used for statues and flowers. In the *chua*, which is divided into three sections, the main altar features a rich pantheon which rises up to the roof beams. Countless lacquered and gilded statues gleam in the muted light, including masterpieces such as a wooden statue of the emperor. The two side altars in the form of a grotto are typical of the 19th century and illustrate the three parts of the universe: in Hell, sinners, robbers and also women who have had abortions suffer drastic punishments; above this are the earthly and the heavenly spheres. The temple festival, on the seventh day of the third lunar month, is celebrated with particular ceremony every 12 years.

Villages in the city-state of Hanoi

The village of **Tan Trieu** (in the district of Thanh Tri) is only a little more than 200 yards (200 m) from Highway 6, the continuation of Pho Thy Son. It has more than 6,000 inhabitants, most of whom earn their living in the weaving trade. Outside the village is a walled spring and a pagoda with a temple for the Taoist mothers. Inside the village gate on the left is a *nghe*, a temple for a guardian spirit without an assembly room, dedicated to Phung Hung, who fought the Chinese Tang Dynasty in 791. On the altar he is symbolized by his sword, and in the room at the back by his robe and crown. A paved path leads past all the sacred places in the village. The tree spirits are worshipped under a large tree; opposite this is a small, open brick building where mourners gather for funeral processions. There is a *mieu*, or ancestor temple, dedicated to the founder of the village, and a 19th-century *dinh*, which is the largest building in the village apart from the concrete administrative block. At the end of the path is a *dien* for the Taoist mothers and, on a hill, another *mieu*. In a hamlet there's a *quan*, a place of assembly for Taoist scholars.

The village is proud of its traditions. Between 1945 and 1980, it was unable to

hold its festival for its guardian spirit, but preserved the garments, musical instruments and palanquins as symbols of this spirit. When the festival was resumed in the 80s, the old men were able to pass the details of the ceremony on to the younger generation. At a festive, slow pace, the procession follows the palanquins. The first of these contains the sword of the guardian spirit; in the second one, garments and a crown represent the spirit's form. A band marches in front, and the dignitaries follow the palanquins. The procession passes through the crowds of villagers from the *nghe* to the *dinh* and retraces its path three days later. This festival takes place a few days after Tet.

The **Dinh Dai Mo** and the **Chua Trung Quan** in the village of **Dai Mo** were renovated in 1994, and April saw the *dinh* festival celebrated again for the

Above: In the ceramics village of Bat Trang (Hanoi): soup bowls are made in a family business. Right: Returning home along the top of a dike, Red River.

first time in many years. In the procession, old Vietnamese costumes were worn, and old customs and games revived. The biggest hit was the *keo lua*, a competition to see who could start a fire with flints in the shortest time.

The pottery village of **Bat Trang** is 10 miles (16 km) from the city center. After the Chuong Dong Bridge in the district of Gia Lam, a path leads off to the right along the top of the dike with a view of the Red River. In the dry season, this sometimes dwindles to an inconspicuous trickle in the middle of its wide bed. Behind the protective dike are imposing farmhouses, surrounded by orchards. An alternative route is along Highway 5 in the direction of Haiphong: after 3 miles (5 km) there is a turn-off which crosses the railway line and leads to Bat Trang. *Bat* means key. Pottery has been produced in this village since the 14th century; the first kilns were built by master potters from Thanh Hoa. There are now around 850 private and state firms producing household crockery, vases and

dishes. Porcelain with a blue-and-white pattern has also been produced here since the 16th century. It is worth paying a visit to one of the family firms, where you can watch the entire process from shaping the clay through painting and glazing it to the final firing, all within a relatively small space. Many of the firms have specialized, and produce soup or tea bowls for everyday use. The village is located on the banks of the Red River, and its *chua* and *dinh* are also worth visiting.

The village of **Phu Dong** (Ke Dong) is in the suburb of Gia Lam, on the left bank of the Red River. At the edge of Gia Lam, after the bridge over the River Duong, a narrow road leads off to the right for 3 miles (5 km) along the top of the dike to the village, which has a population of around 10,000. By the dike, in the middle of a pond, there's a *dinh thuy*, a temple for the guardian spirit of the water puppet players. The plays in this village have a tradition similar to those in the Thay pagoda. Phu Dong was the birthplace of the first hero of Vietnam, Than Giong, in the days of the legendary Hung emperors. Reminders of the hero greet the visitor at every turn. The legend begins in a neighboring village only a short distance away. Here, between the eggplants in her garden, the mother of the hero spied the footprint of a man. She placed her own foot in it and soon afterwards discovered she was pregnant. An unmarried woman, she was driven out of her village and took refuge in Phu Dong, which was then called Ke Dong. She gave birth to a boy and named him Giong. At nearly three years of age, he was not yet talking, smiling or walking. When enemies from the north laid waste to the countryside, the emperor sent out his messengers to look for a hero to drive them out of the country. The envoys also came to Ke Dong and the boy Giong beseeched his mother to bring them to him. When they gathered before him, he began to grow, and demanded a horse, helmet and sword. He ate rice and eggplants by the basketful, and the whole village pitched in to help assuage his hunger. All the horses which the envoys brought him collapsed under his weight, and the emperor ordered a horse to be made out of a mountain of ore. When even his sword split, Giong pulled up a huge bamboo by the roots, and wielded it as his weapon. The nostrils of his horse spewed fire, and the enemy fled or was slain. After the battle, the victor drank a stream dry, then rode to the mountain of Soc. For the last time he surveyed the countryside, then returned on his iron horse to heaven, whence he had come. The emperor built a temple to the heavenly prince Phu Giong, and the village took the name Phu Dong.

The hoofprints of the iron horse became village ponds, which are still pointed out today. In the surrounding area the bamboo, *dong nga*, was singed by the fire from the horse's nostrils, and thus has a yellowish color. You can also see the island in the large spring pond where the hero's mother hid herself until his birth. The **Den Giong**, at the entrance to the village, was founded by the first emperor of the Ly Dynasty, who came from the neighboring village of Dinh Bang. On the main altar is a statue of the hero, surrounded by six generals. All heroes and emperors are depicted with their generals; their power and honor are symbolized by the number of generals. Next to the memorial temple is the oldest *chua* in the village, **Kien So**. The mother of the hero is worshipped as the mother goddess Mau. Outside the village wall is the **Den Mau**, her memorial temple, which was renovated by the village in 1990. It keeps up its traditions: every year on the ninth day of the fourth lunar month, there's a festival at which the story of the hero Giong is performed by young men and women from the village. It is one of the biggest festivals in the Delta, and attracts people from all over the country. Only the people from the neighboring villages are not allowed to come, because it was their ancestors who drove the hero's mother away.

HANOI
Accommodations

Note: Older hotels have a range of rooms in different price categories (from 25 - 160$), and are therefore difficult to classify.

LUXURY: **Heritage**, 80 Giang Vo St., tel. 34 47 27; **Pullman** (Metropole), 15, Ngo Quyen St., tel. 266919; **Hanoi Hotel**, Giang Vo St., tel.25 2240;

MODERATE: **Saigon Hotel**, 80, Ly Thuong Kiet St., tel. 26 84 99; **Thang Loi** (with bungalows), Yen Phu St., tel. 258211; **The Boss Hotel**, 60, Nguyen Du St., tel. 252690; **Bong Sen**, 34, Hang Bun St., tel. 25 40 17; **Eden Hotel**, 94, Yet Kien St., tel. 22 74 65, 22 80 86/7; **Government Guesthouse**, 2, Le Thach St., tel. 25 58 01; **Hawaii**, 77, Nguyen Du St., tel. 22 75 17/8; **Royal Hotel**, 20, Hang Tre, tel. 24 42 33; **Military Guesthouse**, 33, Pham Ngu Lao St., tel. 26 55 40; *BUDGET:* **Bac Nam**, 20, Ngo Quyen St., tel. 25 70 67; **Dong Loi**, 94, Ly Thuong Kiet St., tel. 255721; **Giang Vo**, Am Giang Vo See, tel. 256298; **Noi Bai Airport Hotel**, Noi Bai Airport, tel. 254745;

Restaurants

Nearly every hotel has its own restaurant and bar. Still, you'll find the best food in simple city eateries.

OLD TOWN: **Piano Restaurant**, 50, Hang Vai, piano and violin music; **Kim Ma**, 22, Hang Ca, with roof garden; **Gala International,** 33, Nghi Tam St., tel. 23 42 90, Vietnamese and international dishes; **Five Royal Fish**, 16, Le Thai To St., tel. 24 43 68, view over Lake Hoan Kiem.

AROUND THE TRAIN STATION: **Huong Sen**, 92, Le Duan St., steaks and fish; **See food**, 22 A, Hai Ba Trung Dist., tel. 258759, vietn. specialties, banquet rooms; *French cuisine:* **Le Francais**, 17, Ly Quoc Su Str.; **Le Coq d'Or**, 130, Le Duan Kim Lien St., at Lenin Park, tel. 52 47 13; **L'Élégant**, 66, Hue St., tel. 26 76 39. *Spanish cuisine:* **Bodega**, 57, Trang Tien Str. *Italian cuisine:* **A Little Italian**, 81, Tho Nhuom St., tel. 25 81 67.

ON WEST LAKE AND TRUC BACH LAKE: There are a number of beer gardens and small restaurants on the lakes.

Bars / Disco

Most hotels have their own bars and discos. The bars often serve meals, as well.

International Club, 35, Duong Hung Vuong, by the Ho Chi Minh Mausoleum; **Disco Palace**, 42, Nha Chung Str.; **The Sunset Pub**, Giang Vo St., tel. 35 13 82, with jazz, pop, and piano music. There's dancing on Saturday nighs at the **Thang Loi Hotel** on West Lake.

Cafés

Café and Pastry Shop, 252, Hang Bong (Old Town); **Pagoda Café**, on Hoan Kiem Lake; **Art Café**, 57, Hang No (Old Town); **Artists' Café** 10 A, Pho Bat Dan.

Entertainment

The **Cheo Theater**, Nguyen Dinh Chieu, on Lenin Park, presents traditional operas several times a week. The cinemas screen mainly foreign films. Hotels and travel agencies can give you information about performances of the circus, *rap xiec*, on Tran Nhan Tong St. In the **Russian Palace of Culture**, Tran Hung Dao St., near the train station, there are concerts and ballets. You can see **cock-fighting** on Sunday mornings, and sometimes on Wednesdays as well, in Bach Thuo Park.

Museums / Exhibitions/Temples

Note: Admission to museums stops one hour before closing time. The admission fee is around 2000 - 3000 dong.

Historical Museum (Bao Tang Lich Su), 1, Pho Pham Ngu Lao, open daily except Mon. 8:30 - 11:45 am, 1 - 3:45 pm.

Museum of Fine Arts (Bao Tang My Thuat), 66, Pho Nguyen Thai Hoc, near the Temple of Literature, open daily except Mon. 8 am - noon, 1 - 4 pm.

Museum of the Revolution (Bao Tang Cach Mang), 25, Pho Tong Dan, in the old French customs house. Wed, Thu, Sun 8 am - 4 pm, Tue, Fri, Sat 8 am - noon. **Army Museum** (Bao Tang Quan Doi), 34, Duong Dien Bien Phu, open daily except Mon. 8 am - 2 pm.

Ho Chi Minh Mausoleum, Ba Dinh-Platz, 8 - 11 am, closed Mon and Fri. Sun 7:30 - 11:30 am, admission free.

Ho Chi Minh Museum (Bao Tang Ho Chi Minh), Pho Doi Can, behind Ba Dinh square, open daily except Mon. 8 - 11:30 am, 1:30 - 4 pm, admission free.

Ho Chi Minh House, 48, Hang Ngang, in which Ho Chi Minh drew up the Declaration of Independence in 1945, open daily 8- 11:30 am, 1 - 4:30 pm.

Museum of the Women's Movement, 36, Ly Thuong Kiet St., open daily except Mon. 8 am - noon.

Art Exhibition Center (Trien Lam Van Ho), Vo Ba Trieu, open daily except Mon. 8 am - noon, 1 - 4 pm.

Temples and Monuments

Temple of Literature, open 8:30 am - 4:30 pm. **Den Tan Vu**, open daily 7.30 - 11:30 am, 13.30 - 5 pm. Temples are closed during the midday lunch hour.

Cathedral, built in 1886 on the site of Hanoi's largest temple, Chua Bao Tien. Daily masses at 6 pm, early mass on Sundays.

Additional Information

Banks: National Bank, 47, Pho Ly Thai To, tel. 5 28 31, open daily 8 - 11:30 am, 1:30 - 3:30 pm. Sat mornings only, closed Sun. Best place to change money.

Main Post Office with international facilities (telephone, telex, fax), 75, Duong Dinh Tien Hoang, tel. 5 44 13, open daily 7:30 am - 9 pm;

Shops along Pho Hang Bai; along the south bank of the lake, the main shopping streeets are Pho Trang Thi and Pho Trang Tien.

Vietnam Airlines, city office for international flights, Hang Khong Viet Nam, 25, Pho Trang Ti, tel. 253842, open daily 7:30 am - 4:30 pm. Departure point for the airport bus;

Vietnam Airlines, city office for domestic flights, 60, Nguyen Du St., tel. 25 52 83, 7:30 am - 5:30 pm, Saturdays 7:30 - 11:30 am, closed Sun;

Central train station, *Ga Ha noi*, on Duong Nam Bo. For long-distance travel, it's best to reserve a few days in advance. Open daily 8 - 11 am, 2 - 4 pm. Information desks in the main hall.

International hospital with pharmacy *Benh vien Quoc te*, not far from Pho Kim Lien south of Bay Mau Lake, tel. 6 20 42.

Bookstore of the Foreign-Language Publishers, 46, Tran Hung Dao St., books about Vietnam in European languages;

Foreign Press Club, 10, Le Phung Hieu St., tel. 25 16 97, reading room for foreign papers.

National Library, 31, Thang Thi Str;

Bus Station: Departure points have been moved to two bus stations. Long-distances buses to the south and west depart from *Ben Xe Kim Lien*, about half a mile (1 km) south of the main train station. Buses to the north and east depart from *Ben Xe Gia Lam*, im the district of Gia Lam on the left bank of the Red River, beyond the Chuong Duong bridge. You can reach this bus station with city buses or local trains to Ga Gia Lam.

Minibuses to Hai Phong and Ha Long depart from the north bank of Lake Hoan Kiem.

Regional buses leave from Pho Yen Phu, which is located on the dike along the right bank of the Red River.

Tourist Information

Vinatour, 54, Nguyen Du St. tel. 25 2986;

Hanoi Tourist, 18, Ly Thuong Kiet St., tel. 5 78 86;

Saigon-Tourist, 80, Ly Thuong Kiet St. (in the Hotel Saigon), tel. 26 65 01-5.

THE RED RIVER DELTA

Measuring 5,850 square miles (15,000 sq. km) in area, this fertile rice-growing country is a gift of the Red River. The Delta was once a gulf, which the river gradually filled with alluvial land. And this land became the cradle of the Vietnamese empire and Vietnamese culture.

The land is still pushing out into the sea, and in some places grows 39 feet (12 m) every 100 years. Dai Viet and its capital Than Long (Hanoi) originated at the beginning of the 11th century on the lower reaches of the Red River near its estuary, on the site of a fort built by the Chinese occupying forces.

The Red River is 712 miles (1,149 km) long, 316 miles (510 km) of which are in Vietnam, and is the shortest of the great Asian rivers (the Mekong is 2,790 miles/4,500 km). Its source is in the mountains of Yunan in Southern China. When the snows melt and during the monsoon it carries down more alluvium than the Nile, up to 20 pounds per cubic yard (7 kg/cu. m) of water. The clay contains iron, which colors the water not red but a milky brown.

In the space of 24 hours the river can rise 10-13 feet (3-4 m); in flood it can be as much as 33 feet (10 m) above sea level. For this reason, there are no bridges over the Red River in the Delta, and the three bridges in Hanoi were all built in the 20th century. Floods generally occur between June and October, although it's impossible to predict when they will arrive or how serious they will be; August is generally the worst season for them. It's this time of year which also sees devastating cyclones and typhoons with torrential rains.

In the province of Vinh Phu, near the industrial town of Viet Tri, the Black and the Clear Rivers flow into the Red River.

Left: The mighty water buffalo is a tireless helper for the Vietnamese farmer.

It is here, at the foot of the hills, that the Delta begins, spreading out in a fan to the southeast until it reaches the sea. The Delta includes the city-state of Hanoi and the provinces of Vinh Phu, Ha Tay, Ha Bac, Hai Hung, Haiphong, Thai Binh, Nam Ha and Ninh Binh. Strictly speaking, Quang Ninh Province does not belong to the Delta, but it's included in this section because it is most easily accessible from this region.

The Delta has a complex structure. Limestone hills thrust up from the plain, while the rice fields decline slightly from north to south. Inland, there are places where it's only 5.5 feet (1.7 m) above sea level, while at the coast it reaches height of up to 16 feet (5 m). A dense network of irrigation channels conducts the water to the rice fields.

The Red River is the only river in Southeast Asia which has to be diked in order to prevent the fields and villages from being swamped by water and mud every year. A smaller river, the Thai Binh, comes from the Vietnamese hills and carries less water and sediment; canals link it to the Red River, and enable it to take up some of the larger current's water and mud. In the dry season, salt water from the sea can penetrate some 60 miles (100 km) up the Red River and 30 miles (50 km) up the Thai Binh; the dikes, therefore, also protect the surrounding land from the salt. Many villages extend along both sides of the Red River and its tributaries, behind the protecting shelter of the dikes. In the dry season, the beds of the dried-up rivers on the other side of the dikes are used for the cultivation of rice and vegetables. There are also villages at the foot of the limestone hills, as well as in the hilly country at the edge of the Delta.

Tracks and roads run along the tops of the dikes. The dike system is monitored by control stations; threats include flooding, animals burrowing in the soil, and insects. For centuries, sediment has been steadily building up in the river bed, which has made it, in places, higher than the land on the other side of the dikes. This means that the height of the dikes themselves is constantly having to be raised. The first dike constructions became necessary more than 2,000 years ago, when the Delta was first being cultivated and settled. Extensive dike-building and constant repairs are even described in Vietnamese literature from the 10th and 11th centuries on.

THE DELTA PROVINCES

VINH PHU PROVINCE – Stations of Early History

The round trip of approximately 186 miles (300 km) through the Delta into the hills of Vinh Phu province leads from Hanoi via Co Loa, Thap Binh Son and the Hung temples to the Tam Dao mountains.

Co Loa, capital of the kingdom of Au Lac (BC 258-208) is 11 miles (18 km) north of the city center of Hanoi. To get there, you follow a small road leading off to the right from Highway 2 shortly before the international airport. There are a number of theories as to what the name Co Loa means; the most common translation is Shell City, describing the shape of the citadel. Co Loa, capital of the emperor Au Lac, was first built within the space of a mere 50 years as a citadel. From 938-965 it was the seat of the Ngo Dynasty of the emperor Ngo Quyen, who had won independence from China. All that attests to this second period is a memorial temple, which was built at a later date; the ramparts from the 3rd century BC are, however, still identifiable. The two outer irregular ovals, 8,284 and 6,725 yards (7,600 and 6,170 m) in circumference, followed the contours of the ground and the course of the river; the third wall was rectangular, and smaller. These ramparts were all made of earth

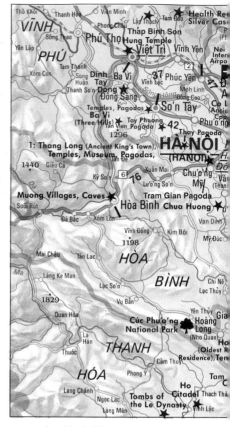

covered with bricks or ceramic plates, 10-13 feet (3-4 m) high and 82 feet (25 m) wide at their base, with watchtowers all along them. The River Hong Giang and its canal system were also incorporated in the citadel, defended by archers whose crossbows were superior to the weapons of the Chinese. Within an area of about 1,000 feet (300 m), archaeologists have found thousands of bronze arrowheads, axes, three bronze plowshares and a bronze drum as well as tiles from the Dai La period.

History and legend complement one another. The story goes that the general of the Chinese Quin Dynasty, who was unable to defeat Au Lac, married his son Trong Thuy to My Chau, the beautiful

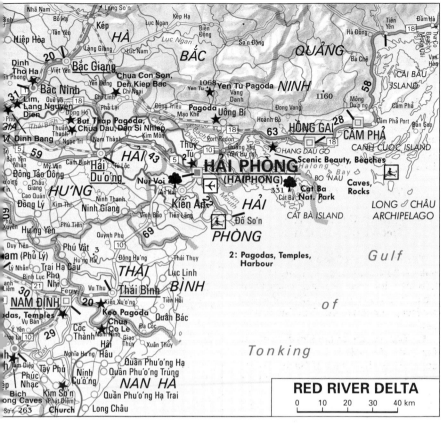

daughter of the emperor of Au Lac. The
prince was assigned to find out why the
Vietnamese archers were so superior.
Out of love for her husband, My Chau
betrayed her father's secret to him. The
golden turtle Kim Quy, the Emperor's
guardian spirit, had given him a crossbow which made him invincible. Trong
Thuy succeeded in exchanging the emperor's crossbow for his own. Soon afterwards he asked for leave to go and visit
his father and My Chau promised to wait
for him. After two years had passed, he
returned with an army and defeated Emperor An Duong, who fled south, taking
his daughter on his horse with him. To
show her husband where they had gone,
My Chau scattered plumes from her dress

along their path. At the boundary of his
kingdom, near Vinh in central Vietnam,
the golden turtle appeared out of the sea.
"Your enemy is behind you," it said. The
Emperor suddenly realized that his
daughter had betrayed the country; he cut
off her head and threw her body into the
sea. It became a small stone which was
carried northwards by the waves. Over-
taken by his pursuer, the Emperor followed the golden turtle into the sea.
Safely returned to Co Loa, Trong Thuy
regretted his treachery and threw himself
into the Jade Spring, where he had often
sat with My Chau.

Today, all the objects that you see in
Co Loa, with the exception of the ramparts, are of more recent date. The **Den**

An Duong was built in the 11th century in the southwestern part of the old rectangular inner ramparts, where the Emperor's palace is thought to have stood. Not far from the temple is the **Jade Spring**. On the main altar of the Den An Duong are garments symbolizing the Emperor. His bronze statue is only shown during the 12-day temple festival which begins on the 6th day of the first lunar month. The **stele house** above the temple dates from the 17th century. The memorial to Emperor An Duong was erected in 1984. Surrounded by a newer, rectangular wall, the Dinh Ngu stands on a site which, according to some theories, was actually the spot where the imperial palace was originally located. The *dinh* roof is supported by massive pillars which, like the roof timbering, are ornately carved. The temple of the guardian spirit at the center of the *dinh* is dedicated

Above: A stone symbolizes the princess My Chau, 3rd century BC, in the citadel of Co Loa, Hanoi.

to the golden turtle. The **Den My Chau** is located behind a massive banyan tree on the left-hand side of the courtyard. A triangular stone, the size of a cowering human figure without a head, fills the room. According to the legend, the river washed up a small stone. Placed in the temple, it grew to such a size that the building had to be enlarged: it is held to be My Chau, who is worshipped in this temple, especially by women, as a symbol of loyalty to one's spouse. The **Chua Bao Son**, which has nothing to do with the history of Co Loa, is situated behind the *dinh* outside the wall. The nuns know tales and legends about many of the statues.

40 miles (64 km) along Highway 2, past the international airport, a rough, unmarked road turning off at Tam Duong leads to a remote region. Some 4 miles (7 km) past the village of Lap Tach, the **Thap Binh Son** sits perched atop a hill. In 1974, all that remained of it was a ruin in a rice field; what fragments had been preserved were moved to this hill and

joined to create this tapering 49-foot high (15 m), 11-story building. The square floors, 43 square feet (4 sq. m) in area at the bottom, rest on a stylized lotus flower. Such tiles as remain, decorated with dragons and stylized chrysanthemums, indicate a probable origin in the Dai La period (11th-12th centuries). In the year 1937, French scientists discovered a second ruined tower on the hill Kim Tou, 6.2 miles (10 km) away; some of the tiles from this are exhibited in the History Museum in Hanoi.

Highway 2 leads to **Viet Tri**, capital of Vinh Phu Province. Near this industrial city, which is also linked to Hanoi by rail, the Black and the Clear River flow into the Red River. From here, the Red River Delta plain spreads out like a fan to the southeast. After Viet Tri, the countryside changes, rising in terraces of rice-fields divided by bushes and trees which soon give way altogether to wooded hills. The Vietnamese call this area the realm of the Hung emperors, or the land of the fathers. A small road leading off to the left from Highway 2 after Viet Tri leads through the woods and ends at the parking lot at the foot of **Nghia Linh Hill**, 572 feet (175 m) high. This hill is said to have been the site of the capital of the realm of Van Lang during the first Vietnamese dynasty of the Hung emperors. Stone tools, pottery and bronze implements found in the 1960s in **Phung Nguyen** at the foot of the hill seem to support this theory. In the 15th century, four temple districts were built at various levels on the hill; these were later renovated in the 19th century. To get to them, you have to ascend 523 steps.

The **Den Co**, Temple of Young Women, at the foot of the hill, also called Den Giang, Temple of the Spring, is built over a spring enclosed in stone. Ngoc Hoa and Tien Dung, the daughters of the 18th and last Hung emperor, are worshipped here. Visitors drink water from the spring and sprinkle it on their heads.

The **Den Ha**, memorial temple for the primal mother Au Co, is approximately 100 steps higher up, in a courtyard entered through a gate with a bell tower. The mother of the Hung emperors and all Vietnamese is represented on the main altar; the left-hand altar is dedicated to the last Hung emperor. On the left of the Den Ha is a *chua*. The steps continue to the **Den Trung** (Middle Temple), the main temple, which dates from the 19th century. It is dedicated to the founder of the dynasty and all other Hung emperors. On the summit of the wooded hill is the **Den Tuong**, the Upper Temple, which is dedicated to the gods of heaven and earth. Lying on the middle altar is the sword of Phu Dong, the country's first hero; another altar is dedicated to the wives and daughters of the Hung emperors. On the hill is a **mausoleum** for the dynasty. Upon the Stone of Oaths here An Duong, founder of the realm of Au Lac, who came from the hills to the plain, swore to defend the land of his fathers.

The temple festival, which begins on the 10th day of the 3rd lunar month and lasts several days, attracts pilgrims from all over the country.

50 miles (80 km) from Hanoi, on the border of Bac Thai Province, is a range of mountains 31 miles (50 km) long, the **Tam Dao** (Three Summits). Its three peaks are frequently covered with cloud. The right-hand summit, Phu Nghia, is 4,578 feet (1,400 m) high, the middle one, Thach Ban, 4,539 feet (1,388 m), and the left-hand Thien Thian 4,496 feet (1,375 m). On the mountainside, 2,943 feet (900 m) up, is a holiday area popular for its pleasant temperatures and scenery. It is usually around 35°F (7°C) cooler here than it is in Hanoi. A summer day on Tam Dao is said to reflect every season. The morning is as cool as in spring, midday is like a summer noon, the afternoon as warm as an autumn day, and night is as cold as winter.

HA TAY PROVINCE

This province surrounds the city-state of Hanoi. Highway 6 leads to the southern part of the province; Highway 2A to the northern part. The **Chua Dau** (Chua Thanh Dao Tu) in the village of **Nguyen Trai** is thought to date back to the 3rd century. It is dedicated not only to Buddha but also to a nature spirit, Phap Vu, and features a pair of dragons from the Tran Dynasty, tiles from the Mac Dynasty, a gong from the Le Dynasty, and a bell tower, complete with bell, from the Tay Son Dynasty. In the pagoda are two statues containing the mummified bodies of two abbots. One weighs about 15.5 pounds (7 kg) and is 22 inches (57 cm) high. In 1931, it developed a crack in the head so that the skull became visible, and a sample could be taken of the wrap-

Above: Statue with the mummy of an abbot in a village temple in the Red River Delta. Right: On the way to Chua Huong, Perfume Pagoda, Hay Ta Province.

pings; in spite of this, no one has been able to establish what method was used to mummify the bodies. The head of the second statue is white, painted with red lips and black eyebrows, a painting style typical of statues containing mummies.

The village **Binh Da** is between the provincial capital of Ha Dong and Van Dinh, 5.5 miles (9 km) from Highway 22. It is famous for its fireworks, notable for their high degree of technical perfection, which are produced by family firms. Many of them require great precision, such as rockets which transform in mid-air into flying dragons or dancers. Duck firecrackers for water puppet plays float on the lake, dive under with a loud bang and resurface with another bang. The main season for fireworks begins in the fall with the Tet festival.

Chua Huong
Perfume Pagoda

Chua Huong (around 37 miles/60 km from Hanoi) is a Buddhist place of pilgrimage with cave temples dating from the 17th century, which were gradually forgotten and not rediscovered again until the 19th and 20th centuries. After the town of Ha Dong, a road leads off to the left which culminates at the river **Ben Duc**. A footbridge crosses the river to the village of the same name, which is the starting point of the pilgrimage to the pagoda. Providing food, accommodation and boats for the pilgrims has made it a prosperous little place. After about half a mile (1 km), the village road curves to the right over a stone bridge to the dock where the boats tie up. Contained by dikes, the canal flows into the **Suoi Yen Vi**, Swallowtail River, so named because of a sharp fork at one point.

The trip to Chua Huong by rowboat takes about 45 minutes downstream, depending on the level of the water, and from 60 to 90 minutes back upstream. The boats glide through the peaceful, ro-

mantic river valley between rocks and mountains which are the subject of many a legend. On the banks and in floating gardens vegetables, cassava and apricots are cultivated, and the peasants bring their produce to the markets by boat.

On the slopes of the Perfume Mountains are two groups of cave temples containing Buddhist statues, some of them carved in marble. The **Chua Huong Tich** is the most beautiful and highest of a group of five caves; the **Chua Tuyet** the most beautiful of a group of seven. According to legend, the youngest daughter of the emperor dedicated her life to Buddha and withdrew into one of the caves, against the will of her father. The emperor ordered the disobedient girl killed; but a white tiger carried her off into a cave and the forest animals brought her food. The emperor contracted leprosy, losing his sight and his hands, and was told he could only be cured by the voluntary sacrifice of the eyes and hands of one of his subjects. The princess heard of her father's illness and was willing to

make this sacrifice. When the emperor recovered, he went in search of his savior, and learned that the person who had sacrificed her eyes and hands for him was none other than the daughter he had believed dead. He, too, became a Buddhist, and from then on lived in the caves and helped transform them into pagodas.

The caves are reached by steep paths through the woods which become increasingly narrow and winding the higher you get. Only the main paths are paved. In order to visit all the temples the pilgrims spend many days in the woods. "Amidha Buddha be praised!" they chant as they walk, a cry which provides some extra encouragement on this strenuous hike. Good walkers will be able to visit the first group with the Chua Huon Tich in approximately 3 hours. Not far from the boat dock is the **Den Trinh** for the white tiger which saved the princess; and the **Tien Tro**, the Heavenly Kitchen, is also at the foot of the mountains. The path then climbs up to the **Chua Tien Son**, which has five 17th-century statues.

In the **Chua Vang** or Hammock Pagoda, the emperor is said to have rested on his way to his daughter. **Chua Huong Tich**, built in 1675, is in a spacious cave with stalactites and stalagmites bearing names inspired by their unusual forms. This cave, which the Vietnamese call the most beautiful cave under the southern skies, is decorated with bronze and stone statues and a Quan Am, goddess of mercy. It commands a good view out over the mountains and river valley.

The princess made her vow in the **Chua Tuyet**. On the way to this pagoda the trail passes the **Chua Hinh Bong**, the **Chua Long Van** and the **Chua Bao Dao**. The season of pilgrimages lasts for a month, from the middle of March to the middle of April. The temple festival begins on the 19th day of the second lunar month, the date when the princess is said to have received enlightenment.

Above: Tay Phuong Pagoda, Ha Tay Province. One of the 18 18th-century La Han. Right: Watchman, Tay Phuong Pagoda.

56 miles (90 km) from Hanoi, in **Kim Boi**, there are sanatoriums around the natural hot mineral springs. The water bubbles out at 96.8°F (36°C). It tastes pleasant, so it can be drunk straight or mixed with other drinks.

Three pagodas in the Red River Delta

Chua Tay Phuong, Chua Thay and Chua Tram Gian (round trip approximately 56 miles/90 km) are three of the most important pagodas in the Red River Delta. You can reach them on Highway 2A, and take in the Den Voi Phuc and the Chua Lang en route.

Chua Tay Phuong is 26 miles (42 km) from Hanoi. 20 miles (32 km) out of town on Highway 2A, a narrow road turns off to the left. Hills covered with vegetation rise up from the plains of ricefields. 5.5 miles (9 km) further on, a path leads off to the right up onto the dike to the parking lot at the foot of Cau Lau, a hill 163 feet (50 m) high. Tall trees shade the Chua Tay Phuong, which belongs to

the village of Thach Xa. 262 shallow steps made of laterite lead up to the gate in the outer wall. On the right of the courtyard is a small temple for the local god of the soil, and at the back, to the right of the pagoda, is a bell tower. In the 8th century the Sung Phuc Tu, a small wooden pagoda, was built on this site. It was enlarged in the 16th century and renovated in the 17th century during the Tay Son Dynasty in the *tam quam* style; since 1794, it's been known by the name it bears today. It was bombed in 1954 and restored in 1958.

The pagoda consists of three buildings one after the other: the entrance hall, *bai duong*; the main hall, *chien dien*; and the building at the back, *hau cung*. All three together are called *tam bao*, Three Jewels. Their high double roofs rest on two rows of pillars, and the upturned corners of the eaves are capped with dragons. On the ridgepoles are colorful images of the holy animals in ceramic. The severe brick walls of the gable sides are broken up by lattice lunette windows.

The Chua Tay Phuong is famous for its architecture and its 62 fine wooden figures. These 18th-century masterpieces include the 18 La Han (called the 500 Lo Han in China and Arhat in India). The Vietnamese legend tells of 18 quarrelsome brothers, rough peasant types, who were killed in disputes. Through the goodness of Buddha they were resurrected and chosen to be his disciples. The legend comes to life in these life-sized figures, which exude a burlesque vitality. No two are alike: some seem to be sunk in meditation; others are full of the joy of life. The attention to detail can be seen in the careful carving of the folds of the garments. These statues are evidence of the dawn of a new flowering in the art of wood carving; there are copies in the Fine Arts Museum in Hanoi and the Thay Pagoda. Every large *chua* has statues of the La Han. The Chua Tay Phuong's 62 wooden figures also include a Buddha of the Future, who in Vietnam is frequently depicted as Di Lac, a fat, happy monk, and eight guardian figures. The Ami-

tabha Buddha on the main altar probably dates from the 17th century. The beautiful Quan Am Thi Kinh to the left of the altar, a female figure in monk's clothing holding a child, is only found in Vietnamese temples. The story is that a woman discovered a hair on the chin of her husband while he was sleeping, and was about to remove it with a razor when he woke up and, thinking she was trying to kill him, drove her out of the house. Disguised as a monk, she entered a monastery. A girl from the village fell in love with the beautiful monk, who however rejected her. When the girl had a child by one of the village boys, she brought it to the monastery and claimed that the monk was the father. Monk and child were turned out of the monastery and eked out an existence by begging. Not until the monk died was it discovered that he was

Above: Chua Tay – Dragon Lake (Long Tri) with Dinh Thuy, temple for the guardian spirit of the water puppet players. Right: Water puppets on the lake.

a woman. She became Quan Am with Child. Quan Am, the goddess of mercy, also appears as Quan Am Toa Son, sitting on a rock, and as Quan Am Tung Te, who hears the prayers of childless women.

The **Chua Thay** in the village of Sai Son is around 6.2 miles (10 km) from the Tay Phuong Pagoda (19 miles/30 km from Hanoi). The road leads across the rice plain, which is dotted with bizarre limestone peaks; in the villages the limestone is processed for use as building material. The village of **Nge Sai**, enclosed by a wall, has a beautiful *dinh*. In the village of **Hung Ngo**, a stone bridge crosses the river. The road then winds its way between the river, canals and mountain peaks until it reaches Sai Son.

The **Thay Pagoda** (Ha Thay Province) lies at the foot of the rocky peak Phat Tich (Son Thay). A steep path leads to the summit; the view from the top is worth the climb. On the summit known as **Cho Troi** (Heavenly Market), the gods are said to play chess on bright moonlit nights.

On **Long Tri**, Dragon Lake, in front of the *chua*, a small temple, **Dinh Thuy**, is for the guardian spirit of the water puppet players. The two covered wooden bridges date from 1602: the one on the right is called *nhat* (sun), the left-hand one *nguyet* (moon). According to legend, a monk called To Lo, who bore the honorary name of Tu Dao Hanh and was also referred to as *Thay*, Master, built the pagoda that is named after him in 1076, and was its first abbot. In addition to Buddhism he also taught the people dancing, singing and water puppetry. He was worshipped as a god, and when he died the faithful interred his bones in a statue made of eucalyptus wood and placed it in a wooden shrine. When the door was opened, the statue rose like a marionette. After his death, a prince was born who was held to be the reincarnation of the abbot. He became the Emperor Ly Thanh Tong, a supporter of Buddhism.

A three-part cult is still exercised in the Chua Thay to the present day: the worship of Buddha, of the abbot Tu Dao Hanh and of Emperor Ly Thanh Tong. On the main altar beneath the three rows of Buddhas are thrones for the emperors of the Ly Dynasty. To the right of the altar is the shrine with the statue of the abbot; in front of this is a statue depicting him as Buddha. In the foreground of the main room, on the right, is an altar for the Ly Dynasty, and at the back, on the left, a statue of Emperor Ly Thanh Tong. In front of this the Emperor is depicted with Cambodian monks.

The Thay Pagoda is built in the *tam cap* style (meaning three stages). It consists of three buildings at three levels on the mountainside with three separate roofs and rather dark interiors. Most of the statues date from the Le Dynasty. Galleries and gardens surround the *chua*. The pagoda festival, which includes water puppet plays, is held on the seventh day of the third lunar month.

The **Chua Tram Gian** (One Hundred Rooms) is about 7.5 miles (12 km) from the Thay Pagoda (17.5 miles/28 km from Hanoi, not far from Highway 6) in the

village of Tien Phuong. It is also known as Chua Tien Lu or Chua Quang Nghiem. Founded in 1185 by the Ly Dynasty, it was restored in the 17th and 18th centuries. The *chua* is situated on the uppermost terrace of a hill under tall trees, its architecture fitting in perfectly with the landscape. Chess competitions are held at the triple gate during temple festivals, while water puppet plays are performed on the lotus pond. Hanging in the bell tower is a large bell dating from 1794. The 153 statues in the pagoda are made of wood or clay; a mummy inside a rattan statue is thought to be that of a highly venerated monk and magician who worked in this pagoda.

Ba Vi –
throne of the mountain spirit

The finest *dinh*, community houses with temples to guardian spirits, are to be

Above: Fishing in an irrigation canal near the rice fields.

found close to the Three Mountains, Ba Vi, (district of Ba Vi in Ha Tay Province; round trip approximately 74 miles/120 km from Hanoi). They date from the 15th to the 17th centuries.

Highway 2A leads past the Tay Phong pagoda turnoff to **Son Tay**. Formerly a provincial capital, this city is now a district capital in Ha Tay Province. As an outpost of the capital Thang Long, it once had a strong fortress. Only fragments of the thick walls and a gate have survived, together with sections of the moat and a stone bridge. The wall was built of laterite, a reddish, porous stone which is frequently used for building in this region. During the wars of independence, much of Son Tay was destroyed.

The area at the foot of Ba Vi is known as the land of the mountain spirit Than Noi, also known as Son Tinh in his manifestation as the guardian spirit of many villages. He lives on the highest of the Three Mountains, Tan Vien (4,238 feet/1,296 m). A legend tells of his competition with the water spirit Than Thuy for the daughter of the legendary Hung emperor. Every year the water spirit, who lost the contest, sends storms and rain to trouble the mountain spirit, as well as the Vietnamese peasants.

The village of **Duong Lam** was the home of Ngo Quyen, who founded the Ngo Dynasty. He drove the Chinese out of the Delta once and for all in 938, and destroyed their fleet on the River Bach Dang. His memorial is located next to the *dinh*. All that has remained of the **Dinh Mong Phu**, which is surrounded by a laterite wall, is the large, open main building. Its high roof is supported by thick pillars, decorated, as are the roof timbers, with fine woodcarvings. The temple to the guardian spirit was destroyed, but is to be rebuilt. In front of the *dinh* is a large square. The farms are hidden behind closed gates. Many important mandarins came from this once very prosperous village, and their families have looked after the *mieu* (ancestor temples) for 13 generations: they still hold the keys to the memorials. The **Chua** and **Den Dung** were built for Nguyen Thi Dung, the favorite of Ngo Quyen. Behind the triple gate, an avenue of trees leads to the ornately carved *chua*. The courtyard is set up for chess; the large carved figures are affixed to bars stuck into holes in the pavement. The temple festival, with chess competitions, takes place on the last day of the twelfth lunar month.

The **Chua Mia** (Sung Nghiem Tu) is one of the delta's most beautiful pagodas and has one of the largest pantheons. It was built in 1632; *Mia* means sugar cane. Half of the 287 statues on the four altars are made of wood, the others of a mixture of earth, straw and finely-ground sugarcane, which was lacquered and gilded. Since wood was expensive in the Delta, large pantheons often included statues made of aluminium oxide or earth mixtures. Next to the main altar, in a shrine, is the statue of the founder. The statue of an Avaloketecvara is particularly beauti-ful. The pagoda also has a bronze bell dating from 1743 and a gong from 1846. The large complex is sheltered by ancient tall trees and enclosed by a wall.

Outside the village at the foot of a hill is the **grave** of the nobleman **Phung Hung**, who led his peasant army against the troops of the Chinese Tang Dynasty in 791 and captured the town of Son Tay. On the altar of his modest grave temple, he is represented simply by a throne. Phung Hung is worshipped in many villages as a guardian spirit. **Lang Ngo Quyen**, the grave of the founder of the Ngo Dynasty (939), is only some 100 yards (100 m) away and is of similar design. The buildings described as *lang* (grave) are in fact memorials; the actual burial site, somewhere in the surrounding countryside, is usually unknown.

The **Den Va** (Den Dong Cung) in the village of **Trung Hung** is a walled complex built for the revered mountain spirit Than Nui. In a grotto in the first courtyard, there's a depiction of the legend of the carp which succeeded with three mighty leaps in turning into a dragon. The second courtyard contains guest-houses for pilgrims, a bell and a drum tower with curved roofs and lunette windows. Stelae and stone lanterns stand in front of the main temple. Inside, in front of the throne of the mountain spirit, stone mandarins keep watch. White and red horses, vases, incense vessels, lamps and ancestor panels with the names of the 18 Hung emperors surround the throne. The temple was founded by the Ly emperors, and has been renovated and enlarged many times since. Foreigners are only rarely allowed access, and photography is not permitted in the interior.

The **Dinh Tay Dong** (Dinh Nam Cung) in the village of Tay Dong, in the Quang Hai district, is the finest surviving specimen from the 16th/17th centuries. On one side, it is bordered by a lake at the foot of the Ba Vi; on the other three sides, it is protected by a wall. Of the original

buildings in the large courtyard, the main building, flanked on either side by a smaller, double-roofed building, has survived. Over the main building is a high roof in four sections, decorated with the four holy animals, dragon, phoenix, turtle and unicorn. The outer gable walls are richly decorated with carving.

Rows of pillars divide the interior into five sections. In the middle of the back wall is the temple of the guardian spirit. The upper sections of the pillars and the roof timbers are decorated with masterful peasant woodcarvings. Scarcely visible on the high roof timbers, the depictions of scenes from everyday peasant life are both animated and accurately observed. The carvings on the right and left sides of the temple to the guardian spirit were executed by two different groups of artists. In the carvings on the right, the lines are more flowing and rounded, and some of

Above: Travelers are regarded with friendly curiosity. Right: Sentry figure, But Tap Pagoda, Ha Bac Province.

the timbers are older. A number of stelae report on restoration work; the most recent was in 1979. The *dinh* festival takes place at the same time as the Tet festival.

Other sacred buildings, such as the **Dinh Vien Chau** in the village of Co Do and the **Dinh Thanh Lung** and **Dinh Phieu**, are also worth a visit.

Dong Mo Lake is 31 miles (50 km) from Hanoi at the foot of the mountains. Measuring about 5,000 acres (2,000 ha) in area, it has 24 islands of various sizes. The shady shores have been turned into a recreation area where people come to swim and hike.

HA BAC PROVINCE – Art and Tradition

To reach this province from Hanoi, follow Highway 1 over the Chuong Duong Bridge and through the suburb of Gia Lam, and continue on Highway 18 in the direction of Hong Gai. To the southern part of the province, take Highway 5, which turns off to the right in Gia Lam and leads to Haiphong. Ha Bac Province is also served by two railway lines.

The first Ly Dynasty ruler (1009-1225), Emperor Ly Thai Tho, came from the village of Co Phap, which today is called Dinh Bang. He was brought up in the village pagoda, and the abbot took him to the court of the Early Le Dynasty in Hoa Lu in Ninh Binh Province. He came to assume a high office at court, and in the 1009 the nobles elected him emperor, making him the founder of the Late Ly Dynasty. In 1010, he moved his capital to Thang Long (Hanoi).

The Vietnamese emperors never lost their ties to their home provinces. Emperors, court and nobility were pious Buddhists and founded monasteries and pagodas in Thang Long and Ha Bac Province. They summoned monks from China to spread Buddhism. Large pagodas were built, while the monasteries developed into centers of learning. While the villages have preserved their traditions to the present day, the province has a reputation for being progressive, open to innovation and reforms.

The village of **Dinh Bang** (Co Phap) is about half a mile (1 km) to the right of Highway 1, and 11 miles (18 km) from Hanoi, in the Tien Son district. At the entrance to the village is a large school building. A narrow street leads between the farms; their gates are firmly closed. The village inhabitants, more than 10,000 in number, are said to have a good business sense. They like to be thought of as city people, and don't want to admit any kind of inferiority to the nearby capital.

Markets are held on the large open square. It was once filled with the walled complex of a community house, consisting of many buildings within a courtyard, sheltered by tall trees. All that has remained of the **Dinh Dinh Bang** is the main building with the assembly hall and the temple – the largest and most magnificent in the Hanoi area. This huge rectangular building is supported on stilts

which are almost completely hidden in the earth. The eaves of the high roof extend down so low that they hide the side walls. Stone animal figures can still be seen on the staircase to the entrance. In the large hall, the roof timbers rest on pillars made of ironwood, which is often used for such supports, and are about 1.8 - 2 feet (0.55 - 0.65 m) in diameter. The pillars and roof timbers, in particular the roof joists, are ornately carved. The peasants who built the Dinh Dinh Bang from 1730 to 1736 were undoubtedly conscious of their independence and power. In the temple to the guardian spirit (*hau cung*), the Ly emperor is venerated, represented by symbols. The *hau cung* is built as an annex in the style of the 18th century, and can be entered from outside through a door at the back of the building. The *dinh* festival is celebrated on the last day of the Tet festival.

Chua Phat Tich (Chua Van Phuc) was built in Phong Hoang, in the hamlet of Phat Tich. The Vietnamese have often fought for their freedom in this area

around the River Day, ever since the 3rd century BC, when Emperor An Duong of Co Loa is said to have led the first battle, after moving from the hill country down onto the plains and uniting his Au empire with that of Lac.

In the 8th century, the Chinese governor Cao Bien built a stupa on a hillside outside the hamlet of Phat Tich; French archaeologists have found statues from this period in the Dai La style. On the same spot, in 1057, Emperor Ly Thanh Tong built the Chua Van Phuc (Phat Tich) with a high *thap* which could be seen from Thang Long. This, the largest and most beautiful *chua* in the Red River Delta, was described in detail by the Frenchman L. Bezacier in his work *L'Art Vietnamien*. It was destroyed in the struggle for independence in 1949. All

Above: But Thap Pagoda, Ha Bac Province: The thousand-armed goddess Quan Am, a masterpiece of woodcarving. Right: The But Thap Pagoda is the largest and most beautiful Buddhist temple in Vietnam.

that remains today are a large stone Buddha statue and some animal sculptures. Copies of this statue, one of the most beautiful in Vietnam, are to be found in the museums in Hanoi. There are plans to rebuild Chua Phat Tich.

Chua But Thap (Chua Ninh Phuc) is in **Dienh To** village in the Thuan Thanh district, 19 miles (30 km) from Hanoi. *But Thap* is the term for a tower in the form of a calligraphy brush. During the Ly Dynasty, the large pagodas had high towers (*thap*), a feature that was not incorporated into later architectural styles.

Since the destruction of the Phat Tich pagoda, the Chua But Thap is the loveliest as well as the most typical specimen of temple building in the Delta. Founded by the Empress Dieu-Vien and a princess, it was built from 1646-1647 by a Chinese monk, Minh Hanh, who also erected a burial stupa for his famous teacher, the Chinese monk Chuyet Cong. A nine-story stupa is said to have existed on this spot as early as the 13th century .

The Chua But Thap has four buildings outside its enclosing wall, and six inside it. Restoration work began in 1990, with some help from the German Federal Republic, in order to check the destructive inroads of termites. Outside the enclosing wall is a triple gate adorned with large, semicircular tiles dating from the 17th century. The two-story bell tower is also outside the wall. On its lower floor is the Jade Emperor, and on the upper floor the Emperor of the Heavens, both with their entourages. The bell, dating from 1815, was donated by Emperor Gia Long, founder of the Nguyen Dynasty. Outside the wall, on the right at the back, is the burial stupa for Chuyet Cong. The Thap Bao Nguiem behind it, 43 feet (13.05 m) high and made of bluish stone with carvings, is the only remaining stone stupa.

The buildings inside the walls are linked to one another by passages or gardens. They contain a wealth of fine wood- and stone-carvings and statues.

The entrance hall (*tien duong*) is of simple design and has statues of sentries, the dragon spirit and an ananda with attendants. The pillars in the Hall of Incense are decorated with dragons, while the gables sport an interesting frieze of animals and inscriptions. Adjoining the open sides of the hall are courtyards with roofed altars for the kings of hell, who are also called judges. This hall leads directly into the main room (*thuong dien*), where you can see representations of Tho Dia, the spirit of the earth, and Bodhidharman, who brought Buddhism from India to China and can be recognized by his black beard and round eyes.

The large pantheon on the main altar is worth closer investigation, but what first catches the eye is the statue to the right of it. The Quan Am, the Bodhisattva Avaloketecvara, with a thousand arms and a thousand eyes, is a unique work. The name of the donor, Truong Van Tao, and the date, 1656 or 1756, can be deciphered on the pedestal. Few statues exude a comparable sense of unease, or a comparable sense of magic. According to legend, Buddha gave Quan Am a thousand hands and a thousand eyes in order to defeat the monster that lies at her feet. The slim figure is surrounded by two semicircles of arms and hands. Those in the first semicircle originally held symbols, which have not survived. Most of the hands surrounding the three heads of Quan Am have eyes in their palms. The middle head has a tiara with the Amidhabha Buddha, the spiritual father of the Bodhisattva, enthroned on top. Her other two heads, arranged pyramidally below the middle one, are also crowned by figures. The statue stands in a half-open room. Her red and golden lacquer invest her with a ceremonial air, and in the play of outside light, her hands and arms almost seem to move. There are copies displayed in museums in Vietnam and Paris. Another marvelous statue, unique in the detail and skill of its execution, is the fasting Buddha to the left of the main altar. These two masterpieces are so fascinating it is hard to tear yourself away to

105

look at the pantheon, which is certainly of equal importance.

Noteworthy, too, is the stone balustrade running around the outside of the building, which consists of 56 panels and carries over into a stone half-moon bridge with panels that represent the best stonework in Vietnam. From the buildings which follow, you can tell that this complex was built by emperors; smaller pagodas don't usually include them. First, there's a temple, its interior practically filled by a prayer wheel typical of Tibetan Buddhism, flanked by two Buddhas. A somewhat plainer prayer wheel is in the nearby Chua Phu Mai; this prayer wheel is supposed to have come from a nine-story stupa built by the monk Huyen Quang in the 13th century. The next building is used by the monks as an assembly room; it contains statues of the royal founders and a stele documenting the building of the *chua*. In one of the last buildings is the statue of the monk Minh Hanh; the Taoist mothers and the gods of the stars are also worshipped here.

Chua Dau (Chua Phong Quang Tri) is 6 miles (10 km) south of the But Thap pagoda in **Khuong Tu** village in the Thuan Thanh district; you can also get there from Highway 5 (Hanoi - Haiphong). The Chua Dau was located in the middle of the old citadel of Luy Lau, which was discovered by French archaeologists, and is thought to be the oldest pagoda in Vietnam (3rd century). In the 6th/7th centuries, the Chinese Sui Dynasty built a monastery with a nine-story stupa. When this was destroyed in 1738, the three-story stupa was built in its place. The Ly and Tran Dynasties undertook restoration work on a number of occasions, and the complex was enlarged by a mandarin in the 14th century. The **Hoa Phong** stupa, 56 feet (17 m) high and occupying an

Right: Dau Pagoda, Ha Bac Province, one of the oldest pagodas in Vietnam with a three-story stupa.

area of 23 x 23 feet (7 x 7 m) was restored in 1737. Stairs flanked by stone unicorns lead up to the entrances on the east and west sides. The sculpture of a sheep next to the staircase, which originally had gilded horns, is evidently very old and, like its counterpart in a neighboring pagoda, must have come from China, since this animal is unknown in Vietnam. Several of the stelae in the courtyard are bevelled at the top, as was the custom in the 19th century, and there is a rectangular stele dated 1737. Judging by their style, the stone dragons by the stairs to the temple date from the 16th century.

Vietnamese Buddhists have no more abandoned their belief in nature spirits than they have their worship of the spirits of Taoism. In the Chua Dau and three other pagodas, nature spirits are worshipped at the incense altars. May, the cloud spirit (Phap Van), is worshipped in the Dau Pagoda of Ha Bac Province and Phap Vu, the rain spirit, in the Dau Pagoda of Ha Tay Province. There's a legend about the pagoda's founding and name: in the village, the river washed up the trunk of a mulberry tree, *dau*. At first, no one paid any attention. Only when the village suddenly became prosperous was this attributed to the tree trunk; a temple called the Chua Dau was built to it, and statues were carved out of the wood.

On the altar in the Hall of Incense is the statue of Phap Van, flanked by her two daughters and her servants. According to a Buddhist legend, the statue represents a pious worshipper of Buddha. The pillars in the main room rest on the typical square pedestals found in 18th-century *chuas*, and some of the roof-timbering dates from the 14th century. The statues composing the rich pantheon – most of which are made of lacquered clay – date from various periods: the three top rows are the oldest. During the temple festival the statues are carried into the courtyard on the two 16th-century chairs which stand behind the altar; the souls of

the gods then remain in the simple wood boxes next to the chairs.

One of the statues in the Dau pagoda contains a mummy. The pagoda festival is on the 8th day of the 4th lunar month.

The **Chua Dan** (Phuong Quang Tu) in the village of **Chi Qua**, near the Chua Dau, also in the Luy Lau citadel, dates from the same period. Here, too, a nature spirit is worshipped. Between the Bhat Thap and the Dau pagoda 6 miles (10 km) away, the road passes the destroyed citadel and the **Den Si Nhiep**, associated with the first Vietnamese governor (187-226) of the Chinese province of Giao Chi. He was held in great respect by the peasants, who called him Si Vuong, King Si. He succeeded in securing for his three brothers the command of the neighboring districts, and in this way extended his dominion over an area that became known as Giao Chau, corresponding approximately to the territory on which the empire of Dai Viet was created in 939.

The village of Lim on Highway 1 is known for its singing competitions for young men and women. In the region, singing competitions are held from the 13th to the 15th of the first lunar months. Groups from the area gather at rivers, on hills and in the courtyards of the *dinh*. Best-known are the antiphonal singing competitions at Lim Pagoda at Lim Hill.

The **Lang Nguyen Dien**, the grave of a military mandarin, also known as the grave of the eunuch, is situated on a hill near the Lim Pagoda and dates from the year 1769. Two gates, watched over by two sentry figures, lead to the grave, which consists of a block of laterite and is covered with a stone slab. Civil and military mandarins keep watch over it, and two stone *ong phong*, slaves from the Cham ethnic minority, kneel in front of it.

The district of Bac Ninh still has interesting *chua* and beautiful *dinh*. Highway 1 leads to the village of **Tho Ha**. On the outskirts of the district capital of Bac Ninh, a small road to the left leads across the railway line between Hanoi and Lang Son to the river. Tho Ha is still known as a pottery village. Originally it produced

Under tall trees on a large, enclosed square, two of the original buildings of the **Dinh Tho Ha**, dating from 1685, are still standing. The small entrance hall, *tien to*, where the sacrifices for the *dinh* festival are prepared, lies directly in front of the assembly hall with its guardian spirit temples. Dances and games are held in the courtyard. The huge 17th-century community house with its richly-decorated interior is impressive evidence of the village's former wealth. The carvings are concentrated on the upper sections of the pillars and on the roof timbering; but the most magnificent, detailed carving is that on the doors of the three-part shrine over the entrance to the temple of the guardian spirit, located in an annex. This spirit, *Thai Ca*, or First Guardian Spirit, is identified as the golden turtle also worshipped in Co Loa. Here, it is symbolized by a throne guarded by two life-sized sentry figures in old Vietnamese dress on either side. The *dinh* festival is held from 20th-22nd of the first lunar month. The three-part **Nghe Tho Ha**, the temple to the guardian spirit without an assembly hall, is also included in the complex.

household crockery and clay figures as toys for children, but these were supplanted by plastic. The kilns have been shut down, and the remaining pottery fragments were used as building material. The village now practices another lucrative activity: pig breeding. Hundreds of these well-fed, grunting animals have virtually taken over the village. They lie on the roads and in the entrances to the courtyards, or root along the river banks. The only place they are chased away from is the market place. They're fattened up for the annual Tet festival, and reach record weights just before it.

The village extends to both sides of the river; there are a number of ferry crossings. You'll get a whole different perspective on the town by taking a boat trip on the river and watching the activity along its banks.

The **Chua Tho Ha** is separated from the *dinh* by a large open square where the pagoda festival and market are held. The statues were gradually stolen from the *chua* after 1954; today, the whole pantheon, and the Buddha, are new. All that remains of the originals are two grotto altars and two statues, Ong Duc, the guardian of the country, and Mother Mau.

The village of **Dong Ho** is one of many in the Delta, but its name is known to everyone in Vietnam. For generations, family businesses here have turned out *Thanh Tet*, New Year's pictures, to the tune of around 500,000 every year. They are also exported, in particular to former East Bloc countries and southern Europe. The motifs of the woodcuts (which measure 9.75 x 11.7 inches/25 x 30 cm) are always the same. They include such

*Above: Pig-farming is the main source of revenue in Tho Ha village, Ha Bac Province.
Right: River dikes in the Red River Delta are themselves transportation arteries.*

lucky figures as Tho, the white-haired old man who is the symbol of long life, and Lao Tse, riding on the black buffalo. Another standard feature is the lucky pig, a sign of prosperity; representations of legends and fables, such as the frog concert, the mouse wedding, or the man with two squabbling wives, are also recurring themes. The greetings and commentaries are usually in Chinese characters. During the Tet festival, every Vietnamese house is decorated with these pictures.

The most talented member of the family cuts the wooden printing block – a separate block is required for every color – and these blocks remain in the family's possession. The other members of the family share the rest of the work. The paper is handmade, dried and colored with natural dyes, which are mixed with pulverized mussel shells to produce a dull gleam. The dye mixture is a secret. Two weeks before the Tet festival, the work is finished and the families take a break until March. The village *chua* and memorial temple are also worth a visit.

The village of **Dong Ky** is one of the three Vietnamese villages where family businesses produce fireworks. These are let off at weddings, on birthdays, to celebrate the opening of businesses and the passing of exams, but especially at the Tet festival. Dong Ky specializes in giant fireworks. On the fourth day of the first lunar month, visitors come from all around to see a competition involving five selected rockets which are transported on carts to a special site. They are judged not only on size – 16-20 feet (5-6 m) is not unusual and some are 3-6.5 feet (1-2 m) in diameter – but also their decoration; they are adorned with the animal sign of the new year. Another criterion is the loudness of the explosion when they are fired.

HAI HUNG PROVINCE
On Con Son Mountain

Highway 18 and the railway run from Bac Ninh in Ha Bac Province through Hai Hung Province to Hong Gai, Haiphong and Ha Long. This isn't the fastest, but it's certainly the most attractive route from Hanoi to the Gulf of Bac Bo.

The hill country starts after Bac Ninh. In Vietnam, outstanding public figures who felt their duty was done often withdrew to the peace and quiet of their native villages or the solitude of monasteries, there to live as philosophers, poets or monks. The lonely mountain of **Con Son** is associated with many a famous name.

Den Kiep Bac in the Chi Linh district is named after the villages Kiep and Bac, which are now called **Phuc Yen** and **Duc Son**. They lie at the foot of the Dragon Mountains, which has a southern range, Nam Tao, and a northern one, Bac Tao, named after the star gods, companions of the king of the heavens, which symbolize north and south. Nam Tao keeps the book of births, Bac Tao the book of deaths. The mountains are popularly known as Duo Son, Healing Mountains.

Den Kiep Bac, near the village of Hung Son, is a memorial temple for General Tran Hung Dao, who defeated the Mongols and the Chinese Yuan Dynasty in the 13th century. In this remote area he prepared his army for battle, and it was here that he returned after victory. His temple dates back to the end of the 13th century and was rebuilt in the 19th century. The seven bronze statues on the main altar depict the general, his wife, his two daughters and his three generals. Separate altars were built for his four sons, also generals. Prior to 1945, the Den Kiep hosted Bac festivals, which were occasions of sorcery, magic, invocations and fortune-telling. The rites were conducted by *ba dong*, shamanistic priestesses. Prohibited in 1945, the festival has now been reintroduced and is held at the same time as that of the neighboring Con Son Pagoda, from the 16th to the 20th of the eighth lunar month.

Right: There are many limestone kilns on the road from Hanoi to Hai phong.

The **Chua Hon** (Chua Con Son), is 3 miles (5 km) away in the same district. The small *chua* with its upturned, curving roof was built in the 15th century on the site of a large complex of 83 rooms.

The first emperor of the Tran Dynasty, Tran Thai Tong, like his descendant Emperor Tran Nhan Tong, sometimes went to Con Son Mountain; and both finally withdrew to the nearby mountain Yen Tu. In the 15th century, Con Son Mountain became the refuge of the statesman and poet Nguyen Trai, who escaped to its solitude from the intrigues at court.

In the pagoda are statues of Nguyen Trai and the three patriarchs of the sects of the bamboo forests; the stele houses contain 14 stelae dating from the 17th century. Behind the pagoda is a spring: Nguyen Trai sat on its flat stones to write his poems describing the beautiful landscape. On the other side are 600 steps leading to the flat summit, which is known as the "chessboard of the gods." The temple festival is held from 16th-20th of the eighth lunar month.

Yen Tu Mountain (Bac Van Son), 9 miles (15 km) from the town of Uong Bi, is in Quang Ninh Province. Uong Bi is on Highways 18 and 10 and has a railway station. Yen Tu, 3,270 feet (1,000 m) high, is often covered with clouds in the winter, and cannot be climbed in the rainy season.

In 1237, Emperor Tran Thai Tong withdrew into the pagoda of Van Tu, having fled in horror from the cruelty of the first prime minister, Tran Thu Do, who wiped out the Ly Dynasty; in the pagoda, he wrote essays on meditative Buddhism. In 1299, Emperor Tran Nhan Tong, who had withdrawn to the Hermitage of the Sleeping Cloud on Yen Tu in 1297, after the victory over the Mongols, founded *Truc Lam*, the meditation sect of the bamboo forest, became its first patriarch, and called himself Hermit of the Bamboo Forest. He was followed by two other patriarchs who lived on Yen Tu.

After the emperor died, his son erected the burial stupa Pho Minh in the dynasty's native town, Nam Dinh, in Nam Ha Province. Subsequent emperors of the Tran Dynasty were buried on Yen Tu. In the 19th century, Emperor Minh Mang of the Nguyen Dynasty erected stelae at their graves.

Along the path to the summit are the **Chua Giai Oan** and the **Chua Lau Dong**. The **Chua Hoa Yen** (Chua Phu Van) was founded by the Ly Dynasty and is a memorial to the three patriarchs.

THANH PHO HAIPHONG –
Port and city-state

Highway 5, from Hanoi to Haiphong (65 miles/105 km) is the fastest route from the capital to the port; but there are also rail and air connections. The roads and bridges are to be repaired and extended, with some help from Taiwan, since they can no longer cope with the heavy traffic. In the future, the Hanoi, Haiphong and Halong Bay region is to become the focus of economic and industrial activity and tourism in the northern part of the country. Helping in this drive are a population of over 18 million people, valuable mineral resources, fertile agricultural land, and tourist attractions.

Hai Phong means "outpost by the sea," and was first mentioned in the first century. The city is located in the northeastern part of the Red River Delta where the hills begin, and, like Hanoi and Ho Chi Minh City, Thanh Pho Haiphong is a city-state. With an area of 586 square miles (1,503 sq. km) and more than 1.6 million inhabitants, it has a population density of around 2,500 inhabitants per square mile (960 per sq. km).

The inner city and harbor lie on the Cam, the Forbidden River. 16 rivers and tributaries run through the city; together, the Cam, Thai Binh, Bach Dang and several smaller rivers form an estuary. As a result of the alluvium that these rivers deposit, the harbor has to be dredged at regular intervals. In colonial times and

during the Franco-Viet Minh War and the Vietnam War, Haiphong played a key role as the largest harbor in north Vietnam and as a naval port. In 1872, a French expeditionary force landed in Haiphong to take the northern part of the country, and in 1955 members of the last expeditionary force in Vietnam left from the same place. During the Vietnam War, city, harbor and factories were bombed frequently and suffered heavy damage.

Visitors en route to Halong Bay seldom take the time to stop off in Haiphong. However, this busy city, with its active arts scene; the lakes and greenery of the surrounding countryside between the hills and the sea; the sea resort Do Son and the offshore islands, deserve more attention. In 1888, the French built a cement factory here, which was followed by factories producing machinery, glass and tobacco. Fish factories process

Above: Coal transport ship in Haiphong.
Right: Renovation of the famous Sat market, Haiphong.

the catches of the fishing fleet along the 58 miles (94 km) of coast. The city and its surrounding villages are well-known for marble and metal processing, basketwork, the production of woolen carpets, lacquer and inlay work, and souvenirs made of shells, tortoiseshell and coral. The village of **Bao Hai** has produced woodcarvings since the 17th century.

Sights in and around Haiphong

The **city center** consists of three districts: Hong Ban, Ngo Quyen and Le Chan. The harbor, streets and colonial-style buildings have the atmosphere of an oriental port. Early risers should look in on the fish market. In general, the city's markets, particularly the **Sat Market**, sell anything and everything which this city-state produces. In 1991, investors from Hong Kong helped to start a large project involving the creation of 430,400 square feet (40,000 sq. m) of space for a department store in a 5-story building. Three floors were earmarked for the Sat

Market, the two upper floors for a hotel. Three stories have been completed, but there has been a hold-up with the hotel part. In April, 1994, only 215,200 square feet (20,000 sq. m) of shops had been let.

The **Den** and **Nghe Le Chan**, a memorial and a guardian spirit temple on Hai Ba Trung Street in the Le Chan district, are dedicated to two female generals under the Trung sisters, the first national heroines of Vietnam (40-43 AD). Their abundant woodcarving makes them the most beautiful temples in the city center.

The **Dinh Hang Kenh** (Dinh Nhan Thong) and **Chua Du Hang** at Du Hang 121 are in the southern part of the same district, an area with many lakes bordering the hills of Trung Kenh. Inside the 13th-century *chua* are many statues and bells, while burial stupas dot the garden. Other religious buildings of interest are the **Chua Nguyet Quan** (Chua Dong Khe) in the district of Ngo Quyen, built between 1608 and 1705, and the **Chua Hai Ninh** (Chua Dong Thien) in Vien Nien village, founded by the Le Dynasty.

The coastal resort of **Do Son**, 13.5 miles (22 km) from the city center on a peninsula in the estuary, dates back to the colonial period. It extends along a ridge 2.5 miles (4 km) long called Cuu Long, Nine-Headed Dragon, because of its nine hills. On Ngoc Son Hill is the **Chua Truong Long**, dating from the 11th century, which was put up in place of an older stupa: its bricks were used to build the citadel of Tran Hai Duong.

On Doc Hill, the **Den Be Ba** is a memorial to a girl who was betrayed. With its long white beach, rows of palm trees, villas and good hotels, Do Son has an atmosphere all of its own. Its only drawback is that the sea is sometimes muddied by alluvium from the Rivers Cam and Thai Binh. There are also ambitious plans for Do Son. Along the coast, a planned stretch of two-level, graded road more than 1,200 yards long (1,100 m) and 25 feet (7.7 m) high is to ease the flow of traffic. By the end of 1994, it is to be used by 3,000 vehicles a day (at present 275 per day). An international tourist

113

and recreation center extending over an area of 110 acres (44 ha) of land and water is also to be completed by the end of 1995.

The village of **Trung Lap** in the district of Bao Vinh has an outstandingly beautiful building, the **Den Cuc Chuc**, which contains statues made of wood and clay, mostly of animals. The village festival attracts many visitors who come to watch the water buffalo fights, fireworks competitions, and especially the water puppet plays.

The **Cat Ba Archipelago** lies in Bai Tu Long Bay, shielding the harbor and city from the winds. It consists of the large island of Cat Ba (78 square miles/189 sq. km) and 366 smaller islands – some of them minute – plus isolated rocks, and includes among its attractions unspoilt beaches, caves and

Above: Sunset in the bay of Ha Long, Vietnam's loveliest coastal region. Right: a fishing-boat goes out for the day in Luc Hai, the Blue Sea.

grottos, and many different species of flora and fauna. On the island of Cat Ba, 50 miles (80 km) from Haiphong (12.4 miles/20 km from Do Son), 1,425 acres (570 ha) have been declared a national park. In places the island rises to a height of 654 feet (200 m); it also has a road. Motorboats cross to Cat Ba and some of the other islands and beaches; while the ferry ride to Halong Bay is an enjoyable and memorable trip.

QUANG NINH PROVINCE –
Halong Bay and the Blue Sea

Although this province is in the northeastern part of the country, it's easy to reach from the Delta. The route from Haiphong to Halong Bay (46 miles/75 km) involves two car ferry rides. It takes around 6 minutes to cross the River Cam, and around 10 to cross the Bach Dang; what takes time is waiting in line to board the ferries. The romantic scenery around the River **Bach Dang** with its steep limestone cliffs make this area a Halong Bay

in miniature. On this river the Vietnamese succeeded three times in destroying the Chinese fleet and checking their invasions. The first victor, in 938, was Ngo Quyen, who won independence for his country; in 981 it was Le Hoan, a Dinh Dynasty general, who defeated the forces of the Chinese Song Dynasty; and the royal prince and general of the Tran Dynasty, Tran Hung Dao, destroyed the fleet of the Chinese Yuan Dynasty in 1288. They all employed the same strategy, one commonly used in Vietnam: the Vietnamese forces in light sailing vessels lured their pursuers up the Bach Dang at high tide. The Chinese let themselves be distracted by skirmishes with the Vietnamese. At low tide, however, their heavy junks got tied up in ironwood rods which the Vietnamese had rammed into the river bed. The shallow Vietnamese boats and troops on shore then made short work of the immobilized enemy fleet.

The name of the bay, **Halong**, means Where the Dragon Descends to the Sea.

Legend goes that a dragon mother came down from the mountains with her children, armed with rocks, and killed a monster that had been frightening the people. The rocks remained in the sea as islands to commemorate the dragon battle.

More and more hotels are springing up around the bay. The natural harbor in Halong Bay can take ships of up to 30,000 G.R.T.; most of the ships which dock here are Japanese coal freighters. A contrast are the fishermen's junks, sails patched gray, red, and black, which go out at night with lighted lanterns. From the cliffs, there's a good view out over the bay's 585 square miles (1,500 sq. km), dotted with a couple of thousand islands and limestone rocks. If you see a typhoon, you won't soon forget it. Waves of up to 98 feet (30 m) have been recorded in the Gulf of Bac Bo.

A round trip through the islands offers constantly changing scenic vistas. Only 15 islands are inhabited year-round. Fishermen camp on some of the others during the fishing season, but most are inhabited

solely by hordes of apes or colonies of birds. Some of the islands and rocks are very close together, but no two are alike. Many have names derived from their bizarre shapes – Fighting Cocks, Turtle, Stone Fisherman, Sleeping Maiden – and with a little imagination, it's easy to think up a few more. And there are countless legends: stories of the beautiful girl who preferred loneliness and death to life with a rich, wicked man; of tigers; and of fairies who rewarded helpful fishermen with large catches.

Trees grow on some of the islands, while the rocks are bare or covered with scrub. The caves, of all sizes, are particularly interesting, and often have stalactites and stalagmites which sound softly, like bells, when touched. There are cranes on the island of **Bo Nau** (Cave of Birds); while the 654-foot-long (200 m) cave of the **Island of Luon** is large

Above: Ha Long Bay, Bo Nau, the Cave of Birds. Right: Coal carrier in the port of Hong Gai.

enough for boats to pass through. In the large caves on the island of **Hang Dau Co** (Gia Go), "Hiding Place of the Wooden Rods," General Tran Hung Dao is said to have hidden the ironwood rods before they were rammed into River Bach Dang. The caves are so large that there is room for a considerable number of people inside.

Hong Gai, the provincial capital, lies at the foot of a chalk cliff 3 miles (5 km) from the hotels on Halong Bay, and can be reached by ferry. Its more than 500,000 inhabitants work in the coal mines and the harbor, make souvenirs of shells and coral, or live as fishermen. Until the end of 1978, many members of the Chinese minority, Hoa, worked as miners or fishermen. They then went to China, but many have come back; others went on to the Philippines. Hong Gai still has *hoi quan*, Chinese temples with community houses. The fish market in the port offers 18 different types of fish from coastal waters and 20 deep-sea fish, as well as seaweed, coral and shellfish.

Luc Hai, Blue Sea, is the name of the ocean between Haiphong in the south and Kap Ngoc, Jade Cape, on the peninsula of Tra Co in the north, close to the Chinese border. Of the numerous islands off the coast, around 1,600 have names. Many have long, unspoilt white beaches and some have hills up to 1,300 feet (400 m) high, but none of them, whether large or small, has a freshwater spring or sufficient rainfall to give a supply of drinking water. If they were to be made habitable, the water problem would have to be solved first. Until then, there will be a limit to tourism and the mining of the existing mineral resources. Winters in Luc Hai are cool and misty and the sea is rough and gray during the northeast monsoon, but the thermometer drops to a few degrees above freezing for only a short time, and in the hot months the climate is all the more pleasant.

Three archipelagos and 600 islands lie off the shores of the aspiring district town of **Cam Pha**, in the hard coal basin 17 miles (28 km) north of Hong Gai. Shell-fish are bred in 500 lakes and ponds. Most of the mineral resources found on the islands are suitable for mining. The harbor Cai Rong is being extended. The **Den Cua Ong**, on a hilltop in the district of Cua Ong, was built for the second son of General Tran Hung Dao, who was also a famous general.

Highway 18 runs north along the coast to the Chinese border, affording many views of the sea and islands on the way.

High-quality anthracite is mined in the coal basin around Muong Duong. The mountain region of Quang Ninh Province is rich in iron ore, antimony, bauxite, mercury, kaolin and clay; while on the islands, gravel and sand are extracted for the production of crystal. Two harbors, Cua Ong and Cua Luc, take ships of up to 10,000 G.R.T.

Alluvial terraces have formed on the banks of the rivers; mangroves grow on the coast. Inland, in the hills, the woods have long since been felled, and only grass and bushes have grown in their place. In the mountainous part of the

117

province live ethnic minorities, the Nung and the Thai, while the coastal plains were settled by the Chinese minority, the Hoa, some of whose villages were abandoned when their inhabitants went to China in 1978.

The border town of **Hai Ninh** (Mong Gai) on Bac Luan is known for its pottery. The bridge here sees active border trading, not to say smuggling, which was interrupted by the punitive expedition of 1979, and was not resumed again until 1989. The sea resort of Tra Co lies on an elongated peninsula; its southern tip is washed by the clear green sea, and is therefore called Jade Cape. The 6 miles (10 km) of empty white beach form perhaps the most beautiful beach in the north, which can be well over 325 feet (100 m) wide, depending on the tides (along the coast of Bac Bo, these can run about 13 feet/4 m); but the infrastructure

Above: The simplest, most common way to irrigate a rice field. Right: Post office in Thai Binh Province.

does not yet meet the requirements of most foreign tourists.

THAI BINH PROVINCE AND THE KEO PAGODA

Highway 10 from Haiphong to Thai Binh has rough stretches and involves the use of several ferries. It is currently being extended, and a direct connection from Hanoi to Thai Binh has also been commenced. At present, the fastest route from Hanoi to Thai Binh is still via Highways 1 and 21 and the car ferry in Nam Dinh.

This province, with a capital of the same name, is the main source of rice in the south of the Red River Delta, and the richest province in northern Vietnam. With about 3,600 inhabitants per square mile (1,400 per sq. km), it is also the most densely populated. 68.5% of its gross product comes from agriculture. Other crops besides rice include sugar cane, vegetables, fruit, peanuts, soya beans, jute and rushes. The plain extends in an unbroken line only a few meters above sea level, and includes the lowest point in the country. Additional boosts to the region's prosperity are deposits of natural gas and oil. Artisan firms and small-scale industry are on the rise, producing mats and baskets for home use from jute and rushes, as well as wool rugs, silk and embroidery.

There is fishing on the rivers and the 31 miles (50 km) of coast, and the mangrove forests are ideal for fish and shellfish cultivation. Salt is extracted from the sea. There are also plans to develop holiday and bathing resorts on the long beaches for recreation and water sports.

The village of **Kho** is known for its traditional terra-cotta toys and religious figures, produced by family businesses. Some of the most popular lucky charms are figures of roosters; their morning crowing drives out evil spirits. The small figures are still sold at pagoda markets.

Chua Keo (Thanh Quang - Holy Light) in Vu Tu district in the village of **Duy Nhat** on River Nhi Ha, a tributary of the Duong, is one of the most beautiful pagodas in Vietnam (71 miles/115 km from Hanoi via Nam Dinh, Highways 1 and 21). After the car ferry over the River Duong in the town of Nam Dinh, a small road follows the top of the dike and turns off to the left after 9.3 miles (15 km); from there, it's about a mile (1.5 km) to the pagoda.

The **Chua Keo** complex was built in 1608 on 70 acres (28 ha) of land, replacing a small pagoda. Within the large walled complex are 16 buildings of various sizes, which you can see clearly from the dike. The finely-structured, three-storey wooden bell tower dominates all the other buildings, although behind them, because of its height (38 feet/11.5 m). A large *tam quan* triple gate in the outer wall leads into the complex. The middle gate dates from the 17th century, and features a finely carved pattern of clouds and dragons, dominated by a

sun with jagged rays. In the first courtyard is a half-moon lake. The next two groups of buildings are laid out in the shape of an H and consist of two rectangular buildings, the entrance hall and the main temple, which are connected by the almost square Hall of Incense. In the second courtyard, the *chua* is followed by a smaller memorial temple (*den*) in the same style.

The eaves of the entrance hall, *tien duong*, curve up sharply and are adorned at the corners with unicorns, symbols of cleverness and compassion. The ridgepole is crowned with dragons. In front of the hall, stelae at either side document the restorations. The pillars of the *tien duong* (and also those of the triple gate) rest on low stone pedestals shaped like lotus flowers, a design influenced by Cham art.

In the main temple, the large pantheon with its dully gleaming lacquered statues comes as something of a surprise. Most of the figures date from the 19th century, and only the Avaloketecvara in the second and the Quan Am in the third row

from the top have survived from the mid-17th century; their crowns feature the projecting floral decoration typical of this epoch. The Amitabha Buddha in the fourth row dates from the 18th century. The seated old man to the right of the altar with white hair and beard is Tho Dia, who protects the ground on which the pagoda stands. On the front of the altar to the left are the Emperor of the Heavens with his companions, the gods of the stars, who hold on their knees the book of births and the book of deaths.

Behind the *chua* is the **Den Minh Khong**, for a famous abbot at the time of the Ly Dynasty who promoted Buddhism and ultimately attained enlightenment. In the courtyard behind the memorial temple is the bell tower, a testimony to the skill and artistry of 18th-century woodcarvers. The roofed side galleries along the walls of the courtyard house the

Above: Textile workers in Nam Dinh, Nam Ha Province. Right: Chua and Thap Pho Minh near Nam Dinh.

large rowboats which are used for festival competitions, a tradition which has only been retained in a few temples. In the courtyard grow tall old Bo trees. Buddha received enlightenment under a Bo tree, and in Vietnam Bo trees are also a place where the spirits meet. The Keo pagoda has two festivals, one on the fourth day of the first lunar month and the main festival, when rowing competitions are held, on the 10th-16th days of the ninth lunar month.

In **Song Long** village in the district of Vo Thu, the **Chua Hoi** and the **Den Thuong** are worth a visit, as is the **Mieu Hai Thou** in the village of **Xuan Ha**.

NAM HA PROVINCE –
TRAN DYNASTY TEMPLES

Nam Dinh, capital of Nam Ha Province, was a textile center in colonial days, and whole sections of its streets are lined with colonial-style buildings. During the Vietnam War, part of the town and its industrial plant was destroyed by bombs, and the access roads were pitted with bomb craters. After 1975, its economy gradually recovered, and today its silk industry is once again exporting to France and Germany.

The **Chua Vong Cung** suffered the same fate as other buildings in the town. Located in the center of Nam Dinh, it provided Emperor Gia Long (1802-1820) with accommodation during inspections. It was damaged during the struggle for independence, and renovated from 1948-1950. Bombing raids on the town started in 1965, and in 1972 the *chua* was badly damaged and repaired. Since then, it has been the headquarters of the province's Buddhists. The kite market in Nam Dinh is worth a visit.

The **Temple of the Tran Dynasty** is 3 miles (5 km) from the town center set in the midst of rice fields. Archaeological findings, including crescent-shaped tiles typical of the 13th century and the remains of a 700-year old water conduit, indicate that this was the site of the hereditary seat of the Tran Dynasty, *Tuc Mac*, the Golden City. The Tran were a hard-working clan of fishermen who rose to become prosperous and powerful; given the fact that fishermen represent the lowest stratum of Vietnamese society, their achievement is all the more remarkable. When the Tran were drawn by marriage into the succession disputes of the Ly Dynasty, they were able to place a powerful private army at the disposal of the weak claimant to the throne, which drove the invading Khmer and Cham armies out of the country.

Chua Thap Pho Minh, surrounded by a wall and sheltered by tall trees, is visible from a long way off with its 69-foot (21 m), 13-story tower. The pagoda was built in 1262 by the Tran Dynasty and in 1305 Emperor Tran An Tong built the Thap Pho Minh with a lotus pond on either side for the ashes of his father, Emperor Tran Nhan Tong, who had founded the meditation sect of the bamboo forest

on Yen Tu Mountain. This tiled building rests on stone slabs; its tiles are decorated with dragon motifs. During the colonial era it was restored and covered with stucco. Some of the tiles have been found to be marked 1305, which was the year the emperor died.

A staircase flanked by two dragons leads to the temple. The original heads of these figures are in the Guimet Museum in Paris. The richly carved ironwood door is also a copy: the original is in the History Museum in Hanoi. The simple building is decorated with abundant carving. On its altar is a reclining Buddha, worshipped as Emperor Tran Nhan Tong, who attained enlightenment. The bell dates from 1792.

The **Den Tran**, the memorial temple for the Tran Dynasty, sits under a group of trees some 1,650 feet (500 m) away. Within the walls are two buildings, the temple dedicated to the dynasty and to the right, set back a little, the memorial for the royal prince General Tran Hung Dao, who defeated the Chinese Yuan Dy-

nasty in the 13th century. In the dynasty temple, the sword on the throne symbolizes the power of the Tran emperors. A large main altar is dedicated to the whole dynasty, with individual altars to the 14 rulers behind it. The statues of the rulers are not in chronological order: those who defeated the Mongols and the Yuan Dynasty have been placed at the center.

In the **Den Hung Dao** the main altar is dedicated to the General, who is represented with his brothers to his right and left. Behind him in the middle are the statues of his parents, with statues of his four sons on the sides. Of the three generals in front of his throne, the most important is Pham Ngu Dao, son of a poor family whose abilities were tested by Tran Hung Dao in a prolonged rivalry before he was elevated to be his comrade-in-arms.

Above: Co Le Pagoda near Nam Dinh; Thap Cun Pham on the back of a turtle. Right: Rice farmers near Ninh Binh.

Chua Co Le, founded by the Ly Dynasty, lies 12.5 miles (20 km) southeast of Nam Dinh on a fertile rice plain. It was built entirely without nails; and the bricks of its walls were also laid without mortar. The 69-foot (21.20 m) statue of the Buddha is one of the largest in Vietnam, and is supported inside by four copper pillars. The pedestal is decorated with the armorial emblems of the Tran Dynasty, lotus flowers and clouds. This statue was erected in honor of the monk Minh Khong, who did much to help spread Buddhism in Vietnam and attained enlightenment. Behind it, steps lead up to a platform where a glass case contains an 800-year old Buddha statue made of sandalwood.

In the garden in front of the temple is the **Thap Cuu Pham**, which rests on the back of a turtle. Legend has it that it was originally in the temple, but it began to grow, and the turtle carried it outside. Next to it is a bell cast in 1945; many of the faithful are said to have added their jewelry to the molten metal. The temple festival takes place on 13th-15th of the ninth lunar month.

The **Chua Keo** in Nam Ha Province, some 9.5 miles (15 km) from the Chua Co Le, is in no way comparable to its namesake on the other side of the River Duong in Thai Binh Province.

NINH BINH PROVINCE – OLD IMPERIAL CITY HOA LU

The provincial capital of the same name can be reached from Hanoi on Highway 1 (62 miles/100 km) and by rail on the Hanoi - Ho Chi Minh City line in 3 hours. Highway 10, which is currently being extended, links Ninh Binh with the provinces of Nam Ha, Thai Binh and the city of Haiphong.

Between the towns of Nam Dinh and Ninh Binh, Highway 10 crosses the railway bridge over the River Day. To the right, perched on a cliff above the river,

are the remains of a French fort. The Vietnamese call this spot the Gateway to the Old Kingdom, which lay in Hoa Lu. When her husband died, the wife of the Dinh Emperor waited on this cliff in the pavilion of Non Nuoc (Beautiful Breeze) for General Le Hoan to come back after his victory over the Chinese in order to offer him the throne.

The route to the **Royal City of Hoa Lu** passes through countryside known as the Dry Halong Bay. This region was once a gulf, which dried up, leaving only bizarre rocks. Hoa Lu was the capital of the Dinh Dynasty from 968-979 and of the Early Le Dynasty from 980-1009.

Ngo Quyen, who fought for the independence of Vietnam, did not succeed in uniting the twelve Vietnamese tribes, and after his death the twelve principalities threatened to split apart. Dinh Bo Linh, the son of a prefect from Hoa Lu, won the war of succession and as Emperor Dinh Tien Hoang ruled with a strong hand and tough laws. A pious Buddhist, he united the kingdom, which he called Dai-co-

Viet (Dai Viet after 1254), and in the remote valley of Hoa Lu established a uniform administration system for the whole country and a powerful army. He first had to secure his northern boundary by paying voluntary tributes to China, and it was only at the end of his rule that he sent General Le Hoan to fight against the Chinese Song Dynasty.

Dinh Tien Hoang and his sons fell victim to violent disputes over the succession to the throne, and only a six-year-old son survived. In 980, the court chose General Le Hoan, the Empress's favorite, to be the next ruler. As Emperor Le Dai Hanh he founded the Early Le Dynasty (980-1009), married the wife of his predecessor, and continued the latter's good work. The following Ly Dynasty was able to transfer its capital from the protection of the mountain valley to Thang Long (Hanoi) in the open countryside of the Delta.

The royal seat of Hoa Lu was protected on three sides by mountains and on the fourth by a river. Chinese travelers re-

ported that the palace lay at the foot of Ma Yen Hill (Horse Saddle Hill); the hall for imperial audiences was in front of it. The officials and military lived outside the royal city, and the army base was by the river.

To visitors familiar with the imperial court in China, the palace in Hoa Lu was a simple affair. In Vietnamese descriptions, however, it is a splendid construction with its red-lacquered, carved pillars and high roofs with colored tiles, fragments of which have been found. As a sign of royal power a cage and a bronze cauldron stood in front of the palace. Punishments were hard: the king's enemies were either put in the cage containing wild animals or thrown into the cauldron of boiling oil.

On the site of the former audience room are the memorial temples for Emperor Dinh Tien Hoang and General Le

Above: Landscape near Hoa Lu. Right: Den Dinh in Hoa Lu; statue of Emperor Dinh Tien Hoang.

Hoan. The road first passes the Den Le Hoan, then that of the emperor, the Den Dinh. It is the Vietnamese custom to visit the emperor's temple first.

Dating from the 11th century, the **Den Dinh** is surrounded by a wall. Inside, the dominant feature is the throne of the emperor, who is surrounded by his sons. During the temple festival the throne is placed on a stone pedestal in front of the building, with an incense burner in front of it. Offerings were placed on the slanting stone decorated with dragons, called the dragon board. 300 steps lead up Ma Yen Hill to the grave of the emperor, from which you can look out over the river valley.

The somewhat smaller **Den Le Hoan** memorial temple for the victorious general was not built until the 17th century by the Late Le Dynasty. At first it contained only the statue of the general; that of his wife, who had previously been empress of the Dinh Dynasty, was put up on the right-hand altar at a later date. To the left of the main altar is the statue of the son of the Le emperor and empress. In the opposite corner is an empty throne for the empress's daughter by her first marriage. The colorful festival of the two temples takes place on the third day of the third lunar month.

Tam Coc, Three Caves, is situated near the town of **Ninh Binh**. From the hamlet Dam Khe, which belongs to the village of Ninh Hai, small rowboats take visitors along the river. This river forms large pools between the high walls of rock, which can only be reached through the caves, each of which is around 330 feet (100 m) long. As the boat passes through the two last caves, neither entrance nor exit are visible for some minutes (take a flashlight). Apes and mountain goats populate the bizarre limestone cliffs; while rice and vegetables are cultivated on the river banks. In this remote spot there were fierce battles in 1953 during the struggle for independence.

The **Chua Bich Dong** is also in the hamlet of Dam Khe. Around 1.2 miles (2 km) from where the boats tie up is a steep cliff where, in 1228, two monks built pagodas in three caves. Just before the cliff, which is part of the Truong Yen Mountains, a 200-year-old stone bridge leads off to the left. The three pagodas are on different levels: the **Chua Ha** lies at the foot of the steep limestone cliff, the **Chua Truong** is halfway up and the **Chua Thuong** is on the summit. They were enlarged during the Le Dynasty in the 15th century, and the large bell also dates from this period. Further extensions were made from 1740-1781. On the stone wall in the Chua Truong are the words Bich Dong, written in large Chinese characters. On the left is a stele. The view from the top of the cliff is a payoff for the rather arduous ascent.

The **Nature Preserve of Cuc Phuong** is around 62 miles (100 km) from Hanoi. From Highway 1, a side road 25 miles long (40 km) leads to the edge of the

park. This primeval tropical forest was discovered in 1959. Extending over approximately 625,000 acres (25,000 ha), it is a veritable open-air museum of the flora and fauna of Vietnam, with around 200 species of trees and plants, including many medicinal herbs. 50 animal and bird species live here, as well as 36 different kinds of reptile. There are giant trees up to 32 feet (10 m) in circumference, and tall tree ferns; some species of tree are as much as 43 feet (70 m) high, while others have spreading branches that form a canopy 37 feet (60 m) in diameter. *Mo*, a local sweet wine, is distilled from apricots and wild honey.

The *Kim Giao* tree is only to be found in this primeval forest area. A legend recounts that the boy Kim and the girl Giao, whose families came from different social classes, didn't want to separate, and threw themselves into a river. Soon afterwards a tree grew on its banks which no one had ever seen before, and it was named the Kim Giao tree. Medicines were made from its leaves, flowers and

roots. Chopsticks from its wood are in demand all over the country. At the royal court, they are said to have been used to test for poison: when they came into contact with poisonous food they changed color.

The **Cathedral** in **Phat Diem** is around 74 miles (120 km) from Hanoi (11 miles/18 km from Ninh Binh). In the year 1891 the Vietnamese priest Sau built a cathedral in the village of Luu Phuong, which is today part of the town of Phat Diem. Like other Christian churches, the edifice is built of stone, but like other Vietnamese religious buildings it occupies almost 2.5 acres of land (1 hectare). It was badly damaged in the Vietnam War, but was subsequently restored.

Highway 1 leads on to Thanh Hoa Province, which is outside the Red River Delta and belongs to the northern part of the country.

Above: Jackfruit are nutritious and taste good.

VINH PHU PROVINCE
Accommodations (Area code: 84 21)
VIET TRI: *BUDGET:* **Song Lo-Hotel**, A 7 Street, Viet Tri, tel. 4 63 18; **Tam Dao Hotel**, in the spa of Tam Dao, tel. 463 06.
Tourist Information
Vinh Phu Tourist, 289, Quang Trung St., Viet Tri, tel. 2 45

HA TAY PROVINCE
Accommodations (Area code: 83 41)
HA DONG: *BUDGET:* **Song Nhue Hotel**, Ha Dong, tel. 2 43 40; **Huong Son Hotel**, District My Duc, tel. 46, near the Huong Pagoda. During the pagoda festival it's impossible to find accommodations, and the provisional accommodations are not recommended.
Getting There/Transportation
Buses toward the Huong Pagoda, 37 miles/60 km from Hanoi, to the town of Ben Duc; from there, continue by boat to the pagoda. Highway 2A leads to the three Red River Delta pagodas: Tay Phuong, Thay, & Tram Giang Pagoda. Round-trip day excursions, 56 miles/90 km.
Tourist Information
Ha Tay-Tourist, 24, Tran Hung Dao St., Ha Dong, tel. 2 43 09

HA BAC PROVINCE
Accommodations (Area code: 8 44 24)
BAC GIANG: **Bac Giang Hotel**, Nguyen Van Cu St., Bac Giang, tel. 5 43 05; **Song Thuong Hotel**, Xuong Giang St., **Bac Giang**, tel. 5 48 53: In Bac Ninh, there are a number of smaller hotels and guesthouses along Highway 1.
Tourist Information
Ha Bac-Tourist in Bac Giang.

HAI HUNG PROVINCE
Accommodations
HAI DUONG: a number of simple hotels.

HAI PHONG PROVINCE
Accommodations (Area code: 84 31)
HAI PHONG: *MODERATE:* **Hong Bang Hotel**, 64, Dien Bien Phu St., tel. 42353; **Hotel de Commerce**, 62 Dien Bien Phu St., tel. 47206. *BUDGET:* **Hoa Binh Hotel**, 104, Luong Khanh Thien St., tel. 423.
DO SON RESORT (12 miles/20 km from Hai Phong on the coast): *BUDGET:* **Hai Au Hotel**, 2, Khu, beach, tel. 6 12 21; **Hai Yen Hotel**, 1 Khu, beach, tel. 6 13 02.
Further Information
The Old Town is in the west of the city. The largest markets are the **Cho Tam Bac** (food and

produce) and **the Cho Sat** (all kinds of products). **The museum** (Bao Tang Hai Phong) is located in a building from the colonial period on Dien Bien Phu St.; **international bank**, 4, Nguyen Tri Phuong Str; **main post office**, 3, Nguyen Phuong St., open daily 7 am - 9 pm; **opera**, Luong Khanh Thien St.; **library**, Dien Bien Phu, corner Minh Khai St.; **hospital**, on Hai Ba Trung St.

Getting There/Transportation
Ferries of the **Binh ferry line** run to Hong Gai on Ha Long Bay (46 miles/75 km) and to the island of Cat Ba (15 miles/25 km).

The **train station** is on Luong Khanh Thien St. The **airport** Cat Ba is 4 miles/7 km out of town in the direction of Do Son; **Vietnam Airlines** city office, 12, Tran Quang Khai - corner of Minh Khai St., tel. 4 76 68.

The **bus station** is opposite the opera on the corner of Nguyen Duc Canh and Tran Phu St.

Tourist Information
Hai Phong-Tourist, 15, Le Dai Hanh St., tel. 4 29 89; **Unitour**, 39 Tran Quang Khai, tel. 4 22 88;

It's about 12 miles/20 km to **Do Son**, the bathing beach of Haiphong. Buses run to the bus station on Lach Tray St. In the district of **Vinh Bao**, 19 miles/30 km south of the city center, is the Dinh Cung Chuc. Don't miss the water puppet shows and the water-buffalo fights held in the village of Trung Lap during the Tet and Dinh festivals.

QUANG NINH PROVINCE
Accommodations (Area code: 84 33)
HA LONG BAY: *MODERATE:* **Ha Long 1 Hotel**, Bai Chay St., tel. 4 63 21; **Quang Ninh Post Office Hotel**, Bai Chay St., tel. 4 62 05; **Vuon Dao Hotel**, Bai Chay St., tel. 4 64 27; *BUDGET:* **Ha Long 2 Hotel**, Bai Chay St., tel. 4 6321; **Ha Long 3 Hotel**, Bai Chay St., tel. 46321.

Further Information
The **main post office** is located in Quang Ninh Hotel.

The **marketplace, ferry harbor** and **bus station** are on the shore road. At the north end of this, there's a ferry across to the capital, Hong Gai.

Getting There / Transportation
Bus station, regional and long-distance buses: reserve ahead! Ferries run over to Hai Phong (3 hours). The tourist office can book round-trip excursions through the bay, which last around 3-4 hours if you visit several islands and caves, and stop off for a swim (bring swimming things and a flashlight). The fishing-boats from the junk harbor also run to the islands in the bay. All traffic northward, including ferries and buses, leaves from Hong Gai.

Tourist Information
Quang Ninh-Tourist, Bai Chay St., tel. 46321
Accommodations
HONG GAI: *BUDGET:* **Hai An Hotel**, Khai San St. **Hong Ngoc Hotel**, 36, Le Thanh Tong, tel. 2 63 69

Getting There / Transportation
From Hong Gai, boats run along the coast through the islands and archipelagoes up to Hai Ninh (Mong Cai) on the Chinese border and the bathing resort of Tra Co, which hasn't yet been opened up to tourism, a total distance of around 62 miles/100 km. All the islands have wonderful beaches, but as of yet no boat connections or accommodations.

THAI BINH PROVINCE
Accommodations (Area code: 84 36)
THAI BINH: Huu Nghi Hotel, Ly Bon St., tel. 7 89; **Dong Chau Hotel**, on the beach of Dong Chau, 7 miles/12 km from Thai Binh.

Tourist Information
Thai Binh-Tourist, Ly Bon St., in the Huu Nghi Hotel, tel. 2 70

NAM HA PROVINCE
Accommodations
NAM DINH: *BUDGET:* **Giao Te Hotel**, Han Thuyen St., tel. 4 93 88.

Tourist Information
Nam Ha-Tourist, 115 Nguyen Du St, tel. 49439.

NINH BINH PROVINCE
Accommodations (Area code: 84 35)
NINH BINH: Ninh Binh Hotel, 2 Tran Hung Dao, tel. 71337; **Hoa Lu**, 39 Hoa Lu St., tel. 71217.

Getting There / Transportation
Train station, Le Dai Hanh St., on the Hanoi - Ho Chi Minh City Line.

Bus station, express and regional buses near the train station at the Lim Bridge.

Further Information
Post office on Tran Hung Dao; no money exchange.

Hoa Lu with a memorial temple and small museum, 7 miles/12 km. From here, there are river trips with visits to grottoes, lasting some 3 hours; **Tam Coc**, three grottoes, 2.5 miles/4 km away. Boat ride through the grottoes takes about 2 hours (bring a flashlight); from here to **Chua Bich Dong**, three cliff caves, and **Chua Linh Coc** 1.5 miles/2.5 km.

Cu Phuong National Park (primeval jungle), 27 miles/44 km from Ninh Binh. Accommodations in hotel or bungalows.

TRUNG BO
Central Vietnam

FROM THE RED RIVER DELTA
TO CLOUD PASS
FROM CLOUD PASS TO THE
MEKONG DELTA
THE COUNTRY OF THE CHAM
SOUTHERN HIGHLANDS

FROM THE RED RIVER DELTA
TO CLOUD PASS

In the colonial period, the middle part of the country, Central Vietnam, was called An Nam. The Chinese used this term, which means Liberated South, after 679 for the General Protectorate of An Nam, the Red River Delta and the northern coast of Trung Bo. In the 14th century, the Vietnamese used "An Nam" to refer to the territory south of the Ngang pass, conquered by the Cham. Today, the central part of the country is called Trung Bo, and you hardly encounter the name An Nam at all.

Northern Trung Bo extends from Thanh Hoa Province at the southern edge of the Red River Delta to Cloud Pass.

During the Chinese dominion over the Red River Delta, this area was a battleground between the Giao Chi and Champa, and a border between Chinese and Indian culture. To the south, Trung Bo extends from Quang Nam - Dan Nang Province at Cloud Pass down to Binh Thuan Province at the northern edge of the Mekong Delta. The mountains here are known as the Southern Highlands.

Preceding pages: Fishing port on the Yatran River, Nha Trang. Left: Fruit at the Han River Market, Da Nang.

Vietnam has been compared to the yoke which its peasants use to bear their burdens. In this analogy, Trung Bo is the long thin bamboo rod on which hang the two laden rice-baskets of the Red River Delta and the Mekong Delta. Dominating the landscape are the mountains to the west and the section of the Pacific known as the China Sea, which the Vietnamese call simply East Sea.

The mountains up to the river Ca in Nghe An Province are foothills of the high mountains to the northwest. South of the Ca, the Truong Son extend nearly 620 miles (1,000 km) from north to south, reaching heights of between 3,000 and 6,500 feet (1,000-2,000 m). In the north, they're comprised of crystalline stone; to the south, chalk and sandstone are overlaid with basalt in many places. They fall off steeply to the east and have the effect of a separate chain of mountains; thus, they're also known as *Giang Man*, Hanging Cliff. In fact, however, this is not one mountain chain, but several, with spurs extending eastward in several places, forming a barrier and falling sharply into the sea. The mountains also serve as a climactic barrier, blocking off the cold north wind from the area. From late summer into the autumn, the coast down to Nha Trang, in the south, is exposed to typhoons. On the eastern cliff

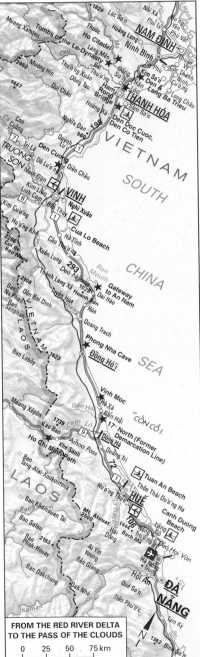

**FROM THE RED RIVER DELTA
TO THE PASS OF THE CLOUDS**

0   25   50   75km

of the Truong Son, where the monsoons fall, grows lush tropical rain forest. To the west, the mountain slopes gently down to the highlands of Laos. The highlands lie between deep gorges; the border with Laos runs along the summit.

The coast here is one of the loveliest in all Asia, generally undeveloped, with clear, unpolluted waves breaking gently on its shore. In Central Vietnam, tides run about 3-6 feet (1-2 m); the salt content of the sea water is 34%, less along the coast and around river deltas. The coastline itself is varied; steep cliffs alternate with lagoons, offshore islands, rocky crags, and long, empty beaches of white sand.

In Trung Bo, wooded heights are the dominant feature of the landscape. These are sparsely populated with members of the Muong, Thai, Dao, Meo, Van Khieu, Ta Ku, Ka Tu, and other minorities. The population of the hills and plains is largely Vietnamese; around Hue and to the South, there are also a number of Cham. Apart from a few unfertile patches, the plains see the cultivation of rice, sugar-cane, corn, soy beans, peanuts, and sweet potatoes.

On the coast and along the rivers, people both catch and breed fish. In areas, salt is filtered from the sea water. The mountains, on the other hand, produce wood, herbs, coffee, tea, and spices; and contain a wealth of natural resources such as chromium, manganese, apatite, iron, zinc, phosphates, and gold. In some areas, the sand of the dunes is used in the manufacture of glass.

THANH HOA PROVINCE

Highway 1 and the railway line from Hanoi to Ho Chi Minh City both follow the line of the coast. While the road crosses over passes through foothills of the Truong Son, the train frequently resorts to tunnels to bypass the heights. The main attraction of this part of the country are its scenic beauties, but it's also full of

memories of battles and resistance to the Cham and the war of independence against the French and Americans. The Song (river) Ma, 237 miles (382 km) long, and the Song Chu form a delta and, together with 20 other rivers large and small, irrigate the province.

Ceramics have been manufactured in Thanh Hoa since the Neolithic period. There were famous kilns here, and artists from the region were even summoned to the royal court in Thang Long. Until the end of the 14th century, Vietnamese rulers focused their care and attention on their native territory, the Red River Delta. When the Chinese controlled Gioa Chi Province, Cuu Chau was a border province and an arena of battle against the Champa Empire. From 549 on, it was known as Chau Ai, and later, under the Tran Dynasty, province and capital were again rechristened, receiving the name Thanh Hoa. But these were not given

Above: Peasants and merchants carry loads on yokes across their shoulders, quan ganh.

equality with the delta until the beginning of the 15th century, under the dynasty of the Ho, Le, and Nguyen, who came from Thanh Hoa themselves.

Halfway between Ninh Binh and the province's capital, Thanh Hoa, on Highway 1, in the Hau Loc district, on the left side of the road, is the village of **Phu Dien**. Atop the Nui Voi, Elephant Hill, stands **Den Ba Trieu**, a memorial temple for Trieu Au, a national heroine who lived in the 3rd century. When her brother fell in battle in the year 248, the 25-year-old gentlewoman from Cuu Chau led the army against the Chinese, riding in atop a fighting elephant in a palanquin of gold. After her defeat, she killed herself; her grave lies near the temple. Not long ago, a bronze sword dating from the Dong Son epoch was found atop the hill, as well.

The Ham Rong Bridge, or Dragon's Jaw (*rong* is an old term for dragon) leads across the river Ma. Not far from the city of Thanh Hoa, it spans the river, which swells to a torrent in the rainy season,

divided himself in two to help both the people on land and the fishermen at sea. At the end of the chain of mountains is the Den Co Tien, a temple to a goddess, which commands a panoramic view of the area. The rocky island of Trong Mai is associated with a legend about a man and a woman who didn't want to part, and died together in a storm.

On the mountain of Do, the village of Dong Son lies 5 miles (8 km) west of Thanh Ho on the road to the Le graves in the Ma river valley. Between 1924 and 1930, and again from 1935-1939, French researchers from the École Française de l'Extrème Orient in Hanoi excavated here to investigate Bronze-Age culture in Southeast Asia, soon dubbed Dong Son culture because of the wealth of finds at the site. Today, the site is no longer being excavated, but artifacts and objects from it are displayed in museums in Hanoi, Ho Chi Minh City, and Paris.

Located about 25 miles (40 km) north-west of Thanh Hoa, the Le Dynasty graves lie in a lovely wooded area near the village of Lam Son in the Tho Xuan district. This village is the birthplace of the first emperor of the Le dynasty, Le Loi, son of a landowner, who drove the Chinese Ming dynasty out of Dai Viet in 1427. The graves, laid out on the model of Chinese imperial graves, demonstrate Vietnamese grave architecture of the 15th - 17th centuries, but are in poor condition. Best preserved is the grave of the first Le emperor, reached through a more recent gate behind a canal. This large complex is surrounded by a wall. On the west side of a lake is the **Vinh Lang Stele**, dating from 1433, bearing a proclamation of victory over the Ming dynasty written by the statesman, strategist and poet Nguyen Trai, an ally of Le Loi. All that remain of the memorial temple today are the foundation walls and a statue of the Emperor from 1522. Leading up to the Emperor's grave hill, surrounded by walls about 3 feet (1 m) high,

from the cliff of Ngoc to the cliff of Rong. In 1904, the French built a bridge here 523 feet (160 m) long. Between 1945 and 1954, this was badly damaged, necessitating a course of renovation in 1964. In the Vietnam War, it played an important role for supply lines to the south, and after 1964 it was attacked more than 100 times by the American air force, defended by the Vietnamese, and finally destroyed altogether in 1972. In 1973, it had to be rebuilt a third time. The city of Thanh Hoa, as well, was badly damaged in the war, and later rebuilt.

The seaside resort of Sam Son, 10 miles (16 km) east of Thanh Hoa in the district of Xuong Quang, bears the name of the coastal mountains which form the southern border of 9 miles (15 km) of white, palm-shaded beach. Atop the mountains, the temple of **Den Doc Cuoc** is dedicated to a one-legged divinity who

Above: Heavily-laden buses traverse the country. Right: Farmers drying rice on Highway 1.

is a spirit avenue lined with statues of guards. Eleven other graves nearby are laid out on a similar pattern, but are smaller and in far worse condition.

The **Ho Citadel**, with the palace of the Ho Dynasty, lay 19 miles (30 km) north of the Le graves in Vinh Loc district, between the rivers Ma and Buoi. When attack from the Ming Dynasty seemed imminent in 1397, the regent Quy Ly had the city of Tay Do (Western Capital) built in a matter of months in the shelter of the mountains. In 1398, he forced the Tran Emperor to move from Thang Long, which he called Dong Do (Eastern Capital), to Tay Do; and he founded the Ho Dynasty in 1400, removing the last few Tran heirs from his path with remarkable cruelty. His reforms were good, but came too late. The aristocracy, mandarins and common people refused to follow him on the grounds that his reign was not legal. He had already surrendered the capital when the Ming Dynasty invaded the country. In 1407, the citadel fell, and the Ho Dynasty was at an end.

All fortifications in Vietnam were built of earth or tile. Because of the need for haste, however, Ho Quy Ly had his citadel built of stone blocks, huge boulders up to 20 feet (6 m) long, 5.5 feet (1.7 m) high, and 4 feet (1.2 m) wide, weighing up to 16 tons. The walls were 16 feet (5 m) high and 10 feet (3 m) thick. Not until the 18th century were the walls breached, when the troops of Tay Son completely destroyed walls and palace, leaving only stones, the ruins of a gate, and a few sculptures of animals to be seen today. The statues are ornamented with a floral pattern reminiscent of the Dai Lai style. Inside the citadel, the space between the foundation walls of the palace was used for growing rice. From here, you can see all the way to the mountain Nui Noi (451 ft/138 m), 10.5 miles (17 km) away.

NGHE AN AND HA TINH PROVINCES

The provinces south of Thanh Hoa are among the poorest in Vietnam. In the val-

ley of the Song Ca, Highway 7 runs to Laos; Highway 8 leads from Vinh to Laos. After 1975, these roads were often the only link between the Communist, landlocked country of Laos and the sea. Since then, Laos has resumed diplomatic relations with its neighbor beyond the Mekong, Thailand, and these roads have diminished in importance. The Laos border, however, is still not open to tourists.

Winters here are cold, and the salty sea air chaps and cracks the skin of the local peasants. The people, especially those in Ha Tinh, are poor, and rely on secondary jobs to survive, making pots and dishes or breeding silkworms. Nghe An, Vietnam's third-largest province, is called the province of scholars and teachers. It's said that students there study by the light of glowworms because they're too poor to buy candles. It's also known as a homeland of strategists and revolution-

Above: The larva spins its cocoon from silken threads. Right: The train from Hanoi to Ho Chi Minh City.

aries, Ho Chi Minh among them. People from this province are known for being industrious, ambitious, and unpretentious, and are not very well liked, especially in Hanoi. In bygone days, their zeal and stubbornness enabled them to reach high court office; today, they hold similar positions in political administrations.

The region has been a battlefield from time immemorial, from conflicts with the Champa Empire to the Vietnam War, when the 17th parallel marked the border between North and South Vietnam. Cities, roads and bridges were destroyed; you can still see traces of the damage.

Den Cuong, 18.5 miles (30 km) north of the provincial capital, Vinh, was built in the 3rd century BC for Emperor An Duong of the Au Lac Empire. Legend has it that he ended his flight at this site. To the left of Highway 1, a steep stairway leads up to this temple, founded in the 10th century by the Ly Dynasty; today's building, however, dates from the 19th century. Like many Nguyen Dynasty temples, it's decorated Chinese-style,

with paintings on the inner walls. Few of the statues have survived.

Vinh, the provincial capital, was expanded into an industrial city during the colonial period, receiving such amenities as a power plant. During the war of independence, it was a center of resistance, and was thus heavily damaged. Patched up again, it was destroyed anew in the Vietnam War. After 1975, the German Democratic Republic got the electricity, water works and sewers going again. The city is still growing, and the maintenance systems, harbor, airport, and train station are to be expanded or rebuilt by the year 2000. Vinh is known for its theater troupes or singing companies, which often go on tour; try to catch a performance when you're in town.

The beach of **Cua Lo**, 12 miles (20 km) from Vinh, has a lot of white sand but no real tourist facilities to date. In summer, the fishermen catch around 20 different kinds of fish in the offshore waters; in winter, they voyage out to the warmer deep-sea regions. Fish factories process a portion of the catch into fish sauce, *nuoc mam*, which is a part of every Vietnamese meal. There are many different kinds; the *nuoc mam* from Vinh is one of the most popular. The fish are put up in earthenware vessels, salted, and fermented. This process results in a sauce which is then bottled.

In the village of **Chua** (Hoang Tri), 12 miles (20 km) west of Vinh, Ho Chi Minh was born; and he spent his early years in the neighboring village of **Kim Lien** (Sen). Both villages now sport memorial plaques. They sit in the valley of the Lam, the Blue River, as the Ca is known in the region near its delta.

Den Mai Tuc Loan, in the district of Nam Dao west of Highway 8, was built for the chieftain of the Muong minority, a Vietnamese national hero who fought against the Chinese Tang Dynasty in the 8th century. Some ruins remain of his fortress **Hoa Chau**. On the mountain Ru Thanh, the **Den Le Loi**, commemorating the 15th-century freedom fighter, celebrates the province's largest festival

every twelve years. On this mountain, Le Loi tested out the strategy of mountain paths, a wartime tactic with which the Vietnamese have been successful even into the 20th century. Southeast of Vinh in the district of Nghi Xoan, the **Den Nguyen Du** commemorates the poet Nguyen Du (1765-1820), who, at the court in Hue, wrote the verse novel *Kim Van Kieu*, paving the way for modern Vietnamese literature. His works have been translated into many languages and are even known in Europe.

The province's traditional festivals are often linked with boat competitions. Asking for rain and good harvests, the long rowboats move in counterclockwise circles, following the course of the sun, while drums imitate the roll of thunder.

Ha Tinh, capital of the province of the same name, the poorest of the coastal provinces, was virtually destroyed in the war of 1954. All the pagoda statues which could be rescued were brought to **Chua Hop Tu** (Chua Vo Mieu) in the district Nam Ha on the Thanh Dong road.

In the south of Ha Tinh Province, the **Hoanh Son**, an eastern spur of the Truong Son, form a barrier 3,335 feet (1,020 m) high. Sloping sharply down to the sea, it acts as a windbreak for the south. Highway 1 leads over **Deo Ngang** pass, which the Vietnamese call the Gate to An Nam. When the Cham were forcing their way south in the 13th century, An Nam (Liberated South) lay before them. At the top of the pass, a milestone lists distances: it's 136 miles/219 km to Hue, 369 miles and 124 miles (595 and 200 km) to the Chinese borders. A winding road leads 6 miles (10 km) to the plains.

QUANG BINH AND QUANG TRI PROVINCES

Mieu Ong and **Dinh Chan Duong**, the Memorial for a Worthy Gentleman, was

Above: Hien Luong Bridge over the river Ben Hai, at the 17th parallel (border between North and South Vietnam, 1954-1975). Right: Grave, Ho Chi Minh Trail.

built by the villagers of **Canh Duong** at the mouth of the Ron river for a whale that had protected the village. Later, this whale was brought into the temple in the village *dinh* as a guardian spirit.

Where the river Giang breaks through the limestone mountains, north of the city of Dong Hoi, there are caves running for about a mile (1.5 km) at the foot of the mountains. Notable among these is the cave of **Phong Nha** (bring a flashlight).

Dong Hoi, capital of Quang Binh Province, was destroyed in the Vietnam War and has since been rebuilt. It bears the name of its fortification wall, Dong Hoi, hotly contested in the 17th-century civil wars. The river Song Giang forms the border between north and south; a bit south of the city, it's never been spanned by a bridge. Today, there are often long lines waiting to get on the car ferry.

The narrowest point of the country, which is not marked, lies near Dong Hoi and is – statistics vary – between 28 and 32 miles (45 and 52 km) wide.

The 1954 Geneva Conference set the river of Ben Hai as the provisional border between North and South Vietnam, and it remained thus until 1975. Crossing the river is the new **Hien Luong Bridge**, 582 feet (178 m) long; the river itself flows from its source in the Truong Son into the East Sea.

Until 1975, **Quang Tri Province**, with its capital **Dong Ha**, belonged to South Vietnam, and saw heavy fighting and resistance. The **Citadel of Quang Tri**, in the village Tha Ca Hoa, was built in 1824 by Emperor Minh Mang of the Nguyen Dynasty. Its wall is nearly 3 miles (5 km) long, and was later reinforced with a wall of brick. In 1972, the citadel was heavily damaged in a bombing attack.

Vinh Moc, the underground village, lies on the coast in the district of Ben Hai. In the Vietnam War, it became a symbol of resistance. Between the villages of Vinh An and Thua Luat there was once a border marker (*moc*) on a bay (*vinh*); thus

the little fishing village, with about 1,000 residents, was called Vinh Moc. It suffered under constant bombardments from the American air force, as it lay at a strategically important point as a link to the island group of Con Co, from which supplies were routed to the south. Some 5,200 cubic yards (4,000 cu. m) of earth were shifted to create a system of tunnels. At first these were 10-16 feet, then 16-32 feet deep (3-5/5-10 m); finally, the whole village of Vinh Moc was laid under the earth. People worked day and night for 600 days while a rain of bombs fell all around them. 17 children were born in the underground village. Huge amounts of ammunition and food could be brought over to the islands and transported, from there, farther south. Today, you can visit the tunnels (bring a flashlight).

By **Dong Ha**, 56 miles (90 km) north of Hue, the Americans installed an impassable electric barrier, the McNamara Line. Supply lines to the south had to be moved across the border into Laos and Cambodia. Thus, the **Ho Chi Minh Trail** was born. People, cars, weapons, ammunition and equipment were transported under constant bombardment along this network of paths through forests and hills, 12,400 miles (20,000 km) long.

From Dong Ha, Highway 9, built by the Americans, leads through the **Cam Lo** valley to southern Laos. The border town is **Lao Bao** (46.5 miles/75 km); but the Laos border is not open to tourists. The mountain regions around Cam Lo are home to the Van Kieu, Ka Tu and Bruus minorities, who live in pile dwellings and cultivate spices, coffee, tea and fruit. There are still traces of napalm bombing and chemical weapons; a monument commemorates the war. About 7 miles (12 km) further on, a side road about 2 miles (3 km) long leads to the former American base, of which only rubble remains. Further along Highway 9, you can see the Rock Pile, an observation tower. The **Dak Krang Bridge** (31 miles/50 km) was rebuilt with help from Cuba. Behind it begins the Ho Chi Minh Trail, which can only be made out today with difficulty.

Behind the Aihoa Pass (40 miles/65 km) is **Khe Sanh**. You need a permit to visit the border territories around this town. From Aihoa, there's a direct road to Hue (38 miles/62 km). Van Kieu, Pa Ko and Ta O dwell in the highlands. The French laid out extensive coffee plantations on this plateau. The Americans built up a strong foothold here. In 1968, they experienced the same fate here that Dien Ben Phu had in 1954; the Vietnamese mountain path strategy, tested by Le Loi in the 15th century on the mountain of Ru Thanh, proved its worth once again. Long preparations were required to transport weapons into the mountains above the fortress. The area around Khe Sanh was ceaselessly carpet-bombed by the

Americans. 40,000 Vietnamese fought against them for 75 days, from January to March of 1968, before Khe Sanh fell. In Hue and other areas of the front, as well, the Tet Offensive (New Year's 1968) demonstrated to the Americans the futility of the Vietnam War. Bombings continued until 1972, but the war was increasingly left to the Vietnamese, and peace negotiations were begun in Paris.

HUE – THE LAST IMPERIAL CITY

Topography and History

Hue (Phu Xuan), capital of Thua Thien - Hue Province, is 405 miles (654 km) from Hanoi and 667 miles (1,076 km) from Ho Chi Minh City, located on Highway 1 and the railway line from Hanoi to Ho Chi Minh City.

The city of Hue lies in the lovely countryside of the Huong Giang, the Perfume River. In the north, like a defensive wall, is the mountain **Ngu Binh**. From this rise, about 3 miles (5 km) out of town, you can see over the city and river to the white beach of Thuan An on the ocean – making it well worth a visit at any time of year or day. It's loveliest when the mists rise from the valley at dawn, or around sunset. About a mile away (2 km) is the hill of **Ngam Muc** (Beautiful View).

The source of the **Huong Giang** is some 37 miles (60 km) away in the Truong Son, where aromatic wild ginseng grows. There are two source rivers: the longer Ta Trach, which forms no fewer than 50 rapids and waterfalls before the point near Huong Phu where it joins the Huu Trach, which falls down fourteen steps, and becomes the Huong Giang. From Hue, it flows another 11 miles (18 km) before reaching the funnel-shaped mouth of the Thuan An, taking in the river Bo along the way. Boat rides along the Huong Giang or Bo are quite rewarding.

Right: Fisherman on the Perfume River, Huong Giang, in Hue.

Hue is closely linked with the history of the Nguyen. As lords from 1667-1775, and as Emperors from 1804-1945, they had a decisive effect on the life of the city. In 1593 two families of aristocrats, Trinh and Nguyen, reinstated the toppled Le Dynasty. Den Trinh managed to gather for himself the reins of power in Thang Long. At the end of the 16th century, the Nguyens tried, as governors, to create a sphere of influence in the south. Fifty years of civil war (1627-1673) between north and south ended with a *de facto* separation of the regions of influence along the river Giang at Dong Hoi. But Trinh and Nguyen had learned from history that usurpers in Vietnam were doomed to fail, as the people always followed the rightful ruler, who was thought to have a mandate from Heaven. As feudal lords, they had the power of potentates, but reigned in the name of the Le emperors. Dai Viet remained nominally a country. The Nguyen had their first seat as governors of Thuan Hoa Province in Ai Tu, north of Quang Tri. In

1520, they extended their rule across Cloud Pass and moved to Tra Bot; in 1620, to Phuoc Yen, 9 miles (15 km) north of Hue on the river Bo; and in 1634 to Kim Long, a village some 2 miles (3 km) west of today's citadel. In 1687, they moved their palace to Hue; but this was destroyed by the Trinh lords in 1775, and the Nguyen clan was obliterated. Only the non-rightful emperors and the rightful heir, Nguyen Anh, were able to flee to the Mekong Delta. From 1789-1801, the Tay Son dynasty ruled from Hue. In 1802, Nguyen Anh managed, as Emperor Gia Long, to found the last Vietnamese royal dynasty after 20 years of struggle, and moved the capital from Thang Long (Hanoi) to Phu Xuan.

City of Tradition

The royal court was oriented on the model of the Imperial Court in China. Architecture, administration and legislation followed the Confucian tradition; and the Emperors were scholars of Con-

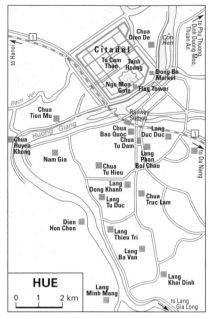

HUE

0   1   2 km

fucianism. Mandarins dictated court procedures; and Vietnamese court traditions also continued to develop. Artisans and artists from the old capital now worked in Hue, creating enamel and silk paintings, fine ceramics, and the famous blue Hue porcelain. Music, theater, poetry and literature saw a new flowering. The emperors commissioned exhaustive works of history and geography; they also had legends and folk poetry, customs and traditions brought to paper. The National Academy was moved from Thang Long to Hue; tests in classical literature were held there until 1918. The Nguyen encouraged Buddhism, as well, summoning Chinese monks to the country, building pagodas and placing them under royal protection.

During the colonial period, when it was no longer possible to prevent contact with Europe, Hue clung all the more firmly to its old values. Its rulers were shocked by the first great victories of the

Right: At Dong Ba Market in Hue's old city.

missionaries. Although they suspected that an isolationist policy had its disadvantages, they maintained their old traditions stubbornly, with tranquil dignity. With the old royal city of Thang Long (Hanoi), the last Vietnamese royal palace was also lost. In the war of independence (1954) and the Vietnam War (1968), citadel and royal city, filled with irreplaceable treasures, were reduced to ashes. Today, only the ruins are left as a reminder of the former splendor and beauty, sensitivity and extent of a culture which took centuries to develop.

Anything that has remained also suffered after 1945 from the incomprehension of the country's new rulers, who until the late 1980s tried to abolish art and culture, labelling them products of a feudal system. Nonetheless, some tradition remained in Hue which was lost in other areas. Behind the large gardens, mighty trees, and old houses of the neighborhood of **Gia Hoa**, the spirit and atmosphere of old Hue return to life. Both in the city and the neighboring villages, there are small altars in front of the houses where people make sacrifices to their ancestors. On the country roads small offerings are laid out on stones for the *ma*, or restless spirits. Yet progress has not been kept out of Hue altogether.

Modern Hue

More than 300,000 people live on the 132.5 square miles (340 sq. km) of Hue. In 1887, the French built the **Trong Tien Bridge** over the Perfume River; this was destroyed in 1968 and rebuilt in 1971. The same year saw the building of the **Phu Xuan Bridge**; while the railroad crosses the **Bach Ho Bridge** to the citadel. The train station itself is on the south bank. East of the citadel, in Chinatown, the market hall of Don Ba extends to the river. Here, you encounter the bustle and activity of an old Asian city. Motorboats and heavily laden rowboats steer toward

the market; ferries cross the river. Girls and women in becoming *ao dai* move graciously along the street or perch atop their motorbikes. The ao dai is a close-fitting garment slit up to the hip and worn over long silk pants. The upper part, of black, white, blue, lilac-red, or peach-yellow silk, is embroidered with delicate patterns. Completing the ensemble is a *non bai thi*, a large, conical hat made of bleached palm leaves, fastened with a band of the same color as the *ao dai*. It consists of thin bamboo rings with strips of palm leaves woven through them. Between two layers of leaves, the landscape of Hue is painted in pale colors so that is shimmers gently through. The simplicity and elegance of these garments is exemplary of the Hue style. In the last decades, the *ao dai* was banned; but at the end of the 80s, when it was still proscribed in Hanoi, it began to reappear in Hue.

Over the river echo the songs of the riverboatwomen, the *ho hue*. There are two kinds of rowing songs, *ho nai day* and *ho nai nhi*. If the boat is heavily laden

or has to traverse rapids, or if there are heavy waves in the lagoon, you hear the strong, fast rhythms of the *ho nai day*. The melodic, lyric *ho nai nhi* sound like the gentle plashing of the oars, and deal with love and desire; but they can also become calls to rebellion and resistance. In the 14th century, they picked up influences from the melodic music of the Cham. *Ho gia gao* were sung in the country, accompanying sowing and harvest as an expression of *joie de vivre*. At night, a drumming noise rises over the river. The fishermen are beating on their boats with the oars to drive the fish toward the banks. When the sun has set over the Perfume River, Hue offers you a meal with dishes that were common at the court of the Nguyen. More than 60 recipes have survived.

Citadel and Royal City

For nearly 30 years, from 1804 to 1831, indentured laborers worked day and night, by torchlight, on building the

Citadel. It was surrounded by an earth wall 20 feet (6 m) high and 32,536 feet (9,950 m) long, **Phong Thanh**, 6.5 feet (2 m) across at the summit. In 1819, it was reinforced inside and out with brick walls in the Vauban style of French fortress building. This made the surrounding wall 65 feet (20 m) thick; it was studded with 24 bastions. Ten fortified gates led into the citadel, which served both as a defensive edifice and as the royal headquarters. Surrounding it was a moat 13 feet (4 m) deep and 13.5 miles (22 km) long. You can still make out remains of this complex in today's cityscape. It was built by Emperor Gia Long, founder of the dynasty. He had citadel and palaces laid out according to strict rules of geomancy, and in harmony with the aspects of the stars. In Huong Giang, two islands lay auspiciously before the fortress: the Green Dragon on the left, and the White Tiger on the right. Behind the citadel was

Above: Citadel of Hue; the Noon Gate, Ngoc Mon.

a protective chain of mountains. On three sides, the fort's mighty walls were straight; the fourth wall followed the course of the river. Standing on the riverbank is the **Flag Tower**, *Cot Co*, also *Ky Dai*, or Royal Knight, built in 1809 and enlarged in 1831. Often damaged or destroyed in typhoons, it was last rebuilt in 1949. In 1945, the flag of the monarchy was taken down; in 1968, after the Tet Offensive, the flag of the Liberation Army flew over the citadel for three weeks, until the site was reconquered in a major attack of the U.S. Air Force.

Thanh Hoang, the Royal City with the Forbidden City, is still commonly called Dai Noi today. It lies in the southern part of the citadel, surrounded by a wall 1.5 miles long and 13 feet (4 m) high, and consists of nine walled courtyards; gates lead out in all directions. Before the southern **Ngoc Mon**, or Noon Gate, there are eight **cannons**. Emperor Gia Long had these cast from the rubble of his fight with the Tay Son Dynasty. They can't actually be fired; they're simply emblems of power. The Noon Gate is the main entrance to the Royal Palace. The gate's four side entrances are covered in green tiles; the central entrance, reserved for the ruler, is tiled in royal yellow. Atop the gate is the Pavilion of Five Phoenixes, **Lau Ngu Phuong**, where the ruler watched festivals outside the palace walls. On August 24, 1945, Boa Dai, the 13th Nguyen Emperor, had to surrender his sword and seal to government envoys here, ending 1,006 years of monarchy in Vietnam.

In front of the Pavilion of Five Phoenixes you can look out over the large garden, at its loveliest when the frangipani trees are in bloom. At one end stands the restored audience hall of the Emperors, **Dien Thai Hoa**. This Palace of Heavenly Harmony was used only for coronation ceremonies and audiences during the most important festivals of the year. One can hardly imagine what a colorful, splendid picture such occasions presented. Only the Emperor could use the central path through the garden and over the bridge in the lake. The ceremonial court **Dai Trieu Nghi** consisted of three rising terraces. The lower of these were used by the royal family; the one over it was for the lower five ranks of mandarins, and the three upper terraces, nearest the Emperor, were used by mandarins of ranks four to one. Their places are marked by stone tables. For every mandarin rank, there was a military mandarin commanded by a civilian mandarin. The nine ranks were divided into two levels under the Nguyen dynasty, so that 36 mandarins were collected with their entourages in the ceremonial courtyard. Rank was indicated by different shades of their fine silk garments. The civilian mandarins wore four-cornered headgear and bore staves; the military mandarins had hats and swords. Immediately in front of the palace were seats for ministers and generals. From the point of view of the Emperor, who sat at the middle of

the palace, the civilians sat on the right, the military on the left.

Emperor Gia Long actually began building the Palace of Heavenly Harmony in 1803 at another site. In 1808, it was moved to its current location, and the Emperor, who had reigned since 1802, was officially crowned. The mighty roof rests upon 80 columns of red-lacquered oak. UNESCO helped fund the restoration of this damaged building. Behind the palace, separated by a wall, began Tu Cam Thanh, the Forbidden City.

A broad path running westward leads through a destroyed and overgrown section of the palace. From here, a picturesque gateway leads to an ancestor temple within a walled courtyard. Five buildings remained preserved enough to enable them to be restored. **Thai Mieu** is the memorial to the Nguyen lords who began to expand their feudal holdings in the south in the 16th century; **Trieu Mieu** honors Nguyen Kim, first Nguyen prince, who with the help of the Trinh lords reinstated the Le dynasty in the 16th century; **Hung Mieu**, or the Temple of the Father of the Dynasty, is for the father of Emperor Gia Long; **The Mieu** honors all of the Nguyen Emperors; and **Dien Phung Thien** was built for the women of the royal family. The last two of these are open to visitors.

In the dynasty's Ancestor Temple, The Mieu, ten memorial altars decorated with honorary awnings stand in the foreground. Seven of these are lacquered red and decorated with gold; the first two and the last, however, are without ornamentation. These three were built by Diem, head of the government of South Vietnam, in 1954 to commemorate all the emperors who had resisted the colonial power, been banished, and therefore had never been properly honored. Two emperors don't have any altars at all; they reigned for a matter of weeks or even days. The 13th and last emperor, Bao Dai, still lives in France. Small stupas of

little gilded tables at each altar are relics of a Hue court tradition: instead of paper money, the dead were given gold ingots to accompany them into the afterlife. Behind these are altars and tables for the emperors and their consorts. In front of these, beds are set up for the dead, complete with pillows and tea-sets.

Cuu Dienh (Vuong Dienh), the Nine Urns or Royal Urns, are symbols of the dynasty's power. Commissioned by Emperor Minh Mang between 1835 and 1837, they demonstrate the skill of bronze-casters in the 19th century. Their form echoes that of containers from the Chinese Xia Dynasty. The largest urn weighs 5,500 pounds, the smallest 4,180 (2,500 and 1,900 kg); and they're about 4 feet (1.2 m) high. They are decorated with Vietnamese motifs, such as landscapes, animals, and plants. To prepare

Above: Cun Dienh, the nine urns in the Imperial Palace, masterpieces of 18th-century bronze casting. Right: Women in ao dai in the Imperial Palace, Hue.

the moulds on the scale required, it took the contents of some 80 to 90 melting-pots.

To the north, separated by walls and gates, several badly damaged buildings stand in a field of rubble. One is the **Dien Tho Palace**, palace of Long Life, built in 1804 by Emperor Gia Long for his mother. Several families lived in the **Trung Sanh Palace**, which was even more damaged. Three of the buildings were built by Emperor Minh Mang.

Loveliest of the buildings to have survived is the **Long An Palace**. It was built in 1845, and ironwood columns support its roof. The palace was moved to its current location in 1909; in 1923, the 12th emperor set it up as a museum displaying objects from the imperial collections. Opposite the palace was the school for imperial lords, today an army museum.

Tu Cam Thanh, the Forbidden City, lies behind the Palace of Heavenly Harmony, reached through a gate. Located within the royal palace, it was used exclusively by the royal family, concubines, and servants, surrounded by walls three-quarters of a mile (1.2 km) long. After 1968, only a few buildings of the Forbidden City remained that were still in good enough condition to be restored. In the first courtyard, the left-hand building, **Ha Vu**, and the right-hand one, **Huu Vu**, were restored according to the original plans by UNESCO in 1977 and 1988 respectively. The mandarins used these buildings to prepare themselves for private audiences. Forming one end of the courtyard was **Dien Can Chanh**, Palace of the Law of Heaven, the hall for private audiences; this, however, was totally destroyed.

Two large **bronze kettles** have survived in the palace courtyard, symbolizing the Emperor's power over the life and death of his subjects. At places of execution, rebels were thrown into such kettles filled with boiling oil. Behind Dien Can Chanh there begins a bleak field of rubble with the reconstruction of the two-story **library** and the former royal theater of **Duyen Thi Duong**, which has also been restored and now serves as the National Conservatory. In the north of this field, along the outer wall, a part of the **royal gardens**, complete with pools and a little temple for the water spirit, conveys some impression of the site's former beauty.

Up the Huong Giang

The village of **Kim Long**, Golden Dragon, lies about 2 miles (3 km) upriver on the road. From 1636-1687, this was the seat of the Nguyen lords. It had one of the loveliest gardens in Hue, as well as a noteworthy *dinh* and *chua*.

Chua Thien Mu (Chua Linh Mu), the Pagoda of the Goddess of Heaven or the Merciful Goddess, lies on the north bank of the Perfume River. By road, it's 3 miles (5 km) from Hue and about 2 miles (3 km) from the citadel. A ride upriver from Hue in a motorboat takes, depend-

ing on the current conditions, about 40-50 minutes. The pagoda of Thien Mu lies on the hill of Ha Khe. From earliest times, this has been a site honoring the mother goddess. In 1601, the goddess Thien Mu appeared to the Nguyen prince on this spot; he subsequently built her a temple. Like many temples in Hue, this has often been struck by lightning, flooded, or destroyed in typhoons, and had to be rebuilt. Its present form is a result of restorations by the Nguyen Emperors. In 1844, Emperor Thieu Tri transformed the temple into a pagoda and built the seven-story, 69-foot (21 m) stupa **Phuoc Duyen**, with a statue honoring Buddha on every floor. On the stone platform in front of the stupa is a temple that was destroyed in a typhoon in 1904. In the left-hand pavilion behind the stupa is a marble stele 8 feet high and 4 feet wide (2.5 by 1.5 m) supported on a marble turtle's back. On it, Chinese symbols describe the beauty of this spot, from which you have a view of the river. In the opposite pavilion hangs Hue's largest bell,

dating from 1710. It weighs 7,227 pounds (3,285 kg), is 4.5 feet in diameter (1.4 m), and is a true masterpiece of bronze-casting. It used to be struck 108 times every morning at 4; you could hear the sound for a radius of 6 miles (10 km).

Ngu Mon, a triple door with sentry figures built in 1907, leads into the courtyard of the pagoda. Behind it is the monastery. To the left, next to a kiosk, there's an old car with a photo hanging over it; the image is of the first Vietnamese monk who immolated himself in protest, on June 11, 1965 in Saigon. The monk Tich Quang Duc, from Hue, was a guest in the Saigon monastery of An Quang; at a demonstration protesting the Diem government and the increasing involvement of the USA, he burned himself standing next to his car, which was given back to the Hue monastery.

Above: The stupa Phuoc Duyen; a stele in Thien Mu Pagoda. Right: Honor courtyard of the Lang Khai Dinh; tomb of the 12th Nguyen Dynasty emperor.

Dien Hon Chen, the Temple of the Mother Goddess, is 3 miles (5 km) further upriver and extends over three levels of the steep bank. When the river is at its normal height, it's about 13 feet (4 m) deep, but it's 23 feet (7 m) deep in front of the temple. It's here that water was drawn for the Emperor's bath. On the bank, there's a small temple to the god of the river; on the next level, the sun god is honored. Single women pray at the next temple. The main temple on the summit is dedicated to Ho Chen, the mother goddess. Centuries ago, the Cham erected a temple on this site to Po Nagara, mother of the country. There's a lovely view over the river valley. Farther upriver there are two royal graves.

The Imperial Tombs – Lang Tan

The Nguyen were the only dynasty who chose to be buried near their residence rather than in their native province. They came from Thanh Hoa; but seven Nguyen tombs here, dating from

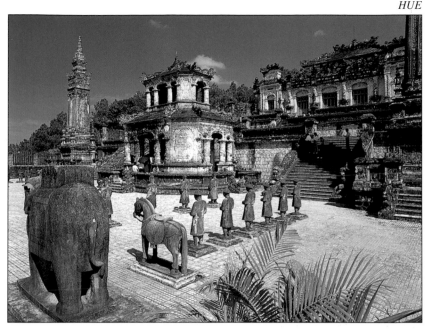

between 1814 and 1920, document a century of tomb architecture and convey some impression of the emperors' personalities.

In Vietnam, the term for architecture conceived of in close harmony with the landscape is *phong-thuy* (wind-water theory). All of the tombs have the same characteristics, with minor variations. Emperors saw their own tombs begun and ended during their lifetimes; and Chinese imperial tombs served as a model. Their close relation to the surrounding landscape, however, reflects the Vietnamese sensibility.

The tombs consist of three parts. First come courts of honor with spirit avenues; animals, mandarins and warriors as guards against demons; and stone stelae on which the living praised the deeds of the dead. In the second part is the temple honoring the deceased emperor and empress. The third part is the grave itself.

Lang Minh Mang, the tomb of the second emperor, lies on the north bank of the river, some 35 minutes upriver from Dien Hon Chen by boat. There's also a little ferry across from the road on the south bank. Minh Mang designed his grave himself, and liked to visit it. His successor, Emperor Thieu Tri, completed it. The generous tomb complex, with gardens, pavilions, ponds and temples, extends over 112.5 acres (45 ha). Some ten buildings have not survived.

Gia Long, the founder of the dynasty, built his tomb, **Lang Gia Long**, in 1814, six years before his death. This smaller complex is in complete harmony with its natural surroundings.

Lang Khai Dinh, grave of the twelfth Emperor, is 6 miles (10 km) from Hue on the right, southern bank of the river; there's also a ferry which runs there from the two abovementioned tombs. This tomb is the record of a very different epoch. It's the only tomb which sits on a hilltop, dominating the landscape. The Emperor had building begun in 1920, and it was finished by the last Emperor, Bao Dai. The juxtaposition of Chinese and French stylistic elements, together with

use of the new building material, cement, resulted in a rather eclectic whole. The traditional three-part organization was preserved, but the three sections were placed on three different levels, linked by steep stairs of 36, 26 and 47 steps respectively. Its best feature is its lovely view of the river valley. The burned earth and leafless forest left in the wake of Agent Orange, a chemical weapon used in the Vietnam War, have since been masked by new brush and undergrowth.

Lang Tu Duc, the tomb of the fourth Emperor, was built in the period of political confusion of the dawning colonial epoch, and gives a sense of the Emperor's personal privation. His reign, the longest of any Vietnamese Emperor (1847-1888) saw the loss of Cochin China and the Treaty of the Protectorate. Tu Duc was the last Vietnamese Emperor who was able to preserve his political and

Above: Lang Tu Duc, tomb of the fourth emperor: Luu Khiem lake and the Xung Khiem pavilion. Right: Tomb of Tu Duc, sentry.

spiritual independence. The childless ruler, who had 100 concubines, was frequently ill. To ensure his succession, he adopted a number of sons from the royal family. But he wrote the text on his stele himself. *Khiem*, mediocre, was his modest term for himself, his government, and his successes; and he excused himself to the people for his mistakes.

Khiem, moderate, was also his term for his tomb. It was completed 16 years before his death, and he often sought refuge in its silence, 4 miles (7 km) from Hue. The section meant to be used by the living took up considerably more room than his grave. Behind high walls with four gates, the diminutive ruler, only 4 feet 10 inches (1.5 m) tall, created a world in miniature with hills, forests, water, animals, and plants. Paths paved with *bat trang* tiles, brown tiles 11 inches (30 cm) square, paved the way to the lake **Luu Khiem**. In the lakeside pavilion **Xung Khiem**, he devoted himself to literature and poetry; on a small lake island, he hunted rabbits and bittern. In this still world, he sought the harmony which seemed to be lacking in his country and his life. He even held court in the temple which was one day to see the ancestor-worship of himself and Empress Le Thien. For his own entertainment, he had plays staged, which continued for up to 100 nights. Hidden in the back of the complex, flights of steps led down to the courtyard of honor and to the stele house. Behind these lies the stone tomb itself. The queen and one of his adopted sons, the sixth emperor, Kieu Phuc, whose reign was but brief, are buried in the forest within this tomb complex.

Not far from Lang Khai Dinh are **Lang Ba Van**, the tomb of a queen mother, and **Lang Thieu Tri**, tomb of the third emperor. Both are small and harmonize well with the surrounding landscape. **Lang Dong Khanh** is the tomb of an adopted son of Tu Duc, whom the French colonial government placed on the throne in place of a less tractable predecessor. Another adopted son of Tu Duc lies in **Lang Duc Duc**; in 1883, after three days in office, he was killed by rivals. Both of these tombs are near the city.

Nam Giao, the Altar of Heaven, was once on the site which is today occupied by the memorial to the fallen. It was laid out on an axis with the royal palace on the other side of the river, and consisted of alternating round and square terraces symbolizing heaven and earth. Every three years until well into the 20th century, the Emperor, the son of heaven, made sacrifices for heaven and earth, asking for good harvests. Contemporary French images of the highest festival in Hue depict ritual dances performed by torchlight.

The Pagodas of Hue

Hue has some 100 Buddhist temples and monasteries. The first were built in the 17th and 18th centuries under the Nguyen lords, but were destroyed when

Phu Xuan was taken by the Trinh lords and in fighting with the Tay Son. As lords and then as emperors, the Nguyen summoned Chinese monks to the country and financed the construction of pagodas and monasteries. In the 19th and 20th centuries, these buildings were renovated many times. Many of their names include the tag "Pagoda protected by the Emperor." The founders and abbots were highly honored. Strict rules of order prevailed within the *sangha*, or monks' community, in monasteries of Chinese sects.

The problems of the modern world and political issues did not stop at the monastery doors. It was, in fact, behind them that the anti-Diem movement developed between 1955 and 1963, a movement which also protested against American intervention and appealed to the international conscience through acts of self-immolation. From 1963 to 1968, monks took an active part in resistance fighting. In Hue, the first institutions for the renewal of Buddhism came into being, as did educational centers for monks and charitable organizations.

The pagodas in Central Vietnam are different from those of Bac Bo. Their roofs are less curved, and don't turn up at the corners. They include Chinese stylistic elements, the tile buildings are higher, often consist of only a single building, and seem larger and lighter from inside. Woodcarvings are rare; the walls are decorated with paintings. The pantheon of gods is much smaller; often, a single large Buddha dominates the room. Most *chua* lie on the southern bank of the river, in the city, or on the grounds around a royal tomb.

Chua Bao Quoc (Chua Thien Tu), on the hill of Ham Long in the district of Duc in the city center, has had its own school of Buddhism since 1940, Bao Quoc, which produced some of the leading figures of the resistance movement. Founded in 1674, the pagoda has often been restored since. The triple entry door dates from 1808. Emperor Minh Mang made it a national pagoda and placed it under his protection. The pantheon is typical of pagodas in Trung Bo. A steep flight of stairs leads up to the *chua*. Behind the main altar is a room with statues of the abbots. Burial stupas stand about in the orchid garden around the pagoda.

In the southern part of the city, **Truong An**, there are several major pagodas. The Le Dynasty founded **Chua Quoc An** (Chua Vinh An), atop a hill, in 1602, and placed it under royal protection in 1689. **Chua Van Phuoc** was founded in 1842 and placed under royal protection in 1937. It's about 650 feet (200 m) from **Chua Tu Dam**, about a mile (2 km) south of the city center, which was founded in the late 17th century. Behind its triple entry gate stands a bo tree which originally came from India. In 1936, the pagoda became the seat of the Buddhists

in An Nam, and in 1951, it hosted the first congress in Central Vietnam for Buddhists from throughout the country.

Chua Dien Duc, founded in 1932, contains statues which were cast in the pagoda. It was also the first place in Vietnam to boast a study center for nuns.

In the village **Duong Xuan**, which belongs to Hue and lies on the way to the Emperors' Graves, there's **Chua Dong Tuyen**, from the second half of the 18th century. Chua Truc Lam, on the hill Duong Xuan, almost 4 miles (6 km) south of Hue, founded in 1903, belongs to the Meditation Sect of the Bamboo Woods, founded in 1903. In 1931, the Union for Studies in Buddhism was founded here, the first institution of this kind in Hue. Among other treasures, the pagoda contains a Chinese edition of the Diamond Sutra donated by the Tay Son Dynasty. The abbess of the Thay pagoda in the Red River Delta embroidered the 7,000 words of the sutras in five colors on silk brocade.

In the village of **Duong Xuan Ha**, 3 miles (5 km) from the city center on the way to the imperial tombs, is the pagoda **Chua Tu Hieu**. This was once the site of the little pagoda An Duong, founded in 1843 by the monk Nhat Dinh. When his mother took ill, he cared for her; Emperor Tu Duc thereupon named him a dutiful son, and the people revered him. The monk died in 1847, and the eunuchs of the royal court took up a collection and donated land to the pagoda, which thus became quite well-off. Many of the eunuchs were buried nearby. Monks from this pagoda also joined the anti-Diem movement.

In the village of **Thuy Xuan**, which belongs to Hue, is the **Chua Tuong Van**, founded in the mid-19th century. The **Chua Tay Thien Di - Da** in the same village dates from 1902 and was originally a small temple with a thatch roof. It was later expanded; since 1935, it has housed a school for monks.

Right: Houseboat on the Huong Giang (Perfume River), Hue.

At the foot of the mountain Thien Thai, in the village **Thuy An**, is Hue's largest pagoda, **Chua Tuyen Ton**, founded in the 18th century. The **Chua Ba La Mat** (1886) is in the village of Phu Thuong. In the outlying district of An Cuu, the **Chua Tra Am**, founded in 1923, lies between two hills in lovely landscape.

The **Chua Dieu De** in the district of Phu Cat is the only pagoda on the northern bank of the river. Built by Emperor Thieu Tri, it's located on Bach Dang Street, near the market hall and east of the citadel. The pagoda features bell- and drum-towers by its entrance and in front of its main building. During the resistence movement, monks from this pagoda joined forces with the population and student protestors. In 1966, the police occupied the pagoda and arrested the monks and their supporters.

Hoi quan are often described as pagodas, but only seldom do they include a Buddhist pantheon. They were built by Chinese clans who immigrated from the south of China and now live in the old city on the north bank of the river by the market hall. Religious and social center of these communities are the community houses, or *hoi quan*. Most of the *hoi quan* are in the Duong Nguyen Chi Thanh. At the full moon in spring and fall, as well as at New Year's, these *hoi quan* host major festivities.

In Hue, only two noteworthy *hoi quan*, complete with temples for the guardian spirits, have survived. **Dinh Kim Long** is in the village of the same name between the citadel and the Thien Mu Pagoda; **Dinh Duong Mo** is east of Hue, also located in the village of the same name and on the road to the bathing beach of Thuan An.

There are also boats which run from the Perfume River to the fine bathing **beach of Thuan An**, which lies 11 miles (18 km) east of Hue.

From Hue, there's a direct road which leads to the Ho Chi Minh Trail, Khe Sanh and the village of Vinh Moc, but it is in a rather poor state of repair, and is therefore only usable in the dry season.

FROM HUE TO CLOUD PASS

From Hue to Hai Van, Cloud Pass, it's about 50 miles (80 km). It's about 2 1/2 hours by car to Da Nang (65 miles/105 km on Highway 1). For reasons of security, you shouldn't cross the Hai Van pass after dark. The road leads along, and close to, the coast. **Phu Bai Airport** is about 9 miles (15 km) south of Hue.

Some 18.5 miles (30 km) from Hue, in the village of **Vinh Hien**, the **Chua Tuy Van** lies on the mountain Thuy Van, surrounded by a swamp, on the coast.

In the morning, there are markets in every village. The marketplaces often lie at river mouths. Between rice-paddies, the road leads through avenues of tall, slender eucalyptus trees. Some 31 miles (50 km) from Hue, on the mountain **Bach Ma**, White Horse (4,722 feet/1,444 m), there's a recreational and spa area with a pleasant climate. It was destroyed and

Above: Beach at the foot of Cloud Pass near Lang Co Village.

has since been rebuilt. The road leads over two smaller passes.

The area's loveliest beach is in **Canh Duong**, 37 miles (60 km) south of Hue, by the picturesque fishing village of **Lang Co**.

Cloud Pass is the highest point on Highway 1. At its crest, nearly 1,635 feet (500 m) high, there are the ruins of a French fort. In the parking place, next to an old temple, a new one for the *ma*, or restless spirits, has been built. Many drivers stop off to lay a small offering on the altar. The pass usually lives up to its name, enveloped in clouds and damp fog. If the sun does happen to break through, however, the view is overwhelming. In the north are the plains of rice, the lagoon, the village of Lang Co and the blue-green sea. The railway follows the steep cliffs of the Hai Van directly along the coast, passing through many tunnels along the way. To the south, the view extends over the bay of Da Nang. Until the 15th century, this was the border between Dai Viet and Champa.

PROVINCE OF THANH HOA
Accommodations (Area Code: 84 37)
THANH HOA: Thanh Hoa Hotel, 215 A, Quang Trung St., tel. 5 25 17;
On Sam Son beach, 11 miles/18 km from Thanh Hoa: **Le Loi Hotel**, tel. 15;
Nha Nghi Cong Doan Hotel, tel. 5 95 08;
Tourist Information
Thanh Hoa Tourist, 298, Quang Trung St., tel. 5 22 98.

PROVINCE OF NGHE AN
Accommodations (Area Code: 84 38)
VINH: *BUDGET*: **Kim Lien Hotel**, 12, Quang Trung St., tel. 4 47 51; **Huu Nghi Hotel**, 41 B, Le Loi St., tel. 4 46 33;
On Cua Lo beach, 12.5 miles/20 km from Vinh: **Cua Lo Hotel**, tel. 13; *nuoc mam* factory.
Further Information
Museum in the citadel.
Bank (exchanges cash only) Le Loi St.;
Post Office on Nguyen Thi Minh Khai St.;
Train and **Bus Stations**, Le Loi St. Reservations advised.
Tourist Information
Nghe An-Tourist, Troung Thi St., tel. 4692.

PROVINCE OF QUANG BINH
Accommodations (Area Code: 84 52)
DONG HOI: Tourist hotel **Nhat Le**.
Further Information
Fisherman's harbor on the Nhat Le river. Beaches and sand dunes to the north and south. Citadel dates from 1825.

PROVINCE OF QUANG TRI
Accommodations (Area Code: 84 53)
DONG HA: **Dong Truong Son Hotel**, 3 km west of Dong Ha on Highway 9, tel. 239; **Dong Ha Hotel**, Tran Phu St., tel. 3 61.
Tourist Information
Quang Tri-Tourist in Dong Ha, Tran Phu St., tel. 5 22 66, fax 5 26 39, (Permits for the border region of Khe Sanh).

PROVINCE OF THUA THIEN-HUE
Accommodations (Area Code: 84 57)
HUE: *MODERATE*: **Hue Hotel** (Century), 49, Le Loi St., tel. 33 90;
BUDGET: **Hue Guesthouse**, 2, Le Loi St., tel. 21 53; **Kinh Do Hotel**, 1, Nguyen Thai Hoc St., tel. 35 66; **Tan My Hotel**, Thuan An St., tel. 33.
Getting There / Transportation
Airport Phu Bai, about 9 miles (15 km) south of town. **Vietnam Airlines**, 12, Hanoi St., tel. 32 49;

Bus Station: Long-distance buses at Nguyen Hue St. about a mile/1.5 km from city center. Reservations required. Tickets sold 5 am-5 pm.
Local buses from the central marketplace;
Train Station Le Loi St.;
Motor- and **Rowboats**: Reserve in the tourist offices, or go to the Tran Tien Bridge or the canal by the Dong Ba Market hall.
Further Information
Citadel, open 6 am- 6 pm; main entrance is the south gate on the river bank;
Museum in the Long An Palace in the citadel opposite the exhibition pavilion. Entrance also through the Hien Nhon gate (East Gate), 3, Le Truc St., 7 am - 6 pm;
Ho Chi Minh Museum, 7, Le Loi St., 7:30 - 10:30 am, 1:30 - 4:30 pm;
Kings' Graves on the north and south banks of the river, 4 - 8 miles (7 - 14 km) from the city, open from sunrise to sunset. On Le Loi St. on the south bank: buildings in the **colonial style**; Quoc Hoc, the famous secondary school for boys, with next to it the Hai Ba Trung school for girls;
Nr.16 **Hospital** and **Pharmacy**, tel. 23 25; all of the major pagodas (except Chua Tang Quang) are on the south bank.
In the center of the southern city at Tran Tien Bridge: **Main Post Office** on Hoang Hoa Than St., open daily 6:30 am - 9 pm (international service); **Bank**, 2, Le Quy Don, 7:30 - 11:30 am and 1:30 - 4:30 pm, closed Sun.;
Cathedral, 5, Nguyen Hue St., masses at 5 am and 5 pm;
Culture House, 43, Hung Vuong St., sporadic theater performances;
Chinese Quarter on the north bank with the Dong Da Market: *Hoi Quans* (community houses) on Duong Chi Long St.;
Beach of Thuan An, 11 miles/18 km east: Tam My Hotel on the bridge to the lagoon; bungalows on the beach. Can be reached either by boat or by road;
In the village of Duong Mo: **Ho Chi Minh's House** and *dinh* (community house).
Village of Lang Co, 60 km south of Hue: **Beach** on the lagoon, nearby church dating from 1954; accommodations in the guesthouse of Nha Kach Tu Lich;
On Highway 1 **local buses**; **train station** (local trains) about a mile (2 km) away.
Tourist Information
Tourist Office of the Province of Thua Thien - Hue, 9, Ngo Quyen St., tel. 32 88, 23 69, open 7:30 - 11:30 am and 1:30 - 5 pm.
Hue-Tourist, 18, Le Loi St., same opening hours as above.

FROM CLOUD PASS TO THE MEKONG DELTA

The Encounter of Chinese and Indian Culture

For information on the period between the 2nd and 4th century AD, scholars of the culture of the Cham have to rely on Chinese annals for information. After the 3rd century, these sources are supplemented by Cham stele inscriptions as well as those of the nearby Fu Nan and Khmer, both also strongly influenced by Indian culture. In the 8th century, Cham architecture and sculpture began to kick in as an additional source of documentation. After the 10th century, another rich source is the written histories of the Dai Viet Empire. The Cham were one of the Austro-Asiatic peoples of the Malayo-Indonesian linguistic family which migrated in several waves from southern Siberia, through China, into southeast Asia.

Indianization began in the 1st-2nd century, intensifying in the 4th-5th century. While India was a seafaring nation engaged in trade, Brahman priests always accompanied its ships. The kings of Indochina appointed these educated Indians to high positions at their courts. Although direct contacts to India were broken off in the 6th century, the groundwork had already been laid for the evolution of an independent Indian-influenced culture in Indochina.

It's impossible to reconstruct Cham history altogether, but it is known that there were two clans, sometimes at odds with each other, which ruled by turns. These clans have been termed Dua, coconut eaters, and Cau, betel-nut eaters, based on the sacrificial finds of golden coconuts in the north and golden betel nuts in the south. Many questions remain

Left: Relief with dancer (late Tran Kieu style) from the Cham museum in Da Nang.

unanswered, however, about the relationship between the northern and the southern kingdoms.

Cham Art and Culture

The northern empire of Dua, called Amaravati, developed south of Hue. During the first Hindu period, from the 4th-8th centuries, the capital was Simhapura, today's Tra Kieu, and My Son was the temple city. This was followed by a period of Buddhism, lasting from the 9th to the 10th centuries. During this time, the capital was the lost city of Indrapura or Champura, while the spiritual center was in the Dong Duong Monastery. This monastery, destroyed in 1954, was located near Tra Kieu.

After the fall of their empire, the Cham moved to Vijaya, about 135 miles (220 km) further south, in the region of today's Binh Dinh. My Son remained the temple city.

The southern Dau empire: Panduranga (Phan Rang), with the temple city of Kauthara (Nha Trang), existed concurrently with the northern empire. With its capital of Virapura in the Phan Rang region, this empire dominated from 749-808. After the end of the Vijaya Empire, the southern empire continued in Phan Rang from 1471-1694. From 1693 to 1822, all that remained were its princes, vassals of the Nguyen lords from Hue.

Today the Cham are a minority group in Vietnam, Cambodia and Malaysia.

For China, the early disputes with the Cham on the border of the Giao Chi province (Red River Delta) were just one of numerous border conflicts along the frontiers of their huge empire. The situation changed in 939 when the Dai Viet Empire was founded and rapidly developed into the leading power within the region. The Khmer from Angkor also reached the zenith of their power during this period. Both states had fertile rice paddies in expansive deltas. Champa, on

the other hand, was comprised of mountainous, less fertile coastal regions and small river deltas. The gold in its mountains, however, awakened the interest of its neighbors. In 446, the Chinese stole a 100-pound statue of pure gold from Vu Xa, northwest of today's Hue, the city of the golden prince Phang Duong Mai. In 603 or 605, the Chinese general Liu Fang quashed a revolution in the Red River Delta and continued on to Simhapura. His booty included 18 bars of cast gold.

The Cham were peasants, fishermen, mariners and warriors. Their fleet controlled the spice trade in the South China Sea up until the 10th century. They rebelled against the Chinese, the Vietnamese, the Khmer and, in the 13th century, the Mongols and the Chinese Yuan Dynasty. Again and again they drove Dai Viet almost to ruin, commandeered the Red River Delta and plundered the capi-

Above: Member of the Cham minority.
Right: Cham temple of Po Klaung Garai near Phan Rang.

tal of Thang Long. The Vietnamese emperors managed to sack the Cham capitals (Indrapura in 982 and Vijaya in 1471), forcing the Cham to retreat south. Champa conquered and destroyed Angkor, the Khmer capital, damaged the Angkor Wat Temple, and succeeded in diminishing the prestige of the god-kings (1179-1181). However, Champa was also forced to submit to Khmer rule for a long period of time and to pay tribute to the Vietnamese. In 1693, the Cham became vassals of the Nguyen lords of Hue.

Religions and God Kingdoms

The peasant folk of the Cham honored fertility gods as well as goddesses of motherhood. The goddess Uroja, whose name means mother's breast, was at the top of their pantheon. She is still honored today as Po Nagara, creator of the world and mother of the country. The Cham viewed menhirs as manifestations of their ancestors, and saw lords as protectors of their fields, crops, and country. **Hinduism**, usually in the form of Shivaism, gradually replaced the old cults. Not in his role as an abstract god of the world, but rather as a local deity responsible for a specific region and lord of the soil, Shiva gradually merged with the figure of the emperor, who was seen as the incarnation of god.

The beginnings of the **god-kings** are to be found in India, but the cult reached its acme in the Indian-influenced regions of Indochina. As the incarnation of both heavenly and worldly power, and as sole owner of all the country, such a ruler also had complete power over the forces of nature. Uniting religious-spiritual and political-secular power, he controlled all of the country's material and spiritual resources, as well as those of his subjects. Assured of this absolute power, these kings could carry out projects which effectively drained the country's strength and resources dry. Thus, the days of the

god-kings were necessarily numbered.

Some of the kings saw themselves as incarnations of Vishnu or of the Bodhisattva Avalokitecvara. This changed the iconography, but not the ruler's basic position. The Cham kings always reverted to the Shiva cult, which was closest to the concept of the god kingdom. Although the Brahman priests successfully introduced Hindu teachings, customs, death rituals, burning of widows and other sacrificial rites into the royal courts, the Indian caste system never took hold. Emperors and nobility saw themselves as *Ksatriya*, members of the warrior caste, and the Brahmans' position as the uppermost caste of society was indisputable. The common people, however, retained their clan structure. It is impossible to say how much influence Hindu thinking had on these common people, since neither their religious sites nor statues of their deities have survived. Among the Cham minorities in southern Vietnam, rudimentary Hindu cults remain, but there are no signs of Buddhist cults.

Buddhism arrived in Champa at about the same time as Hinduism. The monks came to Champa either in the entourage of merchants or as pilgrims travelling between India and China. The influences of Mahayana Buddhism, introduced via China and Dai Viet, were felt in the northern region of the Cham Empire. The south was more under the influence of Hinayana and Vajrayana Buddhism. In the 9th-10th centuries, a Buddhist empire grew up in Indrapura, paving the way for the golden age of Cham art.

Islam played no role in Champa, although Arabian merchants introduced it into the coastal towns. Not until after the fall of Champa did Islam become the religion of the Cham minority. Its modern form, however, which incorporates Hindu deities and cults, is far removed from the teachings of Mohammed.

Champa Art

Stele inscriptions from the 4th century in the temple city of My Son document

the construction of a wooden temple with a lingam or idol. The earliest extant brick structures, as well as sandstone sculptures, are highly developed artistically, and are obviously the culmination of a long period of cultural evolution. From the 8th century on, such brick structures and sandstone sculptures are the basic elements of Cham art.

The Cham architecture that's known to us is limited to royal religious buildings. The Cham built only brick structures, and the building style, up until the 10th century, is similar to that of contemporaneous temples of the Indianized Khmer. Even after the Khmer began turning to sandstone architecture, however, the Cham continued to build with brick, although sandstone ornamentation on the buildings demonstrate that the Cham also knew how to work with this

Above: Bricks are the main Cham building material. Right: My Son: the mandapa D1 is the loveliest Cham building to have survived (today a museum).

material. Throughout their building history, it was used for staircases, friezes on foundations and gables, door and window frames, ornamental elements and cornerstones of the roof structure, or keystones of archways. Ground plans and architectural forms remained basically the same throughout the Cham stylistic epochs; it's only through the decor that one notices the evolution of the art.

Construction materials. The bricks are quite high quality, and have smooth upper surfaces. They were joined seamlessly, without the use of mortar, and decorative and figurative ornamentation was chiseled into the smooth walls after they were built. How these walls managed to stand without any bonding element continues to puzzle the experts even today. French scientists thought that there may have been some kind of bonding element composed of vegetal or animal substances. Another theory postulates that the structures were built from unfired bricks and then fired together, as a whole. In Polish laboratories, scientists are

trying to prove that fired bricks were mortared together using a mass of raw brick as a bonding element, and then fired once again as a complete structure. White bricks were used for the walls around the temple area; red and white bricks for the foundation; and red bricks for the temple building itself.

The **floor plan** did not change significantly over time. Compared with Indian and Khmer temple complexes, those of the Cham are relatively small. The temple city of My Son differs vastly from Indian temple cities. In My Son, each successive emperor built a temple group during his reign. These groups, which were completely unrelated to each other, were each composed of three different types of structure: the tower-like shrine known as the *kalan*, the library, and the hall, or *mandapa*. The **kalan**, with a square floor plan, opens to the east, toward the rising sun. West-facing temples were believed to face the kingdom of the dead, and were used as burial sites. The low, square **library** lies to the south of

the kalan, facing it broadside. The kalans, auxiliary buildings and library are all surrounded by a wall, its four sides broken by small gate or entrance structures. Outside the wall, to the east, and on an axis with the kalan, is the rectangular hall of the **mandapa**. Three tall kalans (triple-tower shrines), built closely together, have also survived, although this type of structure was not found in My Son. Near the temple, not more than half a mile (1 km) away, was a lake which furnished the water with which the statues were cleaned. Many Cham temples are located on hills; others are along the coast. But even those built on flat land dominate the surrounding landscape, unlike the Vietnamese temples, which blend in harmoniously with their environment.

While the basic principles of architectural form remained unchanged, ornamentation and decor did see some transformation. The most important structures, the kalans, ranged between 12.4 feet and 114 feet (3.8 m to 35 m) in height. These kalans hearken back to the

liefs of dance or battle scenes, flowers and animals. Over the course of the centuries, the base has been almost completely covered by earth. It emphasizes the horizontal. Resting on this base is the superstructure, somewhat smaller but also square, which you can walk around. Its brick walls are punctuated at intervals by pilasters and vertical decorative bands chiseled into the brick; these accentuate the vertical. The main portal on the eastern side, which was increasingly emphasized as this style of building developed, became a vestibule. The other three sides have sham portals, richly decorated with figurative ornamentation in sandstone. The corbelled or "false" roof vaultings extend beyond the structure. Roofs are usually three-tiered, sharply tapered, and are about as tall as the building itself. They have also suffered the most from the passage of time, overgrown with plants and shrubs, their wealth of ornamentation lost. Originally, the three tiers had miniature kalans on the corners, and the cornices had animal sculptures. Ornamental friezes displayed figurative and horticultural decor. Particularly in the roof zone, the decor became less opulent in the 12th and 13th centuries, appearing increasingly jagged and bizarre. In the temple city My Son, the roofs were sometimes covered with sheets of gold. The *kalans* are symbols of the holy mountain *meru* from Indian mythology.

cella which were built in India up until the 8th century. The one-room window-less sanctuary with a high roof (*shikara*) is built on a square foundation. In the middle of the interior room is a brick pedestal, usually decorated with sandstone reliefs, on which stands a lingam or idol. Around the base is a channel with a drain leading outside on the north side; this was used to drain off the blood of sacrificial animals, and later for the ritual cleansing water. In the dim lighting from oil lamps placed in niches in the walls, you can hardly make out the corbelled vaulting of the ceiling. All temples had wooden doors. In the walls, you can still see the slots in which the hinges rested.

The kalan is composed of three structural elements: base, superstructure and roof. The high square base is usually set with sandstone panels, decorated with re-

The **library** is a low square building with two interior rooms of equal size in which the temple treasures were kept. The brick facade is richly ornamented with baluster windows, pilasters, and decorative bands. Atop this delicate structure, the roof seems heavy by comparison. It is similar to the roofs of houses depicted on the bronze drums of the Dong Son culture (see page 226).

The **mandapa** is a lengthy hall used to prepare for sacrifices and ritual dances. Inside the larger *mandapa*, there are rows of columns to support the flat roof. Roofs

Above: Nha Trang: the Cham temple of Po Nagara sports lovely decor. Right: Polo player relief, early Tra Kieu style, in the Cham museum at Da Nang.

were made of wood covered with brick or straw. The hall was either open or had a brick facade decorated with baluster windows. In many cases, all that remains of these buildings is the columns.

Styles of Cham Art

This brief summary of Cham styles is largely based on French research, but some data also stems from Vietnamese archaeologists. The specific works cited are in the **Cham Museum** in **Da Nang**, repository of the world's largest collection of Cham sculpture. Other museums in Vietnam, in Hanoi and Ho Chi Minh City, as well as in Paris, have only small exhibits of a handful of individual works.

The **early Tra Kieu style** (late 7th century). Simhapura, capital of the Amaravati Empire, was located in Tra Kieu, 28 miles (45 km) south of Da Nang. Works: 1. Altar with scenes from the Ramayana epic. Apsaras, divine, expressive dancers full of grace and joy. 2. Polo player relief. Figures are very life-like, horses clumsy as in the Chinese Han Dynasty. 3. Animal sculptures, early examples of masterful animal figures. **Features of style**: A highly-developed style, influenced by the southern Indian Amaravati style of the 2nd and 3rd century. Distinctive Cham elements are not yet very evident. **Decor**: Simple geometric forms. **Sculptures**: Natural faces with almond-shaped eyes, accentuated nostrils, and smiling, full lips. **Clothes and jewelry**: Fluttering belts, hair styled into buns at the neck or crown coiffures.

An My style (early 8th century). Named after a temple, now destroyed, 55 miles (90 km) south of Da Nang. **Works**: Statues. **Features of style**: Cham elements starting to crop up. Indian influences. **Architecture**: Three-tower shrine Pho Lai near Phan Thiet, showing Khmer influence. Sculptures: Spiralling hair, hanging loose, framing angular faces with accentuated chins. Wide-open eyes, corners of mouth curved slightly upward. **Clothes and jewelry**: Almond-shaped earrings, many necklaces.

My Son E1 style (early 8th-early 9th centuries). **Works**: 1. Altar from the E1 *kalan*. Opulent reliefs, scenes from the lives of the hermits. Devoted to Apsaras, full of elegance and grace. 2. Gable (incomplete) from E1: Birth of the god Brahma from the navel of the god Vishnu. The ground under the flat arch is harmoniously filled by the reclining Vishnu, with a *rishi* (prophet) at his feet. The idea of placing Brahma on the gable is ingenious, though unusual. 3. Shiva and the elephant-headed god Ganesha. **Features of style**: Encounters between the north and south lead to new forms. The northern empire is still under the influence of the Indian Mathura style. The south is influenced by Cambodia, Java and Dvaravati. Beginnings of a distinct, independent Cham style. **Decor**: Stars, circles and triangles, leaf and vine or-

Above: 15th-century statue, probably Shiva, in the Yang Mum style, Cham Museum in Da Nang. Right: Three-tower shrine of Khong My, early 10th century, south of Da Nang.

namentation spilling out of the niches. **Relief**: High reliefs divided into separate images by pilasters. Flat arches surmounting blind architraves on decorated capitals. The niches, filled with figures, have a monumental effect. **Sculptures**: Slightly slanted eyes, heavy eyebrows, large noses, fuller lips; crown-like hairdos. **Clothes and jewelry**: Knee-length skirts (*sampot*) with a pleated apron at the front. Fluttering scarves emphasize movement, wealth of jewelry.

Hoa Lai style (first half of the 9th century). Three-tower shrine 55 miles (90 km) south of Nha Trang. A destroyed *kalan*. **Features of style**: One distinctive elements are the sham fan arches above the doorways. Simple lines, opulent decor. The structure is visually divided by posts and ornamental bands, emphasizing the vertical. Plant designs well out of the mouths of monsters (*makara*). Steep corbelled vaulting.

Dong Duong style (early 9th - early 10th centuries). Dong Duong Monastery, 37 miles (60 km) south of Da Nang. Discovered in 1902 by the French, completely destroyed in the First Indochina war. **Works**: 1. Large altar from the main shrine of Dong Duong, with reliefs. 2. 30-inch (76 cm) statue in imperial pose, a Buddha, Shakyamuni or Akshobhya (its pendant is in Zurich's Rietberg Museum). 3. Gods and guards. **Features of style**: The iconography displays similarities with the cave monasteries of Dunhuang and Long Men in northern China. Missing in Champa's Buddhist art, however, are elements of renouncing the world or withdrawal. Here, Cham classicism has reached its peak. **Architecture**: Expansive monasteries. Dong Duong Monastery had a royal temple 4,350 feet (1,330 m) long and a monk's cloister of 1,063 feet (325 m). These were linked via the main shrine with its huge altar. **Decor**: Individual reliefs are isolated by means of wide, richly decorated frames; pilasters are topped with flat arches.

Trees in the fields merge with the leafy vines on the frames. Also emerging is the Dong Duong motif, known as the vermicelli or worm motif. **Sculpture**: Lively free-standing statues. War-like sentry figures from the Chinese pantheon. Natural faces, almond-shaped slanted eyes, wide noses and full lips. High, pointed coiffures. New are the compact figures with round faces, bulging eyes and pug noses. Two bronze Buddhas are puzzling. One is from the altar of the main temple, 3.5 feet (1.08 m) tall; its date is contested, probably 4th-6th centuries. Influences of the southern Indian Amaravati style and the early Gupta style from northern India as well as Ceylonese features. Similar statues are common from Ceylon to the island of Sulawesi (Celebes). The statue is in the National Museum in Ho Chi Minh City. The second bronze Buddha was found, carefully buried, 165 feet (50 m) from the main altar. It is 3.7 feet (1.14 m) tall, and robes are pleated in a fashion unknown in Champa. The diamond jewelry and the precious stones of the *urna* and the eyes, as well as the metal jewelry of the robes, have been lost. Thought to be a statue of Emperor Indravarman II, who built the monastery, in his incarnation as Avalokitecvara. The statue is in the museum in Da Nang. **Reliefs**: High reliefs opulently decorated with figures, some of which extend outside the frame; they depict images from the *jakatas* (Buddha legends).

Khuong My style (early 10th century). Triple-tower shrine, 56 miles (90 km) south of Da Nang. **Works**: Well-crafted reliefs with a dancing Shiva and a group of wrestlers. **Features of style**: Architecture and sculptures show Khmer influence, features of the art of Indonesia and elements of the Tra Kieu and My Son E1 styles. Realism and simplicity have returned to art.

My Son A1 style (late 10th century). Kalan A1 in My Son. The structures A8, A9, B3-B8, B11 and B14, as well as C1-C5, D1-D4 and D6 were also built in this style. **Architecture**: The destroyed *kalan* A1 and the restored *mandapa* D1 are

among the most beautiful Cham structures. Khmer and Java influences in the ornamentation (makara heads). Stylistic elements from My Son E1 appear here in more refined form. The structures appear more slender because of their greater height. The roof structures are lower. There's a return of monumentalism. Animal sculptures appear as decorative stones on the corbelled cornices.

Late Tra Kieu style (late 10th century). **Works:** 1. One of the loveliest Cham works – indeed, of Indianized southeast Asia – is the remains of a relief 9.8 feet (3 m) by 3.8 feet (1.15 m); it's so finely crafted that the dancer looks like a three-dimensional sculpture, holding her own in relation to the overhanging cornice. Javanese influence shows in her pearl jewelry and crown coiffure. The effect is graceful, more worldly and sensuous than the *apsaras* of the My Son E1 altar. 2. Lifelike elephants and lions; deer also appear for the first time. **Features of style**: Champa is influenced by Java, and seeks a return to early Tra Kieu and My Son E1 style, with some local influence.

Po Nagara style (11th century). Temple in Nha Trang (Kauthara). **Features of style**: Transitional style. The Cham empire's political crisis is evident in the decor, which is stylized and less opulent. One last high point of Cham art is the temple's main shrine.

Chanh Lo style (11th century): Chanh Lo is 93 miles (150 km) south of Da Nang. **Works**: Well-crafted high reliefs. The dancers and musicians, however, lack elegance and animation. Their bodies are womanly and realistic. **Features of style**: Transitional style. Less foreign influence, Cham features are more dominant. **Sculpture**: Faces have narrow eyes, flat noses and very full lips. The coiffure is a two-part hair crown, decorated with flowers. Bead necklaces like those in the late Tra Kieu style.

Above: Relief on the three-tower shrine of Chien Dan, 10th century, south of Da Nang. Right: Flute-player, altar of the shrine E1, 8th-9th centuries, Cham Museum.

Binh Dinh style (12th-14th centuries). Capital Vijaya (1000-1471). **Features of style**: Tall buildings and raised roof construction. Large structures are built in front of the main portals of the *kalans*. The architecture seeks to preserve tradition, but falls into an experimental vein. The decor declines rapidly.

Thap Mam style (11th or 12th-14th centuries). Thap Mam was the northernmost shrine of the Vijaya Empire. The French date it earlier. They originally believed that this style represented the beginnings of Cham art. **Works**: A relief with dancers, never completed, dates from the initial phase of this style and shows influences of the waning Khmer art. **Features of style**: Attempts to return to the dynamism of earlier art. The lack of conviction is particularly evident in the roof structures. **Sculpture**: Freestanding sculptures are rare. The animal sculptures evolve into monstrous fabulous creatures with a wealth of ornamentation, losing their naturalism. Lion-elephants (*gaja-simha*) and Garuda appear.

Yang Mum style (late 14th-15th centuries). The Cham retreat to Yang Mum in the southern highlands (Dac Lac province). **Works**: Two well-crafted figures. **Features of style**: Influences of the waning Khmer art. The triangular, cowering figures seem foreign; there are no standing statues. There's a wealth of highly stylized decor. The *kut* stones, menhirs with carved faces and hints of clothing, found in the cemeteries south of Phan Rang, probably date from this period.

Cham Sculpture

Sculptures and reliefs went through a number of stylistic developments and were open to foreign influences, assimilating them quickly. Expression and ideals changed, but ultimately, artists quickly returned to their own distinctive ethnic style. The earliest works from the 7th century show a highly-developed

technique, which supports the hypothesis that there had been a long tradition of wooden sculpture. The Cham were able to create free-standing sculptures before the Khmer. The statues demonstrate a great degree of sensitivity and talent for observation. Although they were proficient sculptors, the Cham, like the Khmer, placed more emphasis on high reliefs; these tend to be more expressive because they're telling a story. Cham sculpture reached its zenith during the Buddhist period (9th-10th centuries). After that, the empire moved to Vijaya, and the work became more stylized and simpler, with an emphasis on monumentality. In the 14th and 15th centuries, the art of sculpture deteriorated more rapidly than the architecture, losing its warmth and veracity. Once, the weightlessness and grace of sculpted Cham elephants and lions were without compare; now, animal sculptures seemed to lack movement and harmony. The prevalent unrest, poverty and time pressures were reflected in a loss of force and spirit in the art.

Tropical Vietnam

The Cloud Pass leads over the Hai Van mountains, an eastern spur of the Truong Son. A weather divide, it forms the border between two climate zones. South of the barrier, the temperatures remain relatively constant at 77-81°F (25-27°C).

Tropical Trung Bo is comprised of small fertile river deltas where rice, sugar cane and peanuts thrive. Further south, coconut, rubber and tobacco are cultivated. Trees, spices, coffee and tea grow in the mountains. The best pepper comes from Than Phuc, while the most popular cinnamon-growing region is Tra My. Particularly high-quality silk is produced in Phu Vang. Driving along Highway 1, you can in many places observe the extraction of salt from sea water: huge flat pools in which the water evaporates rapidly. The salt which remains is piled up in mountains along the roadside, awaiting transport. Huge flocks of ducks frequent the ponds, rivers and irrigation canals; in the hills and mountains, cattle are bred for meat and dairy products. The mountains have a wealth of natural resources. Even the Cham discovered gold here, although they panned for it in the rivers rather than mining it.

Along with the Kinh, Hoa (Chinese) minorities live on the plains of southern Trung Bo, as do some 75,000 Cham. In the hills and highlands live Radang, Ka Tu, Co and other mountain peoples.

DA NANG AND ENVIRONS

From Cloud Pass (Hai Van), the road serpentines 6 miles (10 km) down into the valley. It provides a wonderful view across the wide bay of Da Nang, dominated by the mountainous **Son Tra Peninsula**. White beaches line the bay; **My Khe**, the best-known, is only a few miles

Left: The village of Nam O near Da Nang is known for making wonderful fireworks.

from Da Nang. A partially ruined fort and gasoline tanks at the foot of the pass date from the colonial period.

A popular fish sauce is produced in the village of **Nam O**. This is also one of the three villages in Vietnam famous for the production of fireworks. Sometimes you can see the red-violet paper used for wrapping the fireworks lying out in the sun to dry. Nam O's family-owned businesses produce 48 different firecrackers and rockets. Large cemeteries can be seen on both sides of the road, just before reaching Da Nang.

Da Nang, capital of Quang Nam - Da Nang Province, stretches over 370 square miles (950 square km) and has a population of more than 800,000. It lies on the Han River and on a large bay with a huge natural harbor filled with ships. When French warships fired on this bay, just 65 miles (105 km) south of the capital of the Nguyen emperors, in 1847 and 1856, in an attempt to force the country's opening to foreign trade, there were only small settlements lining the bay's shores. These were incorporated into a French base, today's city of Da Nang. In the Vietnam War, American troops landed at Da Nang. The largest American base, used by the army, air force and navy, was located 68 miles (110 km) further south in Chu Lai. The territory between the city and the base was declared a *free-fire zone*, in which anything which moved would be fired upon. The people fled to Da Nang, where the population quickly swelled from 50,000 to 500,000. Today, this industrial city offers few noteworthy sights for a visitor.

The **Museum of Cham Sculpture** (Bao Tang Cham) was built in an open square, in the style of a Cham *mandapa*, in a park along the Han River. It contains 10 rooms with about 300 works, arranged according to stylistic periods. At the end of the 19th century, archaeologists of the École Francaise de l'Extrème Orient discovered the Cham monuments. In order

to collect all the finds in one central location, a storage depot was founded in Da Nang in 1915-1916, and this was opened as a museum in 1939. The works are placed in open rooms, and have to be anchored in the walls. At present, the museum is being renovated and expanded.

The **Cho Han** market on the Han River offers fresh seafood. A bit further inland is the **Cho Con** market, where handcrafts and textiles are sold. Nearby is the largest warehouse and the theater. The **Tuong** and **Cai Luong Theaters** have a long tradition in Da Nang and the surrounding villages, which has been reawakened in the last decade. Songs sung during card games, *bai choi*, have also been collected and are occasionally performed here.

Chua Pho Da (Chua Tam Bao), on Pham Chau Trinh Street, was founded in 1932 and is the largest pagoda in the city. **Chua Phap Lam** at 500 Ong Ich Kien Street, built in 1930, is the headquarters

Above: Cave temple in the Marble Mountains, Da Nang.

of the Union of Buddhists in Da Nang.

Bac My An Beach is about 3.5 miles (6 km) south of Da Nang on the way to Hoa Hai. The mountain village of **Ba Na**, 22 miles (36 km) east of the city, is more than 4,500 feet (1,400 m) above sea level. The French turned it into a resort in 1929. The town was completely destroyed in the war and has been rebuilt as a resort.

Hue, 65 miles (105 km) away, is attractive either as a day excursion or for a more extended visit. A ship route for tourists travelling from Da Nang to the Hai Nan Peninsula in southern China is to open in the near future. Highway 14 leads to the southern highlands.

Tum Ngu Hanh Son, the Mountains of the Five Elements, usually referred to as **Marble Mountains**, are 5 miles (8 km) from Da Nang and can be reached via the Nguyen Van Troi Bridge. Many legends surround these five limestone cliffs; they are said once to have been islands in the ocean, or – in another story – the eggs of a mother dragon. In the evening sunlight, they look like elephants straining to reach the sea. For the Vietnamese, the five elements are *thuy* (water), *kim* (metal, gold), *tho* (earth), *hoa* (fire), and *moc* (wood). Cham reliefs have been found in the caves of Tho Mountain; and there are also caves and grottoes in all the other mountain ranges. It is said that Emperor Le Thanh Tong founded the Tam Thai Pagoda in 1471 after the destruction of Vijaya, the Cham capital. In 1925, the Nguyen emperor Minh Mang came to the mountains, ordered paths built, built and expanded the Tam Thai and Ung Linh Pagodas, and placed them under his royal protection.

The largest number of pagodas is found on **Tuy** Mountain. This mountain encompasses 37,500 acres (15,000 ha), running from east to west. On the southern side, 156 steps lead up to the **Tam Thai caves**, where there used to be golden statues of Buddha. On the eastern side, 108 steps lead to the **Chua Ung Linh**. Narrow paths connect these two sites. From here, trails also lead to the grottoes of **Tang Chan**, **Van Thong** and **Van Nguyen** and to the scenic overlooks of **Vong Giang Da** and **Vong Hai Da**.

Sculptors and silversmiths live in the village of **Non Nuoc**. This seaside resort, located a little less than 2 miles (3 km) from the Marble Mountains and also known as China Beach, has a long stretch of sandy beach. The air and water temperatures remain constant, which means you can swim here all year round. Not surprisingly, therefore, Non Nuoc is being expanded as a tourist resort.

The City of Hoi An

Hoi An (Hai Pho) is about 14 miles (22 km) along a narrow road from the Marble Mountains (19 miles/30 km from Da Nang). Along Vietnam's coastline, much of the land is continuing to grow out into the ocean. In the 5th-6th centuries, the Cham had their harbor at the mouth of the Thu Bon; remains of this harbor have

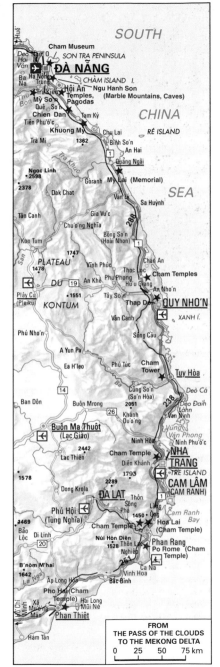

FROM
THE PASS OF THE CLOUDS
TO THE MEKONG DELTA
0   25   50   75 km

171

now been discovered about 2 miles (3 km) inland on Truong Phuong Lake. The Cham capital of Simhapura and the temple city of My Son were also located along the 124-mile (200 km) Thu Bon River. When the water is high enough, you can journey upriver by boat from Hoi An to the rapids just below My Son.

Hai Pho (Hoi An) was known to the seafaring Asians as early as the 15th-16th centuries. The Europeans arrived in the 17th century, bringing missionaries with them, and bowdlerized the name to Faifo. But even before the Europeans came, Japanese and Chinese had set up trade centers in separate parts of the city. In the 18th century, the Tay Son sacked these foreign trading settlements. The Chinese rebuilt theirs; the Japanese abandoned the region. As the heyday of Chinese trade passed, the harbor silted up. Textile industries grew up here in the colonial

Above: Fishermen on the beach of Non Nuoc (China Beach) by the Marble Mountains.

period. In the 20th century, however, Hoi An was forced to relinquish its harbor and industry to Da Nang. In 1930, the railroad came to Da Nang. As Hoi An grew more remote, it fostered a growing spirit of rebellion against the colonial power. The Americans, determined to nip this in the bud, established an outpost in Hoi An for the CIA and the Korean Green Dragon division in 1965. Also here was the province's central prison, holding as many as 4,000 political prisoners. The rebels retreated to the coastal village of **Quan Than**. When the American tanks got stuck in the sand dunes, the air force appeared on the scene, dropping napalm bombs and chemical weapons along 4 miles (7 km) of coastline and throughout the coconut palm plantations. By 1975, Hoi An was a dead city. Gradually, the refugees began trickling back, and started to reestablish the textile industry. In recent years, the Japanese have rediscovered the quaint charm of this city, its streets lined with 19th-century buildings, and would like to develop it into a tourist center. Hoi An has about 20 noteworthy sights from the 18th and 19th centuries.

Near the **Cam Nam Bridge**, there are still French colonial-style houses. **Chua Cau**, a pagoda in the middle of this wooden bridge, dates from 1793. The bridge itself once linked the Chinese and the Japanese parts of the city. Today, nothing remains of the Japanese neighborhood. Two stone dogs watch over the Chinese end of the 59-foot (18 m) bridge, while two monkeys guard the Japanese end. The Japanese began building it in a year of the monkey, and finished it two years later, in the year of the dog.

The Chinese were fishermen and merchants. They came from different southern Chinese provinces and built *hoi quan* (community buildings with temples) for their ancestors and taoistic gods, rarely for Buddhist statues. *Hoi quan* are community houses for people who originally came from the same region. Their floor plan is similar to that of a Chinese house. Almost all of the city's *hoi quan* are located on Duong Tran Phu. The **Hoi Quan Phuc Kien** was founded in 1792 for the Chinese from Fukien (Fokkien). One gate leads into a courtyard with a garden; another leads into a meeting-room with an enormous conference table. Murals depict the goddess of the sea and the six mandarins from Fukien who settled in Hai Pho. Passing through another courtyard, you come to a temple for the sea goddess and her two attendants, *See-All* and *Hear-All*, who report to her when fishermen and merchants run into trouble at sea. Yet another courtyard leads to the ancestral temple, where there are lounges and dining rooms, as well as guest rooms and a kitchen. **Hoi Quan Quang Dong**, founded in 1786 by Chinese from Quang Dong, is dedicated to Ong Quan Cong, a general of the Three Empires period (3rd century). **Hoi Quan Hai Nan**, the assembly hall for Chinese from the Hai Nan Peninsula, has a memorial for 108 members of the community who were executed after being falsely accused of piracy. There is lovely woodcarving in the **Hoi Quan Trieu Chau**, the assembly hall for Chinese from Trieu Chau, dating back to 1776. A *hoi quan* built in 1773 for five Chinese communities is today used for the production of rugs and bamboo curtains. On holidays it is used as a temple. **Mieu Quan Cong**, founded in 1653, is dedicated to General Ong Quan Cong.

There are only two pagodas here, located about half a mile (1 km) outside the city in Duong Nguyen Truong. A Chinese monk founded **Chua Chuc Than** in 1434; the pagoda still houses bells dating from that year. **Chua Phuc Lam**, 325 feet (100 m) away, was founded in the middle of the 17th century. Graves of Japanese merchants from the 17th century can be found a bit further outside the city.

You can also tour three homes of wealthy 19th-century merchants. The **house of the Tan Ky family** of merchants on Duong Nguyen Thai Hoc was built in 1840 and is now in the 6th generation of family ownership. It shows 19th-century lifestyle as well as the typical floor plan of a Chinese house, which alternates house buildings and courtyards so that a house complex reaches from one street to another, to the river or to the fields. In the first house, above the entrance and facing the interior of the house, is the ancestral altar, something found in all Chinese houses. The lovely stone floor, heavy, dark, carved columns and wooden panels covering the roof exude an atmosphere of affluence and wealth. A Chinese merchant built the **house of the Diep Dong Nguyen family**, on the same street, at the end of the 19th century. He once ran a pharmacy here; you can still see some of the furnishings. The **house in Duong Tran Phu** is somewhat older. Featuring beautifully carved walls and roof beams, it seems generally lighter, less serious and ceremonial.

From Duong Phan Chau Trinh, you can reach the **Cham Spring** (*bai le*). The deep wells of the Cham are famous for their clear and clean water. In Hoi An, this water is used to cook the noodles for *Cao Lau*, a local specialty.

Woodcarvers, responsible for the carvings in the city's temples and houses, have been living in Kim Bong village on Cam Kim Island for centuries, as have skilled carpenters who build boats.

The archipelago of the **Cham Islands** is so far from the coast (12 miles/20 km) that its sea swallows cannot collect their nest-building materials from the mainland. Instead, the birds build their bowl-shaped nests from their own hardened saliva. For many years, swallows' nests (*yen sao*) have been collected from five caves on these islands and sold for high sums to Chinese gourmets. Originally, the Nguyen leased out this concession,

Above: Hoi An, house of the merchant family Tam Ky (1840); the woodcarvings in the main room.

but today it's the state that profits. The job of nest collector is difficult and dangerous. Three times a year, after the young swallows have departed, the nests are removed from the caves' inside walls, using bamboo scaffolding. They are then washed and sorted according to size. These swallows' nests are also collected on other island groups south of Hoi An. Currently, plans are taking shape to open up the Cham Islands to tourists.

THE TEMPLE CITY OF MY SON

The temple city of My Son is 43 miles (70 km) southwest of Da Nang. After 28 miles (45 km), a smaller side road leads off to Tra Kieu. From a Christian church which sits high among the rice fields, you can make out the remains of the defensive walls which surrounded the first Cham capital, Simhapura. The cathedral at the roadside has a small museum with Cham works of art, found by peasants in the fields. Tra Kieu is 15.5 miles (25 km) from the Thu Bon River, which is crossed

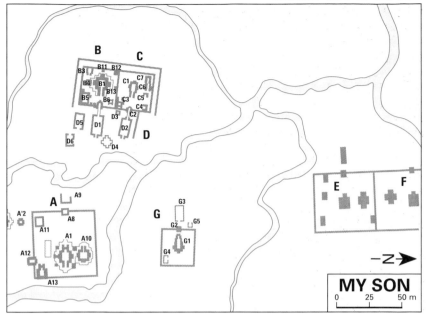

by a small footbridge. It would be unfortunate indeed if the road for car traffic were to be extended all the way to the temple, as it would destroy the serenity of the valley. Currently, you follow a pleasant path through the low jungle growth for 2.5 miles (4 km) to the ruins.

In a hilly valley below the mountain My Son (lovely mountain), also known as hon quap (cat's tooth) because of its overhanging summit, once lay some 70 Cham temples from between the 8th and 13th centuries, described and restored by French architect H. Parmentier at the beginning of the 20th century. My Son lay within the free-fire zone; after U.S. Air Force attacks in 1968, 20 ruins remained. Since 1981, 15 of these have been rescued from complete ruin by Vietnamese and Polish restoration experts, under the direction of the architect K. Kwiatkowski from Lublin. The first step was to clear the area of mines; only then could the jungle growth be cleared, the ruins surveyed and partially restored. After every rainy season, vegetation, moss and mildew have to be removed. Between 1992 and 1994, with support from the German government, the buildings D1 and D2 were restored and opened as museums.

French scientists were responsible for the classification system, labelling the temple groups with letters from A to L, and assigning numbers to buildings within the individual ensembles. The Vietnamese have adopted this system.

The best way to get a good overview of the complex is to stand with your back to D1 and D2, two long *mandapa* (now museums). Temple B will be at your left, Temple C at your right. A gate indicates where the wall around group B once stood. This group's main temple was destroyed, leaving only the foundations. Within them is the temple's lingam, found in 1985. To the left is the 10th-century library, B5, with an elephant relief. The next building, B4, is thought to date from the 9th century. To the right of the main temple, B6 has also survived.

The main shrine of the C1 ensemble is, as an exception to the rule, built on a

175

square foundation. The roof structure of this large *kalan* with its long porch was only one story high. It dates from the 10th century, and has lovely ornamentation on its facade. There's also lovely figurative and decorative ornamentation on the facades of the side buildings, C5-C7. The buildings in the D ensemble aren't really an independent group, but are actually the *mandapa* of B and C. Note the mandapa D1, on your left, which is the loveliest surviving building. Behind you, the A group lies on the other side of the Thu Bon River. The French described the A1 tower, now destroyed, as the most beautiful brick structure in all of Asia. Group E has been surveyed, while Group F has not yet been excavated. The sculptures found at the site are displayed in the D1 and D2 museums, where you can also see the remains of the only grave which has been discovered here to date, found

between the walls surrounding B and C. All of the buildings are brick; only the G group, located somewhat apart from the other groups, is made of laterite, a material which, though available in abundance, was rarely used by the Cham. Even despite the destruction, My Son still provides a vivid impression of the great artistic talents of the Cham.

Three Cham temples near Highway 1 (Da Nang - Quy Nhon), **Bang An**, **Chien Dan** and **Khuong My**, can be easily reached on a one-day excursion from Da Nang (124 miles/200 km round trip) or as a stopover as you make your way south.

17 miles (27 km) down Highway 1, after the road passes over a bridge, a small road on the right leads about 4 miles (6 km) to the single-tower shrine (*kalan*) of **Bang An** (12th century). It is the only octagonal structure built by the Cham. The interesting roof has been badly damaged. Animal sculptures stand in front of the tower; the interior is empty. The newer parts of the wall were reconstructed by French restorers.

Above: My Son, the ruined main temple B with the lingam, recovered in 1985. Right: Member of the Cham minority.

Chien Dan (10th century), 50 miles (80 km) south of Da Nang, is set just 325 feet (100 m) back from Highway 1, past a bend in the road. The three-tower shrine was shored up in 1989/90 and the base exposed, enabling almost 200 reliefs, sculptures and fragments to be preserved. A museum is currently in the planning stages. The outstanding reliefs of the base were also exposed and restored.

Khuong My (10th century), 7 miles (10 km) south of Chien Dan, is on the outskirts of the village of Tam Ky. Just before a bridge, a side road leads right off the main road, running about half a mile (1 km) to the triple-tower shrine. It has *kalans* of different heights built on square bases of varying sizes. Only the middle and southern towers have vestibules. The Khmer influence is evident. Heavy tree growth has damaged the towers, and bricks from the walls have served later generations for the construction of their own paths and houses. The enclosing wall and auxiliary buildings have completely disappeared. A small temple for a local deity stands behind the towers. The lake, located half a mile (1 km) away, provides water for cleansing the statues.

QUANG NGAI PROVINCE

In the year 982, the northern kingdom of the Cham, Amaravati, ended at the southern border of the province Quang Nam - Da Nang. To the left of the road, 68 miles (110 km) from Da Nang, lay the U.S. military base of **Chu Lai**. The Vietnamese have now built a victory monument on the other side of the road.

A little over a mile (2 km) beyond the provincial capital of Quang Ngai, before the bridge over the Tra Khuc, a sign points the way to the My Lai memorial, 7.5 miles (12 km) away. It was in this village that 504 people, mainly women and children, were murdered by U.S. soldiers during a punitive expedition. In Co Ly, near the mouth of the Tra Khuc, was a

Cham fortress. Several sculptures were found here in 1958. The village temple contains a statue of the Cham emperor Po Klaung Gahul. Cham graves have also been discovered in the area. In **Sa Huynh**, a seaside village with a lovely beach, protohistoric finds have been excavated and termed Sa Huynh culture. This region is known for producing salt.

BINH DINH PROVINCE

In this region, the northern Cham empire, Vijaya, was located from the 11th-15th centuries. 12 Cham structures remain from this epoch, scattered around the province's capital, Quy Nhon.

Thoc Loc (12th century), called Golden Tower by the French, is about 25 miles (40 km) before Quy Nhon. A footpath about a mile long (2 km) leads off to the left from the village of Go Gang, on Highway 1, to the *kalan*. This dates from the end of the Vijaya epoch; its roof structures are stylized, and the building has several "false," *trompe l'oeil* stories.

The **Canh Thien** (11th-12th centuries), called Copper Tower by the French, is about half a mile (1 km) from Highway 1, to the right. To get there, you take a small footpath from the middle of the village Dap Da, and across a dam at the cemetery. The tower, once part of the Cham capital Vijaya, has projecting eaves and small *kalans* at the corners. Several other ruins and remains of walls can be found in the area around Canh Thien.

Four structures of the larger temple group **Banh It** (11th century) are still standing on a hill, visible from afar. 11 miles (18 km) before Quy Nhon, a road to the left leads to the foot of the hill. A gate on the side of the hill was part of the surrounding wall, aligned on an axis with the main tower. The *kalan* has a large vestibule. On its south side is a library with a barrel roof.

Also 11 miles (18 km) before Quy Nhon, Highway 19 branches off into the southern highlands toward Play Cu. This road was fortified by the Americans as a strategic route. After 15.5 miles (25 km), in Phu Phong, a small street leads off right across the Co River dam. Rade and Sarang minorities live in this region. A memorial with a temple and museum is found in Tay Son, the birthplace of the Tay Son brothers. As a tribute to the fighting techniques of the youngest brother Nguyen Hue, who later became Emperor Quang Trung, the sport of cockfighting, *Tay Son Vo Si*, was developed, a discipline in which small men had a realistic chance to beat large opponents. Today, you can arrange to see *Tay Son Vo Si* demonstrations in the museum. On the fifth day of the first lunar month, young people show their skills in this martial art during a festival.

Duong Long, a triple-tower Cham shrine from the 12th century, is 6 miles (10 km) from the memorial, in the village

Right: Morning exercises on Nha Trang beach.

of Trung Dinh. This monumental ensemble, in the middle of the rice fields, shows evidence of Khmer influence, particularly in the use of sandstone in the opulent decor. The form here shows signs of simplification, but does not yet signify the decline of Cham art.

Of the three towers of the shrine **Thap Doi** (12th/13th centuries), two now remain. The shrine was originally located on a lagoon between the sea and the mountains. Today it is in Quy Nhon, 3 miles (5 km) from the city center, on the left side of the road amidst houses and marketplace. The interesting roof structures have been restored.

Quy Nhon, capital of Binh Ninh province, is at the estuary of the Song Cai. It has a harbor for ocean-going vessels and a long beach lined with palms, which is to be opened up to the tourist trade. The region has a great deal of rainfall, and the dampness seeps into the walls of the houses, covering them with grey algae and greenish moss. The **Chua Long Khanh** dates from the 17th century. **Cho Lon**, the large marketplace, forms the city center. The **Truong Theater** has, without a doubt, the best troupe of actors in Vietnam. There are also *Tay Son Vo Si* demonstrations Quy Nhon.

PHU YEN PROVINCE

The route from Quy Nhon to Nha Trang (150 miles/240 km) is the loveliest stretch of Highway 1 south of Cloud Pass. After 25 miles (40 km) of rice fields and lanes lined with eucalyptus trees, you reach the 4-mile (6 km) **Deo Cu Mong** Pass, which leads through bright bamboo forests. The road climbs to an altitude of 800 feet (245 m), providing a lovely panorama across the sea. **Tuy Hua**, capital of Phu Yen Province, is the headquarters of the sugar industry. Beyond the city, on a hill, is **Bao Thap**, a Cham tower. At the foot of the hill is the **Chua Ba Sat**. Another pass, the 7.5 mile (12 km) long **Deo**

Ca, winds its way up the mountain, offering a beautiful view of the valleys at its foot. The cliffs on the high peak to the left of the street are called **Hon Vong Phu** (Waiting For the Husband). According to legend, a fisherman's wife stood here holding her child, waiting for her husband to return from the sea, until finally she turned to stone. From the top of the pass, the sea, with its islands and bays, comes into view. The railroad also runs along this stretch, passing through seven tunnels, one of them the longest in Vietnam (about half a mile/1 km). A picturesque fishing village in a large bay lies at the foot of the third pass, **Deo Dai Lang**.

The **O Loan Lagoon** is a paradise for nature lovers, gourmets and travelers with plenty of time. O and Loan are legendary birds from which the lagoon takes its name. Freshly-caught fish, crabs and mussels are grilled over charcoal fires right on the fishing boats, or cooked into soups. Not far away are the **Vung Dieu Lagoon** and the **Bai Ngo Beach**.

KHANH HOA PROVINCE

The smaller **Deo Co Ma**, or Horseneck Pass, is located 51 miles (83 km) before Nha Trang. From here, a road branches off to the resort village of **Dac Deu**. Highway 26 leads from Ninh Hoa, 20 miles (32 km) before Nha Trang, into the southern highlands. One final pass, **Ro Tuong**, 17 miles (27 km) before Nha Trang, provides a scenic panorama of the sea. On a hill outside the city stands the grave of Alexandre Yersin (1863-1943), a French doctor of Swiss heritage who established the **Pasteur Institute** in Nha Trang in 1899.

Nha Trang is the capital of Khanh Hoa Province. The name hearkens back to the Cham term Yatran. Fishing here is among the best in Vietnam, and swallows' nests are collected on the islands off the coast. The 6 miles (10 km) of sandy beach is well set up to accommodate tourists. Divers and snorkelers will appreciate the conditions here, particularly around the offshore island of **Hon**

Above: Po Nagara, Cham shrines from between the 7th and 13th centuries, Nha Trang.

Mun, where, when the sea is calm, you have a visibility of some 82 feet (25 m) through the crystal-clear waters. A boat trip of 15 minutes brings you to the island of **Tri Nguyen** with its long expansive sandy beaches. It was turned into a resort in 1971, and houses aquariums where fish, turtles and crustaceans are bred.

Po Nagara (Thap Ba), dating from the 7th-13th centuries, was formerly the temple city Kauthara in the southern Cham empire. It perches on a hill above the fishing harbor on the Yatran River. 14 columns of a former *mandapa* line the pathway up to the temple. The shrine was first documented in the 7th century, while the most recent structure dates from the 13th century. Four of the 10 temples still remain. In 774, the Javanese plundered the temple, destroying it and taking a golden mask of Shiva as booty. In the year 930, it was sacked by the Khmer. Po Nagara, mother of the country and a local goddess of this city, is worshipped by both the Vietnamese and the Cham. The main shrine houses a statue of Bhagavati, one of Shiva's wives, and part of the cult of Po Nagara. The main temple, 74 feet (22.5 m) high, has a three-story roof and well-crafted brick walls. Bhagavati, with her ten arms, sits on a lotus throne in the dimly-lit shrine. The southern temple, with its non-integrated roof structure, is the only one built on a square foundation. The oldest *kalan*, in the northwest, also has a well-preserved facade. The temple festival is held on the 23rd day of the 3rd lunar month.

The **Dam Market**, built in 1972, is the largest in Nha Trang. Families from the harbor area to the south produce souvenirs of coral, tortoiseshell, mother-of-pearl and mussel shells. **Bach Dinh**, the white palace on a hill overlooking the harbor, was a residence of the last Vietnamese king, Bao Dai; today, it serves as a hotel. The **Marine Biology Institute**, built along the harbor in 1922, has collections of fish and other aquatic life. The **Chua Long Son**, at the southern end of the city, has a large Buddha on a hill behind the temple. Today's temple building dates from 1971, but is on the site where an older temple once stood. Going on excursions from Nha Trang to Buon Ma Thuat in the southern highlands, you take Highway 26, a rather poor road.

From Nha Trang to Phan Thiet

Between Nha Trang and Ho Chi Minh City, Highway 1 crosses no fewer than 257 bridges over rivers and streams. Mango groves, plantations of coconut palms and tobacco begin on the other side of Nha Trang. Vietnam's best natural harbor is found in **Cam Ranh** Bay, 13.5 miles (22 km) long and 2.5 miles (4 km) wide. It was leased to the Americans until 1975, serving as an important naval base. After 1975, it became a Soviet base.

The region is inhabited by the Darley minority group, dark-skinned hunter-gatherers who carry their baskets on their backs. 750 acres (300 ha) of land here are used for extracting salt from seawater. Water buffalo and herons roam the fields. Plows here are pulled by yokes of two animals. Huge flocks of ducks cavort in the ponds and irrigation canals. The less fertile regions are used for livestock cultivation: the cattle come from Cuba, cows from India, and pigs from Yorkshire.

Hoa Lai (8th-9th centuries) was a triple-tower Cham shrine. The third tower was destroyed during the war of independence. The decoration of the smaller, southern tower is the more attractive of the remaining two. Both shrines are becoming overgrown.

Phan Rang - Thap Cham, capital of Ninh Thuan Province, served as the seat of the last Champa empire. You still encounter Cham minorities on the street; the men sometimes wear robes and turbans and carry large shoulder baskets. The Muslim Cham have four mosques in

Phan Rang. **Ninh Chu**, a deserted beach, is located 3 miles (5 km) south of the city.

The Phan Rang - Thap Cham train station is 5 miles (8 km) east of the city. From 1930 to 1964 a cog-wheel train ran from here to Da Lat, a resort in the southern highlands. Powering it was a locomotive built in Germany in 1929. After the train was discontinued in 1990, the locomotive and train cars were transported to Switzerland. Today the only link to Da Lat is a winding, uneven mountain road.

Po Klaung Garai (13th century) is a Cham shrine with three remaining structures. Along the road to Da Lat, on the other side of the train tracks, you can see the temple, which the Cham call Chok Hala; a road leads up the hill. The Cham use the temple for four different religious festivals. They climb the hill and pass through the gate which is on an axis with the main temple. This temple has a large vestibule with a statue of the steer Nandi. Emperor Po Klaung Garai can be seen inside the temple in the form of a muchalingam. For the Cham, this phallic form with the face of Shiva, which originated in India, is often seen as representing the idolized king.

The simplification and loss of ornamentation in later Cham structures is apparent in the temple roof. In the lateral temple, called fire temple by the Cham, incense sticks are lit during religious ceremonies and carried into the main temple in honor of the Emperor. During these festivals, held between planting and harvesting, the Cham sing their traditional songs and dance ritual dances.

Villages of Cham minorities are found along Highway 1, between Phan Rang and Phan Thiet. Only a few farms are still set up along matriarchal lines with the house of the mother of the extended family in the middle. South of Phan Rang live the last surviving descendants of the Cham emperors. A Cham cemetery, located near the village of Tai Son, still has *kut* stones. These are menhirs with faces

carved into them, seen as manifestations of the idolized ancestors.

Po Rome, called Cham Da Lai Thuom by the Cham (16th or 17th century), is the last Cham temple. It is 9 miles (15 km) south of Phan Rang near the village **Huu Phuoc**. It is 3 miles (5 km) back from the road, on the right side, on one of two adjacent hills 165 feet (50 m) high. The roof decor is so simplified that it appears square. The structure must have been built in a great hurry; even the bricks are laid without the usual accuracy.

Huge boulders are piled atop one another along a half mile (1 km) stretch of the **Ca Na Beach**. It is said to have been a fishing bank of the Cham.

Since 1948, the famous mineral water has been bottled near the village of **Vinh Hoa**, 1.2 miles (2 km) back from the road. The springs were holy sites during the time of the Cham emperors.

The fishing village of **Mui Ne**, with its beach and dunes, is located on a peninsula about 12 miles (20 km) before Phan Thiet.

Pho Hai (8th century), a triple-tower shrine and the southernmost Cham temple, is located 4 miles (7 km) before Phan Thiet, directly on the ocean. It dates from the early days of the southern empire and displays similarities with Khmer structures of this period. The beach extends to the city limits of Phan Thiet.

Phan Thiet is the capital of the southernmost province (Binh Thuan) of Trung Bo. The fish sauce, *nuoc mam*, from Phan Thiet is said to be the best in the country. Fishing boats anchor on the Phan Thiet River at the entrance to the city.

Highway 1 continues on to Ho Chi Minh City, becoming better and better the further south one travels. It passes by gardens of spices planted with clove trees, climbing pepper bushes, and coffee trees, as well as tea plantations. The countryside here is not suitable for rice cultivation, but in the last decades it has been used intensively for livestock breeding.

Above: Boatyard, Nha Trang.

QUANG NAM-DA NANG PROVINCE
Accommodations (area code: 84 51)
DA NANG: *MODERATE to BUDGET:* **Bach Dang Hotel,** 50, Bach Dang St., tel. 2 36 49; **Hai Chau Hotel,** 177, Tran Phu St., tel. 2 27 22; *Am Non Nuoc beach (China Beach),* 7 miles/11 km from Da Nang: Non Nuoc Hotel complex with tourist center, tel. 2 14 70.

Getting There/Transportation
Airport 4 miles / 7 km from the city center. **Vietnam Airlines,** 35, Tran Phu St., tel. 2 11 30, 7 - 11 am, 1:30 - 4:30 pm except Sun.; train station half a mile / 1 km out of town, reserve ahead! **Bus station** 2 miles / 3 km fromthe city center on Dien Bien Phu St., daily 1 - 5 pm; **local buses** from the bus station on Hung Vuong Str.

Further Information
Trade Bank, 46, Le Loi St., 7:30 - 11:30 am, 1:30 - 3:30 pm except Sun and Thu and Sat afternoons; main **post office,** 46, Bach Dang St., daily 6 am - 9 pm (international services).
Hospital, Ngo Gia Tu St.; **Museum of Cham Sculpture,** Tran Phu St., 7 am - 3 pm except Mon.

Tourist Information
Quang Nam - Da Nang-Tourist, 68, Bach Dang St., tel. 2 14 23, fax 2 28 54. **Hoi An-Tourist,** 100, Tran Phu St., tel. 72

QUANG NGAI PROVINCE
Accommodations (area code: 84 55)
QUANG NGAI: Song Tra Hotel with restaurant, tel. 26 64/5;

Tourist Information
Quang Ngai-Tourist, in the Song Tra hotel, tel. 38 70.

BINH DINH PROVINCE
Accommodations (area code: 84 56)
QUY NHON: *BUDGET:* **Quy Nhon Hotel A** and **B,** 8 and 10, Nguyen Hue St., tel. 22401; **Phuong Mai Hotel,** 14, Nguyen Hue St.;

Further Information
Phu Cat **Airport,** train station in Dieu Tre, 6 miles / 10 km west, local trains bring you there; **bus station** on Tran Hung Dao St. in the west of town; **regional buses** to the station and airport from Phan Bou Chao St.; **bank** 148, Tran Hung Dao Str. (cash only); **post office** Hai Ba Trung St.; **Tay Son Museum** with guesthouse ca. 28 miles / 45 km on Highway 19, toward Play Cu.

Tourist Information
Tourist office of the province is **Binh Dinh-Tourist,** 10, Nguyen Hue St., tel. 2 25 24; **Tourist office** of the city of **Quy Nhon,** 41, Nguyen Hue St., tel. 22 82.

PHU YEN PROVINCE
Accommodations (area code: 84 57)
TUY HOA: Phong Lan Hotel, Nguyen Hue St., tel. 31 81; **Huong Sen Hotel** with restaurant, Tran Hung Dao St.

Further Information
Post Office on the marketplace.

Tourist Information
Phu Yen-Tourist, 137, Le Thanh Ton St., tel. 2 33 53.

KHANH HOA PROVINCE
Accommodations (area code: 84 58)
NHA TRANG: *MODERATE:* **Bao Dai's Villa,** Tran Phu St., tel. 2 24 49; **Hai Yen Hotel,** 40, Tran Phu St., tel. 2 29 74; **Thang Loi Hotel,** 4, Pasteur St., tel. 2 22 41; *BUDGET:* **Thong Nhat,** 18, Thong Nhat St., tel. 22966.

Getting There/Transportation
Airport south of the city. Train station on Thai Nguyen St., 8:30 - 10 am, 2 - 4:30 pm, reservations advised; **bus station,** Le Hong Phong St., for express buses, 46, Le Thanh Ton St., 6:30 am - 4:30 pm; **regional buses** depart between the river bridges.

Tourist Information
Khan Hoa-Tourist, Nha Trang, 1, Tran Hung Dao St., tel. 2 27 53, fax 2 19 12.

NINH THUAN PROVINCE
Accommodations (area code: 84 68)
PHAN RANG - THAP CHAM: Huu Nghi Hotel, 2, Hung Vuong St.; **Phan Rang Hotel** and **Thong Nhat Hotel,** on Thong Nhat St.; *on the beach of Ninh Chu* (3 miles/5 km south): **Ninh Chu Hotel,** tel. 22.

Further Information
Bus station on Thong Nhat St.; **train station** Thap Cham, 4 miles / 7 km west near the Cham temple.

Tourist Information
Ninh Thuan-Tourist, Thong Nhat St., tel. 2 25 42.

BINH THUAN PROVINCE
Accommodations (area code: 84 62)
PHAN THIET: Phan Thiet Hotel, 276, Tran Hung Dao St., tel. 2 16 94; On the beach north of town: **Vinh Thuy Hotel,** 1, Ton Duc Thang St., Tel 26 22;

Further Information
Bus station on the river bridge; train station of Muong Man 7 miles / 12 km west, access trains.

Tourist Information
Binh Thuan-Tourist, 82, Trung Trac St., tel. 2 24 94.

SOUTHERN HIGHLANDS

In the Land of the Mountain People

The southern part of Truong Son is known as Tay Nguyen, the Southern or Western Highlands. Its three mountain ranges run north-south, descending sharply, in the east, toward the coastal plains. To the south, in Song Be Province, the mountainous terrain dwindles into the hill country at the northern edge of the Mekong Delta. Along the top of the mountain ranges runs the border with Laos and Cambodia.

From a geological and structural point of view, southern Truong Son differs not only from the mountains in the north, but also from those of northern Truong Son. Like the mountains of lower Laos, northeastern Cambodia and Thailand, it is part of the Indochinese Massif. The limestone lies under a layer of slate, laced with veins of granite and basalt. About 65% of the mountainside is wooded, and there are a number of inactive volcanoes and volcanic lakes. Over 70% of the region's reddish soil is suitable for the cultivation of rubber trees, coffee and tea. Rice is grown in the irrigated river valleys or as dry rice in the mountains.

The mountains are sparsely populated. In Kon Tum Province, only 230,000 people live within 4,516 square miles (11,580 sq. km). As well as Vietnamese, 32 of the country's 54 minorities live in the southern highlands, extending across the borders in the neighboring states. In the Vietnam Wars, both the French and Americans took advantage of the mountain tribes' antagonism, training them to fight in border warfare and against the Vietnamese. The hostile feelings still remain. At the end of the 1980s, the government policy of settling Vietnamese in

Left: 32 of the 54 minorities live in the Southern Highlands. Above: Many spices come from this region.

the New Economic Zones, created after 1975, led to further unrest.

Standards of living and civilization among the various minorities vary greatly from group to group. Many villages of hunter-gatherers with huge families of children, who eke out a living by practicing primitive agriculture in burned-out clearings, suffer from atrocious poverty. Other tribes farm their land, use its timber, or raise livestock. Additional sources of income include fishing the lakes and rivers or artisan crafts, particularly weaving.

In addition to utilitarian and fine wood, herbs and spices, one of the most valuable resources in the mountains is the wealth of wild elephants which are captured, tamed and trained as work animals. They are used to transport logs out of the mountains. Until the war disrupted the profitable elephant trade, buyers from Burma and India came here for their elephants. A large number of rivers have their sources in the highlands, flowing down into the East China Sea. These

could be harnessed for irrigation and for the production of electricity.

Several roads lead from the coastal plains up into the highlands. Every plateau has an airport. The provinces are linked by Highway 14, which runs from Da Nang in the north. It meets Highway 20 in Da Lat, and Highway 13 in Son Be Province. Both of these highways lead to Ho Chi Minh City.

KON TUM AND GIA LAI PROVINCES

The province of Kon Tum (Cong Tum), with its capital of the same name, and the province of Gia Lai, the capital of which is Play Cu, are on the Kon Tum - Gia Lai plateau.

Kon Tum, which covers 4,545 square miles (11,650 sq. km), is the 7th-largest of Vietnam's 50 provinces. With only 18

inhabitants per square kilometer, it is the most sparsely populated. The city of Kon Tum, 193 miles (312 km) from Da Nang, is 1,753 feet (536 m) above sea level. The plateau is surrounded by mountains, which are older than the massifs to the south. **A Thuat** rises to 8,175 feet (2,500 m), the Mang measures 5,559 feet (1,700 m), and the Ba Da 4,797 feet (1,467 m). Noteworthy sights in Kon Tum include a wooden **cathedral**, about 200 years old, and the **Ba Ai Pagoda**. **Yaly Waterfall** is located 13.5 miles (22 km) to the south-west. The minority groups call the pile houses they live in *rong*.

Play Cu (Pleiku), capital of Gia Lai Province, is 29 miles (46 km) from Kon Tum on Highway 14. You can also reach it from Quy Nhon on Highway 19, a well-built road which crosses the Mang Giang Pass (113 miles/182 km). Play Cu also has an airport. With its 40,000 inhabitants, this town is an important market for the highlands. Coffee and tea are grown in its red soil. The plateau, surrounded by mountains, is 2,300-2,600

Above: Tea grows throughout the Southern Highlands; the Vietnamese prefer to drink green tea.

feet (700-800 m) above sea level. Abundant in fish, **Tu Truong** Lake is a volcanic lake 6 miles (10 km) from the town.

27 minority groups live in this province. Around Play Cu, the main minority group is the Jarai.

The minorities celebrate traditional festivals with *Mnam Thuon*, buffalo sacrificed on special occasions. The festive meal of new rice eaten in every household after the harvest is called *Hua Esei Mrao*. The largest festival, *Pothi*, honors the dead; people go to the cemeteries so that the living can visit the dead.

Since 1994, the tourist office in Play Cu has been offering interesting excursions and sightseeing trips. Wild elephants are trained in the village of **Nhon Hoh**, also called Elephant Village; you can watch the training sessions, and even try riding on an elephant's back.

Other points of interest include **Ayun Ha** Lake, the **Da Trang** (white stone) River, the fire king in the village of **Pleioi**, Mount **Ham Rong**, **Ya Bang** Lake, the tea plantations of **Dau Cam**, the village of **Bia**, **Da Che** mountain, the village **Xa Nam** (Am Khe), the town of **Dan Chu**, the woods of **Kon Cho Rang**, and the former battlefield of Pleme.

DAC LAC PROVINCE

Buon Ma Thuot on the Dac Lac plateau is the capital of Vietnam's largest province (7,722 square miles/19,800 sq. km). It is 122 miles (197 km) from Play Cu on Highway 14. Highway 26, a road in bad condition, leads from Nha Trang over the Deo Phuong Hoang, or Phoenix Pass, into the elephant mountains of Nui Voi (113 miles/183 km). Buon Ma Thut also has an airport. The plateau and the capital are both 1,635 feet (500 m) above sea level, a good 650 feet (200 m) lower than Play Cu. This means that the climate here is warmer. It is surrounded by mountains; the highest, **Chu Yang Sinh**, measures 7,983 feet (2,442 m).

SOUTHERN HIGHLANDS

0   25   50   75   100 km

In the language of the Ede minority, Dac Lac means savannah; and this plateau is mainly covered with sparse woods and savannahs. Rubber trees, coffee and tea are grown in the basalt-rich soil, which is also suitable for raising livestock. After the Vietnamese, most of the population are Ede, a minority which grows rice and corn in the irrigated river valleys. The Ede are also known for raising work elephants. Almost every family in the Ede villages owns an elephant.

In the village of **Buon Don**, the land of the elephants, some elephant hunters manage to capture several hundred of these animals over the years. It takes about two to three years to tame and train an elephant to work in the mountain woods. There are severe penalties for anyone caught killing elephants for their ivory. In the spring, during the traditional

annual competitions, drivers and elephants demonstrate their talents. More than 50 elephants take part in the races, lumbering over a 1,635 foot (500 m) course. Visitors come from near and far, making it hard to book accommodations and plane reservations. The road continues through the picturesque Ede village of **Buon Tua**, with pile houses, to the **Dray Sap** waterfall. To the south is the 1,250-acre (500 ha) Lac Lake, at an altitude of 1,308 feet (400 m). Nestled among the towering mountains, it is a refuge for storks and cranes. With its abundance of fish, it is known as the fish pot of the highlands; and you can enjoy both fishing and boating on its waters. The Ede demonstrate traditional dances, sing songs and sell home-made rice wine. Buon Ma Thuot has a small but very interesting **museum** of minority groups.

Above: House of the Ede tribe in Dac Lac province. Right: Ede grave in Dac Lac province. Far right: Peasant woman in the highlands near Da Lat.

LAM DONG PROVINCE

Da Lat is the capital of Lam Dong Province, which has three large plateaus.

188

Lam Vien, on which Da Lat is located, is at an altitude of 4,907 feet (1,500 m); **Don Duong - Lien Khuong** is at 3,270 feet (1,000 m); and **Bao Loc - Di Linh** is at 2,616 feet (800 m).

Da Lat is 155 miles (250 km) from Buon Ma Thuot along Highway 14, and 186 miles (300 km) from Ho Chi Minh City on Highway 20. Although it's only 76 miles (123 km) from Phan Rang, the road is very poor, leading around sharp curves and over steep mountains, including the pass **Deo Song Pha**, 12.5 miles (20 km) long and 3,270 feet (1,000 m) high. After crossing the second pass (4,905 feet/1,500 m), the road reaches the plateau. There's a waterworks, built in the 1960s and fed by the river Da Nhim, on the mountainside above Phan Rang. The cog-wheel train which once serviced this steep route no longer runs.

With its mild climate, Da Lat is often referred to as the city of eternal spring. It was discovered in 1893 by the French scientist Yersin. His countrymen retreated here in the hot summer months, enjoying the mountains' cool climate and many lakes. Da Lat reminded them of a European city, and they nicknamed it Little Paris. Although visitors may be enchanted by the town's charm, it doesn't seem very Vietnamese; some travelers might prefer the more traditional atmosphere around Dac Lac and Gia Lai to the land of love and honeymoons, as the Vietnamese call Da Lat. In the language of the mountain peoples – Kho, Lat, Chit, Kahor, Sre, Baja, Nop Maug, Chill, Ma and Chum – *da* means land or water. Da Lat is thus the land of the Lat. The mountain people call the plateau *Nang Biang*. The name commemorates Nang, a young boy, who could not marry the girl Biang because they came from different mountain tribes. Retreating into the jungle in desperation, they both took their lives. All of the animals came to their funeral, crying so many tears that the river *Da Nhim*, Water of the Eyes, was formed. Only one lion arrived too late. Turned to stone, he now stands, eternally mourning, by the road to Ho Chi Minh City.

Da Lat has a well-developed tourist infrastructure, with hotels built by the French and accommodations in villas. The city is an Eldorado for lovers of flowers, particularly orchids; you can see wild orchids and countless hybrids in the nurseries and gardens. Horse-drawn wagons take visitors to the golf course or to the town's most scenic sights. A promenade leads around **Xuang Huong Lake** with its outdoor restaurants and cafés.

The temples and churches as well as the *hoi quan*, the Chinese community houses, all date from the 20th century. Loveliest among these are the **Hoi Quan Thien Vuong** (Chua Than), built in 1958, and the **Hoi Quan Minh Nuyet Chu Sy Lam**, from 1962. The **Chua Linh Phong** was constructed in 1952. Da Lat has two noteworthy structures from the 1930s: the cathedral and a villa which was the summer residence of the last Vietnamese emperor, Bao Dai, and which is now open to the public.

Above: The Cham Ly waterfalls near Da Lat.

The **Nuclear Institute** built by the USA was rendered inoperative in 1975. The Soviet Union has since turned it into a center for research in medicine, geology and agricultural technology.

20 minority groups live on the plateaus and in the mountains, generally in pile houses. Some practice animistic, nature religions; others are Protestants or Catholics. Several of their villages are easily reached from Da Lat. A small **museum** in Da Lat provides insight into the lifestyle of the mountain peoples. On Sunday mornings, the tribes sell their products at the marketplace by the large **market hall**. Everything which grows on the plateaus can be found here, including coffee, tea, potatoes, vegetables and a variety of fruits, particularly pineapples, as well as plants and flowers. The market hall itself, and the shops around it, is a shoppers' paradise for everything which is produced in Vietnam.

Da Lat has a large number of waterfalls, though they are only impressive after the rainy season. The **Cam Ly Falls** are just over a mile (2 km) from the center of town. Most famous is the **Prenn Falls** (Thien Sa), 8 miles (13 km) south of Da Lat on the road to Ho Chi Minh City. Other falls, which drop from 50 to 100 feet (15 to 30 m), are worthwhile for their picturesque settings. The **Ankroet Falls** are known as the Golden Current. The **Da Tanla Falls** are 3.5 miles (6 km) south of town, thundering over the towering cliffs in two separate cascades. 18.5 miles (30 km) further on are the **Lien Khuong Falls** and the **Gougah Falls**, also known as O Ga Falls. The latter, 23.5 miles (38 km) from Da Lat, tumbles down over 65 feet (20 m). The **Pongour Falls** are hidden away in thick forest, 31 miles (50 km) from Da Lat; they're said to be the most picturesque of all. Another popular site for excursions is the Valley of Love with its lovely lake **Than Tho**.

From Da Lat to Ho Chi Minh City

The journey along Highway 20 from Da Lat to Ho Chi Minh City, a distance of 186 miles (300 km), takes about six hours. About two hours into the journey, around the town of **Bao Loc**, it is not unusual to see members of the Ma minority carrying their baskets secured on a headband. They are also fishermen, hunters and plantation workers; the women are weavers. Around the town, 25,000 acres (10,000 ha) have been planted with mulberry trees. In Vietnam's largest silkworm breeding grounds, crossbreeding has produced hybrids which can withstand the cooler climate. The production of silk in Vietnam is a tradition dating back more than 1,000 years.

At the 124-mile mark (200 km), near the village of **Duc Trong** (Dienh Quan), bizarre cliffs tower above the road on both sides. Below these sits the stone lion of the legend, described above. At the beginning of the expressway, 18.5 miles (30 km) outside Ho Chi Minh City, Highway 20 merges with Highway 1.

KON TUM AND GIA LAI PROVINCES
Accommodations (area code: 84 59)
KON TUM: only simple lodgings.
PLAY CU: **Play Cu Hotel**, 54, Le Loi St., tel. 2 46 28.
Tourist Information
Gia Lai-Tourist, Play Cu.

DAC LAC PROVINCE
Accommodations (area code: 84 50)
BUON MA THUOT: **Hongkong Hotel**, 30, Hai Ba Trung; **Thang Loi Hotel**, 1, Phan Chu Trinh, tel. 5 23 22; **106 Hotel**, 106, Ly Thuong, tel. 5 23 22.
Tourist Information
Dac Lac-Tourist, 3, Phan Chu Trinh St., tel. 5 23 22.

LAM DONG PROVINCE
Accommodations (area code: 84 63)
DA LAT: **Anh Dao Hotel**, 52-54, Phan Chau Trinh St., tel. 2 23 84; **Da Lat Hotel**, 7, Tran Phu St., tel. 23 63; **Duy Tan Hotel**, 83, Duy Tan St. tel. 22 16; **Ngoc Lan Hotel**, 54, Nguyen Tri Phuong St., tel. 2 21 36;
Palace Hotel, 2, Tran Phu St., tel. 22 03; **Tran Hung Dao Villa**, 25, Tran Hung Dao St.
YOUTH HOSTEL: Lang Bian, 6, Nguyen Thi Minh Khai St.;
CAMPGROUND: on Lake Tuyen Lam.
Further Information
Airport 18.5 miles/30 km south of the city.
Vietnam Airlines Da Lat, 5, Truong Cong Dinh St.; **bus station** between the central marketplace and Xuan Huong Dam, ticket sales: 4:30 am-5:30 pm, reserve in advance! **Money exchange** in the Palace Hotel; main **post office**, 14, Tran Phu St.
Villa Bao Dai, 2, Le Hong Phong St., 7-11 am, 1:30-4 pm;
Flower & orchid gardens, 2, Phu Dong Thien Vuong St. on Xuan Huong Lake, 7:30 am-4 pm;
University can only be visited by prior arrangement, tel. 22 46;
Cathedral, Tran Phu St., masses: 5:30 am and 5:15 pm, Sun. 5:30, 7:00 am and 4 pm;
Music center in the former Lycée Yersin, 1, Hong Van Tu St., tel. 2 55 11;
Former **residence** of the French Governor-General (with hotel), Tran Hung Dao St., 7 - 11 am, 1:30 - 4 pm;
The **golf course** is supposed to be repaired and reopened.
Tourist Information
Lam Dong-Tourist, Da Lat, 12, Tran Quoc Toan St., tel. 2 21 25.

NAM BO
The Southern Region

NAM TIEN - THE MOVE
SOUTHWARD
DONG NAI
HO CHI MINH CITY
MEKONG DELTA

NAM TIEN –
THE MOVE SOUTHWARD

"Go to Gia Dinh, where the water is pure and the rice is white," sang emigrants in the 17th and 18th centuries. Gia Dinh is the name of the delta created by the Mekong. Because of its nine mouths, the Vietnamese call it Cuu Long, Nine-Headed Dragon. In the Red River Delta and in Trung Bo, or central Vietnam, agricultural land had been scarce for a long time. More and more rice fields were taken over by feudal lords, estates and monasteries. In addition to the havoc of nature, there were wars, rebellions and tax debts which led to a state of servitude. It took a lot to make the farmers leave their villages and land, the graves and memorials of their ancestors and demigods, and the guardian spirits in their *dinh*. They took them along on the long journey and built new temples for them wherever they settled down.

In the southern delta, until the 6th century, there was an empire influenced by India, Funan. After the 9th century, this

Preceding pages: Hustle and bustle on the nine mouths of the Mekong, called "Nine-Headed Dragon." Left: Confident and modern, the Vietnamese woman drives a Honda and dreams of a Mercedes.

became nominally part of Cambodia, but it was only sparsely settled by the Khmer, who had no lack of land. With the Dai Viet empire in the 10th century, *nam tien*, the southward migration of the Vietnamese, had begun. This led to battles with the Champa empire from the 10th to the 17th centuries. In the 14th century, the Viet came as far as the Hoanh Son Mountains. The Le dynasty secured the conquered land in the 15th century by establishing 42 military colonies. During the civil war in the 17th century, the Vietnamese left the combat zone by ship and moved up the Dong Nai river all the way to Bien Hoa. After 1693, when the Nguyen lords from Hue had destroyed the last Champa empire in Phang Rang, many Cham fled to the delta. In 1697, 50 junks with 3,000 Chinese soldiers on board were spotted off the coast. They were supporters of the Ming dynasty who had been persecuted by the subsequent Qing dynasty. The Nguyen from Hue allowed them to settle in Ban La on the Dong Nai River and in My Tho on the Mekong River. Mac Cuu, also a supporter of the Ming, established an autonomous territory in Ha Tien. Also starting in 1697, the Nguyen managed to intervene in the Khmer struggles for the throne, and gradually took possession of the delta. In the 17th and 18th centuries,

195

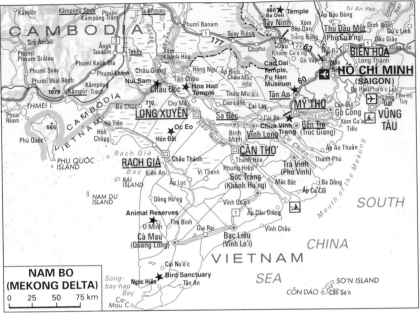

DONG NAI PROVINCE

the Vietnamese transformed it into arable land, settled it and set up administrations. At first they defended the fertile land, covering over 15,600 square miles (40,000 sq. km), against the Siamese (the Thai). When they lost their land to the Tay Son, the last Nguyen heir started a long battle in the delta, which he continued for 20 years, until he reached the Red River Delta in 1802. The Vietnamese defended the Mekong Delta against the French, who turned it into the Cochin China colony; against the missionaries, who dreamed of a Asian Christian state; and finally against the United States during the Cold War. As of 1975, Vietnam is once again an independent state, from the mountains in the north to Cape Ca Mau in the south. And, despite differences in mentality, living conditions, and political and economic systems, the Vietnamese, north and south, have remained one people.

Right: Rickshaws and cyclists don't have an easy time in the business district of Saigon.

The northeastern section of Nam Bo is not part of the Mekong Delta. It is the watershed basin for two rivers, the Dong Nai and the Be. Volcanic basalt cliffs, some 350-650 feet high (100-200 meters), rise up from the alluvial soil of the plain, covering 1,560 square miles (4,000 sq. km). Ho Chi Minh City lies on the southern edge of this plain, 50 miles (80 km) from the ocean as the crow flies. The rivers Van and Co Dong irrigate the fertile rice fields from Ho Chi Minh City to Long An province.

Highway 1, coming from central Vietnam, goes through rubber plantations. Only the neighboring province of Song Be produces more rubber than Dong Nai. In addition, it furnishes one-third of the country's soy beans, a dietary staple.

The large nature preserve **Cat Tien**, 25,000 acres (10,000 ha) in size, lies at the juncture of Song Be, Lam Dong and Dong Nai provinces. Here, you can find rare plants and animals, pythons, cro-

codiles, and several Asian rhinoceroses, which are almost extinct.

Xuan Loc, 37 miles (60 km) from Saigon, was the site of the last battle between North and South Vietnamese troops. Today, **Long Thanh** has become a popular place for excursions from the big cities of Ho Chi Minh City and Bien Hoa.

Bien Hoa, the capital of Dong Nai province, 18.5 miles (30 km) from Ho Chi Minh City, is one of the oldest settlements from the 17th century. It was founded by immigrants who came up the Dong Nai river. Today, it is an important industrial city in Nam Bo. The Dong Nai river forms the **Tri An Falls**, located 22 miles (36 km) from the city. There is a **high-capacity power station** on its reservoir which provides electricity for the region's industries and cities. Bien Hoa now has 400,000 inhabitants; this number is expected to increase to 700,000 by the year 2000, and industry is to increase proportionately. The main industries are electronics, construction machinery, textiles and consumer goods. In 1958, the Americans expanded Highway 1 between Bien Hoa and Saigon, turning it into a multi-lane throughway, linking their military bases with Saigon. A ring-road passes around the industrial area, paid for by the Americans and built by South Korean troops; it is called **Korea Road**.

In the villages to the left and right of the expressway, you can see modern churches of the North Vietnamese Christians. Many of these migrated to the south in 1954 after the Geneva conference, which guaranteed free choice of residence.

GIA DINH, SAIGON OR HO CHI MINH CITY

In the 16th and 17th centuries, the trading center was called Dong Nai, like the river along which the Vietnamese and Chinese settlers entered the country. Later it was called Phan Yen, Gia Dinh and Ben Nghe, Landing of the Water

Buffalo. After the citadel Gia Dinh had been built, the place was called Ben Thanh, Market by the Citadel. On a map from 1815, there is a street called Saigon and a market called Cho Lon, Big Market. The name Saigon is derived from *sai con*, kapok tree, or from the Cambodian *preikor*, city. Under the Nguyen lords, the city, citadel, province and the entire delta were called Gia Dinh.

Before 1859, there were 40 villages here with approximately 40,000 inhabitants. Although many of them fled when the French came, the population of Saigon and Cholon grew to 100,000 between 1865 and 1883. The French pushed across the Saigon River in 1859, capturing and destroying the Gia Dinh citadel. In 1862, Saigon became the capital of the French colony Cochin China, and in 1883 the seat of the French colonial government of Indochina. Under French colonial administration, the city and colony received more economic support than the An Nam and Tonkin protectorates. Harbor, shipyard, streets and the railroad system were expanded.

Saigon remained under French rule until 1954, and became South Vietnam's provisional capital after the Geneva conference (1954). The last Vietnamese emperor, Bao Dai, who had been dethroned in 1945, governed South Vietnam from Saigon in 1948-65, until overthrown by the Catholic Diem. In 1962, the Americans took the place of the French.

On April 30, 1975, the North Vietnamese Liberation Army marched into Saigon. Hanoi has been the capital city since reunification in 1976, but Saigon is the largest city in Vietnam. After the Vietnam War, the conversion from a capitalist economy to a socialist one presented problems. Ho Chi Minh City (HCM) was created, a three-city area consisting of the commercial city of Saigon, the neighboring region of Gia Dinh, and the district Cholon, the Chinese quarter or Chinatown.

198

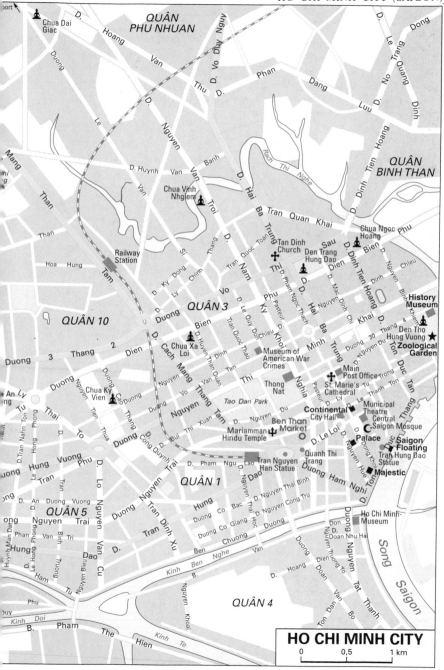

HO CHI MINH CITY

0   0,5   1 km

The Modern City

HCM, often called Saigon once again by the Vietnamese, has close to 4 million inhabitants. Currently it has the largest harbor in Vietnam, located on the Saigon River, a waterway 73 miles (117 km) from the ocean, and the country's largest international airport, Tan Son Nhat. Highway 1 and the railroad link HCM with the rest of the region. The road system in the Mekong Delta is extensive.

Not until the 19th century did villages and marketplaces grow together into a city, a city which took on a European look due to the intervention of French urban planning at the end of the century. It is divided into districts, or Quan. Q1 is the inner city of Saigon, Q5 and Q6 are Cholon. Le Loi Boulevard marks the center of Saigon. There is no old city center; but there is the neighboring, older city of

Above: View of the harbor on the Saigon River. Right: The main post office dates from the colonial period.

Cholon, Chinatown. Artisan shops, merchants and markets have settled in this maze of streets. The *Binh Tay* market stretches down to the river.

Saigon – The Business Quarter (Q1)

Duong Ton Duc Thang is a promenade along the Saigon River, where ocean-going ships anchor. In the middle of the promenade is the memorial for General Tran Hung Dao, who defeated the Mongolians. Boats traverse the harbor or carry people from one side of the river to the other.

Duong Dong Khoi goes from the middle of the river promenade at the Cuu Long Hotel, today known again as the Majestic, to the business quarter between Duong Ham Nghi, the market hall, Duong 30 Thang 4, and Duong Hai Ba Trung. This is the area for hotels, shops, art galleries, artisan shops and restaurants. The **Central Mosque** is only a couple of steps away; turn right on Duong Dong Du. It was built in 1935 by a rich Muslim. Its visitors include Indians, Cham, Vietnamese and businessmen of the Muslim faith who are passing through. The **City Theater**, built in 1900, is on the right at the intersection of the boulevard Duong Le Loi. During the American occupation it served as the parliament building for the Saigon government. It has been a theater again since 1975, and offers a rich program, ranging from classical Vietnamese theater to pop and beat concerts. The square in front of the theater has become a hangout where young people gather or cruise the streets on motorcycles and bicycles. A couple of blocks farther on, somewhat back from the street, the **Main Post Office** is on the right side of Duong Dong Khoi, and on the left is the neo-Romanesque Cathedral called Notre Dame, completed in 1883, with two 131-foot (40 m) towers. At Christmastime, a Christmas market is held around the cathedral, more reminiscent of an Oriental bazaar than its European models.

Thong Nhat (Conference Hall), also called Palace of Unity, is at the end of the street 30 Thang 4. The Norodom Palace, seat of the French governors, once stood on this site. During the Diem regime in 1962 it was bombed by a rebellious South Vietnamese air force officer. President Diem survived the assassination attempt, and the building was rebuilt from 1962-66 in the shape of a T. One hundred rooms on 6 floors, two of them underground, were constructed on an area of 2,392 square yards (2,000 sq. m). The North Vietnamese Liberation Army moved into the palace on April 30, 1975, and took over the city from General Minh, the last president of South Vietnam. It was in this building, in late 1975, that the National Consultation Conference declared the reunification of Vietnam as of 1976.

The North Vietnamese marched into the city along the street 30 Thang 4, or April 30th Street. It runs from the Conference Hall to the **Zoological** and **Botanical Gardens**, with a recreational area covering 83 acres (33 ha). Construction commenced in 1864. Beyond the entrance on the right is **Den Tho Hung Vuong**, the memorial to the legendary Hung emperors. The **National Museum**, on the left beyond the entrance, was built in 1929 and has collections well worth seeing from every period in history. Especially noteworthy are the bronze drums from Dong Son, the findings from Oc Eo (Funan), ceramics, Cham sculptures and clothing, as well as utensils from the minorities of the southern highlands.

On **Le Loi Boulevard**, Saigon's most elegant street, which starts at the theater, is the French **City Hall** (today the City Council). It is located at the intersection of Nguyen Hue Boulevard and was built from 1901-08 in a controversial style. Not until a decade later did the French colonial style adapt to the construction methods and climate of Vietnam. At the end of the boulevard is the equestrian statue of Tran Nguyen Han, who used

homing pigeons to carry messages for the first time in the 13th century. A small monument is in remembrance of the student **Quanh Thi Trang**, who was shot dead in 1963 during Buddhist demonstrations against the Catholic Diem government. On the right is the largest market in the city, **Cho Ben Thanh**, built in 1919, and roofed with a large dome. In front of it is a rectangular bell tower with a clock. The only Hindu temple of the city, east of the market on Duong Truong Dinh, is called **Chua Mari Amman** by both the Vietnamese and the Chinese. They too occasionally call on the miracle-working goddess for help.

Pagodas and Temples

Almost all of the religious buildings are from the 19th and 20th centuries; only a few are worth a visit. In Nam Bo,

Above: Doesn't anyone want to buy peanuts? Right: Selling groceries at the Ben Than market in the middle of Saigon.

the Buddhist pantheon and large statues of Buddha are even smaller in number than the pantheon in the central part of the country. The statues are often surrounded by neon tubes and gaudy light shows. The buildings are lofty and bright and covered with colorful wall paintings. They are similar to Thai pagodas. Because everyone is cremated in HCM, most of the pagodas have rooms for storing urns. In Cholon there are *hoi quan*, Chinese community buildings, where mainly Taoist divinities are worshipped. The Vietnamese Buddhists also have assembly rooms in their pagodas.

Chua Giac Lam (Chua Ho Dat) in the northwestern part of the city (Q11) is one of the oldest pagodas in HCM and the most beautiful (118 Duong Lac Long Quan). It was founded in 1744. The flat wooden construction is unusual. It consists of three parts: the main temple, the room for the urns and altars for the ancestors, and the assembly room. On the main altar, which is surrounded by a carved, golden frame, there is a bronze Shakyamuni Buddha, which is probably the oldest statue of Buddha in the delta. The black brass Child Buddha, surrounded by nine dragons, is not found elsewhere in the southern delta. The *chua* has 153 wooden carved statues, sixty of which are Buddhas. Along the side walls are the Dien Vuong, lords of the underworld, and two groups of the eighteen La Han. The Di Lac Buddha (Maitreya Buddha) in the assembly room is an excellent specimen of woodcarving. The main festival is celebrated on the fifteenth day of the fourth lunar month. Smaller festivals are held on the eighth day of the fourth lunar month as well as on the fifteenth days of the first, seventh and tenth lunar months.

Chua Giac Vien, toward the city center on the same street, is close to a lotus lake. It was founded in the 18th century and is similar to Chua Giac Lam. Next to the figure of a guard is a carved wishing tree with 49 small Buddha figures and 49

small oil lamps. Relatives of sick people hang notes on the tree pleading for the ailing one's recovery, and give offerings of oil for the lamps. Notable is a large incense basin, decorated with dragons.

Chua Phung Son Tu (Chua Go) was built in 1820 on a small hill in District Q11, Duong 3 Thang 2, on Hong Vuong Boulevard. In 1988, Soviet archaeologists were able to prove that it was built on a Funan shrine. It has bronze, wood and ceramic statues, and a pantheon that's unusually large for Nam Bo. In the courtyard is a bronze Buddha on an altar, a lean figure which radiates harmony.
Chua Xa Loi was built in 1958 by the South Vietnamese Buddhist Association. The Hue monk Thich Quang Duc was visiting **Chua An Quang**, seat of the Saigon Buddhists, when he burned himself to death in Saigon at the corner of Duong Cach Mang Than Tam and Nguyen Dinh Chien. The spot is marked by a small plaque. **Chua Ky Vien** (1952) on Nguyen Dinh Chien Boulevard belongs to the Theravada Buddhist sect and has a

stupa for relics, a Shakyamuni and a Parinirvana Buddha. From 1964-73, Buddhists from the north built a stupa in **Chua Vinh Nhgiem** on Duong Nam Ky Khoi Nghia.

On the way to the airport is a Cham mosque. **Chua Dai Giac**, about a mile (1.5 km) from the airport on the left side of the road, has a pink ten-story tower. The Buddha on the main altar is surrounded by blinking neon lights. At **Lam Son**, a lacquer factory and shop for high-quality enamel works on the right side of the street, you can, during business hours, observe the process by which lacquer is produced.

Den Tran Hung Dao, dedicated to the victor over the Mongolians, is in the park on Duong Dien Bien Phu, on the site of a French cemetery in the district Q1. **Chua Nhoc Hoang** (Chua Phuc Hai Tu) is a *hoi quan* for the Chinese from Guangzhou (Canton). It is on Duong Mai Luu, district Q1. The section on the right is dedicated to the Jade Emperor and has a large Taoist pantheon; the section on the left is

a pagoda. With its many rooms and figures from various cults, this is the most interesting *hoi quan* in the city.

Cholon (Q5, Q6)

Tran Hung Dao Boulevard, the continuation of Le Loi Boulevard, leads into the center of the Chinese quarter, Cholon. The largest market hall, Cho **Binh Tay**, is surrounded by market stands. In the evenings, countless small and large restaurants offer Chinese specialities. Across from the **bus station** (on Duong Hoc Lac) is the church **Cha Tam**, where President Diem and his brother found refuge in 1963 before they were murdered. On Duong Nguyen Trai you can get a good sense of life in Chinatown. The *hoi quan* of several Chinese communities are nestled between restaurants. The most beautiful, **Hoi Quan Ba Thien Hau**,

Above: The Chinese quarter, Cholon, reaches to the riverbanks. Right: Entrance to the tunnels in Chu Chi, Ho Chi Minh City.

wrongly called a pagoda, was built in 1847 by Chinese from Canton. Its largest festivals are celebrated during the spring and autumn full moons. Giant coils of incense are then lit; they are supposed to bring the donor luck. The Chinese have wishes written for them on red lucky charms, and some burn paper money as a sacrifice to their ancestors. The bronze bell is from 1830, and rings when a donation is made. The Taoist sea goddess Thien Hau is worshipped here. **Den Ong Quan Cong**, also called Chua Nghia An Hoi Quan, is 980 feet (300 m) farther. It is dedicated to General Ong Quan Cong of the Three Empires (3rd century). To his left and right are a civil and a military mandarin. Ong Bon, the spirit of luck and guardian of the temple, carries a rod in his hand. Even the sea goddess has her place on the altar. There is also a **mosque** on the same street, which was built in 1932 by Tamils from southern India. The sea goddess Thien Hau is worshipped in the **Hoi Quan Ha Chuong** of the Fukien Chinese; she was supposedly born in Fukien. In her honor, four heavy columns painted with dragons were brought from Fukien for the construction.

At the end of Duong Tran Hung Dao in Cholon there is a memorial for Phan Dinh Phung, who fought against the colonial powers.

More *hoi quan*, pagodas and a Cham mosque are on Duong Tran Hung Dao and Duong Hung Vuong, the two big streets connecting Saigon with Cholon. When these institutions celebrate their big festivals with long processions, traffic is brought to a standstill.

Outside of the city in the villages on both sides of the highway are large monasteries and pagodas of the wealthy sects. **Chua Tinh Xa Truong Tam** in the Binh Thanh district was the seat of a Vietnamese mendicant order until 1975. A 39-foot-high (12 m) Buddha statue sits at the center of a temple complex extending over some 59,000 square feet (5,490 sq. m).

In the ceramics village **Thu Dau Mot** (heading out of the city, to the left of the highway) on Korea Road toward Bien Hoa, ceramics, ranging from ashtrays to large water jugs and vats for fish sauce, are formed by hand and fired in the kilns. Bicycles, oxcarts, trucks and barges carry them to every corner of the delta. **Dinh Phong Ong** in the Thu Duc district, circa 9 miles (15 km) from the center of the city, to the right of the highway, is one of the few remaining *dinh* in the southern part of the country. The festival of the guardian spirit is celebrated on the 14th and 15th days of the eleventh lunar month.

AROUND HO CHI MINH CITY

In **Chu Chi**, 22 miles (35 km) from HCM between the Saigon River and the Van River, is a 157-foot-long (48 m) underground tunnel, built during the First Indochina War. Guerrilla troops operated out of this tunnel against the French. In

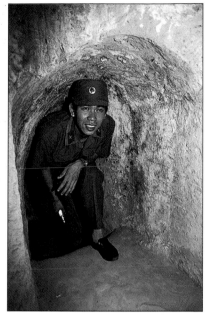

the Vietnam War it was expanded into a tunnel system 12 miles (20 km) long, 16-20 feet (5-6 m) below the surface. Corridors 5 feet high (1.5 m) and 2 feet wide (.6 m) connected the tunnels, which were 33 feet (10 m) apart. There were weapons depots, hospitals, workshops, recreation rooms, kitchens, and even wells for drinking water. On the surface, the area was covered with plants and secured with bamboo spikes. In 1966, the Americans discovered the resistance base and carpet-bombed it. Airplanes spread fast-growing grass seeds and the grass was then set on fire. Napalm bombs and chemical weapons were used. The narrow tunnels were only accessible to the slim Vietnamese, so the Americans sent down soldiers from the Philippines and, later on, 300 German shepherds. This placed the soldiers in considerable danger, until a Vietnamese farmer had the idea which saved the day: simply place pieces of American clothing in the tunnel entrances. This did, in fact, confuse the German shepherds. Losses were

high, also among the civilian population in the surrounding villages. But the rebels did not give up.

Highway 22 leads to Tay Ninh (62 miles/100 km). In Go Dau the road branches off to Cambodia (Ho Chi Minh - Phnom Penh 186 miles/300 km). The **Temple of the Cao Dai**, 2 miles (3 km) from the provincial capital city of Tay Ninh, is nestled on a lake and surrounded by parking lots, rooms and resting spots for pilgrims. The high, angular church is colorful and pompous.

Den Ba Ben is on Black Mountain, an extinct volcano 3,224 feet (986 m) high; you can see it from Tay Ninh. It is also known as Van Son or Nui Mot, Lone Mountain. According to legend, a beautiful girl, Thien Huong, was to marry the son of a mandarin. But because she loved a soldier who was away at war, she fled to the mountain and died there. She is

Above: Caodaist service in the pilgrimage church near Tay Ninh. Right: Vendor on the beach.

worshiped as Ba Den, the Black Lady. The temple is on a slope about 980 feet (300 m) high. The temple festival is celebrated at the beginning of the year.

Since 1979 **Ba Ria - Vung Tau**, Vietnam's 53rd province, has been a *Special Zone*. The peninsula Vung Tau, which has one of the largest ocean harbors in Vietnam, and the 14 offshore islands of the **Con Dao Archipelago**, which the French called Poulo Condor, joined forces because of the supposition that there were offshore oil deposits along the coast. Vietsopato, a Vietnamese-Soviet joint venture, started drilling in 1981 and struck oil in 1984. Vung Tau is the center of the oil industry.

In 1994, Japan promised financial support for the construction of the international harbor **Sao Mai**, in the Chau Thanh district. It is meant to become the largest deep-water harbor in Vietnam for ships of up to 50,000 tons. In addition, the oil harbor on the Ti Van River and the international airport, as well as the entire transportation network, are to be ex-

206

panded. Today, the city of Vung Tau has 180,000 inhabitants; it's supposed to grow to 300,000 inhabitants by the year 2010. The ocean resort Vung Tau, which means Bay of Ships, is Vietnam's most elegant and beautiful bathing resort and meets international standards. It is on a good road 77 miles (125 km) from HCM. Along the 9 miles (15 km) of coastline here, with steep cliffs falling sharply into the sea, are seven bathing beaches. The most beautiful are **Thuy Van** and **Tam Guong**. Constant temperatures around 82°F (28°C) and water temperatures around 77°F (25°C) mean that you can swim all year round. Vung Tau was discovered by the French in 1870 and built into a sea resort. **Bach Dinh**, the White House, was the summer residence of the French Governor General. In 1909-10, Emperor Thanh Thai was imprisoned in this building, and deported from here to the island of Réunion. During the Vietnam War the number of hotels here swelled to 70; and modern hotels are always being added.

During the second half of the 20th century, Buddhist sects founded several temples. **Chua Thich Ca Phat Dai** (1963) was built on Nui Lon, Big Mountain; it has a 20-foot-high (6 m) Buddha on a 13-foot-high (4 m) base. On the slope of Nui Nho, Small Mountain, is **Chua Niet Ban Tinh Xa** with a 69-foot-high (21 m) flag tower in the shape of a lotus flower and a 39-foot-long (12 m) reclining Buddha. **Lang Ca Ong**, on Hoang Hoa Avenue in the city, was built in 1911 as a burial place and memorial for a whale which helped some fishermen. The temple contains three other whale skeletons which washed ashore in 1968. The temple festival takes place on the 16th day of the eighth lunar month.

The island of **Con Dao** is in an archipelago with 14 large and small islands (totalling 28 square miles/72 sq. km), 111 miles (179 km) from Vung Tau. They have a pleasant sea climate; the average temperature is 68°F (20°C). Con Dao is a vacation paradise, but it still does not have a tourist infrastructure. The

islands are 80% hills and forests, surrounded by cliffs and beaches. In 1984, a **nature reserve** was established here; it has 285 types of trees and herbs and 62 species of birds. On the main island, which was under French and American rule for 113 years, prisons remind us of the resistance fighters of this period.

Long Hai (Dong Hai province), on the way to Vung Tau, also has a beautiful sand beach and a cultural center for the minorities. On Minh Dam Hill there are several temples; one of them, **Ding Co**, is for a brave girl who drowned in the ocean when she tried, in a small boat, to bring a letter to the emperor of the Tay Son dynasty, Emperor Quang Trung.

THE MEKONG DELTA

The Mekong, the third-longest river in Asia, is 2,790 miles long (4,500 km) and

Above: Candy is made from the juice of the sugar cane. Right: Rice harvest in the Mekong Delta.

has its source in Tibet. It breaks through the mountains of Yunnan in South China, flowing through Laos, Myanmar (Burma), and Thailand, often forming the border between these countries. Its delta starts in Cambodia. It developed from a gulf which the Mekong had filled up with its fertile mud. In Kratie, north of the Cambodian capital of Phnom Penh, it becomes navigable, a powerful stream which divides near Phnom Penh into the Bassac and the Lower Mekong. It flows 138 miles (222 km) through Vietnam before emptying into the South China Sea. Oceanic currents force to one side a part of the river's sediment; this has given the delta its strange shape, resembling the head of a bird. In some coastal areas the land erodes, but in other areas it continues to grow out into the sea by as much as 8 inches (20 cm) a day.

The water of the Mekong rises in the rainy season, but the Mekong does not need any dikes. It reaches its highest level between September and October; from March to April it reaches its lowest. The floods are calculable, and catastrophes are rare; the typhoons of 1994, with extreme flooding, were the exception in these latitudes. In areas that are always underwater, special varieties of rice have been cultivated, with stems up to 16 feet (5 m) long, and called "floating rice."

In 1957, the *Committee for Coordination of Investigation of the Lower Mekong Basin* was founded with the support of UNESCO. All of the countries along the river were supposed to take part, from Yunnan in the north to Vietnam in the south. The idea is, within an area of 234,000 square miles (600,000 sq. km), with 35 million people, to increase the arable area by 22.5 million acres (9 million ha), to control flooding, to use water for irrigation and energy and to make the Mekong navigable up to the inland state of Laos. Revolutions, wars and lack of funds have meant that reality has fallen far behind expectations. At a conference

in Hanoi in 1994, Vietnam and the Chinese province of Yunnan, which had thereto declined to take part in the project, declared their willingness to join on. Thus fortified, the committee can continue its work with renewed strength.

The Mekong Delta, with its 14,040 square miles (36,000 sq. km) of rice land, is more than double the size of the Red River Delta in the north. In addition, there are another 15,600 square miles (4,000 sq. km) from the deltas of smaller rivers. Thus, Nam Bo has 15,560 square miles (40,000 sq. km) of rice-growing land. The delta plains are 5-8 feet (1.5-2.5 m) above sea level. With artificial irrigation, 2 to 3 rice harvests a year are possible. Unrestricted use of the Mekong waters, however, would lead to salt water penetrating into the tributaries, flooding the land and spoiling it.

There's still virgin land in Nam Bo, especially in the northwestern hill country. Villages and farms are often very far apart. Many of them do not have access to streets and roads, relying on water-ways, rivers and canals. Rice is grown almost everywhere in the delta, but so are vegetables, sugar cane, peanuts, soy beans, bananas, oranges, pineapples and durian fruits. On the coasts, rivers and canals, fish and shellfish are caught and cultivated. The farms were only partially organized into collectives. The favorable climate, constant temperatures and lack of typhoons are all positive factors for agriculture.

The Kingdom of Funan

The first kingdom on the Indochina peninsula that was influenced by India developed in the Mekong Delta. After this mighty state came to an end, all that remained of its settlements and cities, art and culture, were those objects that had been covered over with alluvial earth by the Mekong River. There was no historical writing in Funan, and very few stele inscriptions. Up until the 20th century, researchers had to turn to Chinese annals for information. These documents told of

a people of sailors, merchants, craftsmen and farmers, who were also feared as pirates. From the first to the sixth centuries, they ruled the delta, the coasts of Malaysia, Sumatra, the east coast of the Indochina peninsula, and the seas. The Chinese called the kings of this land Fu Nan, Rulers of the Mountain. The Cham and Khmer, also influenced by India, and the kings of Java also called themselves Rulers of the Mountain. The term Funan was applied to the state and the people; no other terms are known.

The legends of the Funanese, like those of other peoples influenced by India, tell of a Brahmin from southern India who pointed his magic spear at distant shores. With this spear he conquered the Naga Queen (Snake Queen), married her and ruled over her land. As is true in Champa and Khmer, there is no indication in Funan of large groups of Indians immi-

Above: You can eat cheaply and well at the simple cookshacks. Right: Many villages can only be reached by boat.

grating. According to Chinese records, the Funanese were Hindus, but had contact with Buddhism. Their treasures of pearls and gold – they had gold tableware and pearl jewelry – roused the admiration of the Chinese. They described the Funanese houses, built on richly carved stilts. They were more critical in their judgment of their customs, particularly their clothing, which only consisted of a loincloth. They found their appearance strange, and the descriptions of a people with curly hair and dark skin leads one to the conclusion that they were related to the Melanesians.

The Chinese also describe an extensive canal system which was used for irrigation and navigation. This made it possible for sea-going junks of the merchant fleets from Arabia, India and China to sail through Funan and thus avoid the dangerous Cape Ca Mau.

The Funan kings sent tributes to China, and emissaries of the Chinese emperor's court visited Funan. In the 3rd century the reports intensified, but a century later they dwindled. The Funan had withdrawn to the north, to a capital on Pho Da Hill in the south of Cambodia.

In the 6th century, Funan was conquered by its satellite state Chen La. The empire of Chen La was integrated into the Khmer empire around the 9th and 10th centuries. Funanese art is considered to be the predecessor of Khmer art. The political power of the Funan was transferred to the Khmer, as well. Nominally, the delta itself also belonged to the Khmer empire; but the Cambodians only established a few settlements, as they had plenty of land at home. The vastness of the delta was covered by the fertile masses of mud of the Mekong and its tributaries, and sank into oblivion until the Vietnamese made it arable again in the 17th century.

From a helicopter, French scientists were able to discover the outlines of an old canal system and hills over sunken settlements.

Between 1942 and 1944, the French researcher L. Malleret uncovered a settlement in **Oc Eo**, in the present-day Giang An province, which probably was a harbor of the Funan. He named the culture Oc Eo culture, after the place of discovery. Of the houses and temples, only the stilts and brick foundations were found. On the other hand, an abundance of artifacts, coins and utensils from other cultures point to the connections which Funan must have had with the Arabian world as well as the Mediterranean countries.

At new excavation sites during the last decades, Vietnamese archaeologists have also found foundations, burial items, artifacts and a gold treasury. The inscriptions on these objects could help to fill in the missing pieces of the historical puzzle. The museum in Ho Chi Minh City contains objects from the Oc Eo excavations. A small museum in Long Tan (Long An province) displays objects found by Vietnamese archaeologists.

Land of the Nine-Headed Dragon Cuu Long

The vastness of the delta landscape, the mangrove forests, nature reserves and bird preservation areas, beaches and waterways have made Nam Bo an ideal travel destination for nature lovers, fans of aquatic sports, and people looking for general peace and quiet. Only small branches of rivers and canals have bridges, and often these are only "monkey bridges": a tree-trunk or bamboo poles. State and private car ferries carry traffic over the branches of the Mekong. Villages, cities and markets are generally located at points where the waterways intersect.

A round trip leads through the eastern part of the delta up to Cape Ca Mau and back through the western part.

Highway 4, the Rice Road, heads east. All of the waterways between Ho Chi Minh City and Long An Province are branches of Van River and Co Dong River or canals.

Long An is the first province in the delta. In the capital, **Tan An**, there's a **temple of the Cao Dai** sect on the right side of the road; on the left side is the **Provincial Museum** with a number of objects and some gold treasures of the Funan from recent excavations by archaeologists from the province.

My Tho (50 miles/80 km from HCM), located on the Mekong arm Tien Giang, is the capital of Tien Giang province. It was settled by the Chinese in 1697. The **Chinese Quarter** is beyond the **Thu Khoa Huan Bridge**, and here there are several *hoi quan* (community houses with a temple). During the Tay Son rebellion and the Vietnam War, the city was caught in the middle of the battles, and the citadel was destroyed. The first railroad in Indochina – it is no longer in operation – went from Saigon to My Tho. The Cambodian capital city of Phnom Penh can be reached by waterway from My Tho (105 miles/170 km). Life in My Tho centers around the river. The **market** on Duong Trung Trac takes up an entire city quarter. **Chua Venh Trang**, built in 1849 and located outside the city proper, is the oldest temple in the delta. Its construction is based on that of a Chinese house.

Traveling along the Tien Giang, an arm of the Mekong, you don't get an idea of its actual width. The view is blocked by a group of islands; on the other side of the four islands, it's as wide again. The last members of the Dao Du sect live on Phoenix Island, surviving exclusively on coconuts; their temples show the synthesis of various religions. Most of the members of the sect have returned to HCM. There is a Dragon Island, a Turtle Island and a Lion Island, **Tan Thoi**. It is 5.5 miles (9 km) long and half a mile miles (1 km) wide; "monkey bridges" lead to its five hamlets. These are part of

a village with circa 5,000 inhabitants, who plant vegetables and fruit and raise pigs and cattle. The island has a pagoda, two schools and a small hospital.

Boats leave from the district capital of **Cao Lanh**, on the left bank of the Tien Giang, to travel through canals, lakes and lotus ponds of the reed grass plains, an area covered by reeds taller than a man. It is a tranquil world inhabited by waterfowl. Thap Muoi, a 137-foot (42 m), ten-story tower, is marked even on old maps. Its name refers to the name of this province, Dong Thap.

Vinh Long and **Tra Vinh Provinces** are located between two branches of the Mekong, Tien Giang and Hau Giang. Vinh Long can be reached by car ferry. From here you can observe life on the Mekong. Boats travel on the Tien Giang into the canals and to the islands **An Binh** and **Binh Hua Phuoc**, where abundant fruit gardens are found. Hundreds of sampans bring the produce to the capital city. Khmer peoples live in Tra Vinh (50 miles/80 km away); they have retained their traditions. Their pagodas belong to Theravada Buddhism. **Ba Dong Beach**, at the mouth of Hau Giang River, still lacks an infrastructure for foreign tourists, which make its location and beaches all the more beautiful. A shipping line is planned to the island of Con Dao.

Can Tho, capital of the province of the same name, is located on the right bank of the Hau Giang. From Vinh Long, the road leads to Binh Minh, and from there the ferry, which takes both people and cars, goes to Can Tho. Vietnamese, Khmer and Hoa (Chinese) live in the province. Can Tho is the most important city in the southeastern part of the delta. It has an extensive river harbor for ships up to 5,000 G.R.T., and the Ninh Kieu shipyard. A cement factory and a whole series of other industries get their power from the Tra Noc power plant. As well as technical colleges, there is also a university in Can Tho. The province is the lar-

Right: Only simple bamboo bridges cross some canals and streams.

gest rice producer in the delta; but cattle-breeding and fruit growing are also important.

On the main street is **Dinh Long Tuyen** (Dinh Tan), built in 1852. A mandarin from the Nguyen dynasty is worshipped as the guardian spirit. In the back room is a memorial plaque to Emperor Tu Duc. The building on the right in the courtyard, the Mieu Than Mong, was built for the rice god; the temple on the left was built for the mountain spirit Son Quan. The dinh festivals take place from the 12th-14th days of the fourth lunar month, on the 14th day of the 12th lunar month, and at the start and the end of the rice harvest. 2,500 Khmer live on Duong Hoa Binh. They are Theravada Buddhists and have old pagodas.

At the intersection of several waterways, 19 miles (30 km) from Can Tho, is the **Floating Market** of **Phong Hiep**, where hundreds of boats can be found every day. The picturesque village of **Long Thanh** is not far from here. The Khmer close to Soc Trang, 46 miles (75

km) from Can Tho, celebrate their pagoda festival on the 14th day of the 10th lunar month with boat races. Old carved rowboats, up to 65 feet (20 m) in length, take part in the race.

Near Bac Lieu, district capital of Minh Hai province, 73 miles (117 km) from Can Tho, there are mangrove forests close to 2 miles (3 km) wide along the coast, which are home to eleven different species of nesting birds. **Cape Ca Mau**, the southernmost point of Vietnam, is also in Minh Hai province. The province is outside the Mekong Delta and is irrigated by various rivers. The peninsula is a paradise for birds and animals. With an area of 375,000 acres (150,000 ha), it is the world's second-largest mangrove forest – the largest is in the region of the Amazon. During the Vietnam War it was badly damaged by chemical weapons, and is slowly recovering. The province's capital, Ca Mau (124 miles/200 km from Can Tho), is a starting point for trips to the nature preserves: the bird paradise **near Ngoc Hien**, the **Tan Khanh Na-**

213

ture Reserve, where there are bears, apes and snakes (325 acres/130 ha), and the animal preserve **U Minh**.

Rach Gia (rach means canal), the capital of Kien Giang province, is located between two arms of the Cai Lon canal. A deep-sea fishing fleet anchors in the harbor. The market is large and colorful. In the city there are temples of various religions. **Chua Phat Lon** is a Khmer pagoda of the Theravada Buddhists from the 18th century. **Chua Tam Bao** is from the beginning of the 19th century; **Chua Pho Minh** was built in 1967 in the Thai style. **Hoi Quan Ong Bac De** in the center of the city dates from the time when the first Chinese began settling here. **Den Nguyen Trung Truc** was built for the resistance fighter against the French, who was executed in 1868 on the marketplace. He had helped destroy the battleship *Es-*

Above: Many water routes intersect at the Floating Market in Phong Hiep. Right: Who knows what these pretty girls in Ben Tre could tell us.

pérance off the coast of Yung Tau in 1861, and fled to Rach Gia. When the French threatened to shoot hostages, he surrendered. Rach Gia also has a **Cao Dai temple**, a Catholic and a Protestant **church**. You can get to the Oc Eo excavations from here. The city also boasts a **museum** with objects from Oc Eo (21 Nguyen Han Troi Street). The beach is 1.2 miles (2 km) from the city center.

Ha Tien, 56 miles (90 km) from Rach Gia and 4 miles (6 km) from the Cambodian border, is on a peninsula, facing offshore rocks and islands along the coast. There is a pagoda in the **Trach Dong Cave**, 2 miles (3 km) away in the direction of the border. 130 Vietnamese were killed in front of the pagoda by Pol Pot's troops. Between 1975 and 1978 they murdered countless inhabitants in order to add force to their demand that "the Delta belongs to Cambodia." Afterwards, Ha Tien was virtually a ghost town. On the beach, large sea turtles lay their eggs.

A lake, **Dong Ho**, lies picturesquely between the mountain chains Ngo Ho

and To Cau. This strip of coast is the most beautiful in Nam Bo. Vietnamese and many Chinese live here. At the edge of the city there are graves of the Mac, the first Chinese settlers, who created an autonomous territory here in the 18th century.

Dao Phu Quoc Island (222 square miles/568 sq. km), in the Gulf of Thailand, is Vietnam's largest island. It is surrounded by 16 smaller islands, whose sands are used to make glass. Kaolin clay, copper and iron are also worked here. Above all, the Vietnamese know the island for its pepper and its fish sauce, *nuoc mam*, which is surpassed only by the sauce from Phan Thiet.

An Giang Province, with its capital **Long Xuyen**, is on the Cambodian border. It is one of the most important shrimp exporters in Vietnam. In the provincial museum here, you can view objects from the Oc Eo culture. **Oc Eo** is 19 miles (30 km) away on Mount Nui Sap. The ruins of a Funanese harbor were discovered at the deserted site where the ex-cavations took place. The city of Tan Chau produces silk.

During the Pol Pot regime (1975-78) in Cambodia, refugees were pursued onto Vietnamese soil. **Ba Chuc** contains an ossuary with the bones of some 3,000 Khmer, killed after they had fled into the pagoda in 1978. Now there are numerous Khmer settlements in the area.

Chau Doc (38 miles/62 km from Long Xuyen) is close to the Cambodian border, 180 miles (290 km) from Ho Chi Minh City. It lies on the Mekong branch Hau Giang. It can also be reached directly from Ba Chuc. The market stretches along the river bank. Behind it, **Dinh Chau Phu** has a guardian spirit who was a relative of the 15th-century poet and strategist Nguyen Trai. The city has several splendid pagodas and temples.

Nui Sam, Mount King Crab, rises from the rice plains 3 miles (5 km) north of Chau Doc. At the foot of the mountain is a pilgrimage site where various religions have constructed buildings. The oldest is **Mieu Xu Than** (Ba Chua Xu)

215

from 1821; it became a pilgrimage site in 1973. The object of worship is a stone that resembles the figure of a woman; it is painted and dressed in precious robes. The stone is said to have been worshipped for years. Nowadays, believers come from near and far, bringing precious robes, which are stored in side rooms. There's a small temple in front of the entrance for the earth spirit. The temple festival is on the 23rd day of the fourth lunar month.

On the other side of the street is the **Den Thoai Ngoc Hau**, built for a mandarin who was the supervisor of this territory under the Nguyen emperor Minh Mang. In the garden are the graves of the mandarin and his two wives. There is a church located next to the **Chua Tang** (1847).

The **Chua Phuc Dien Tu** (Chua Hang), on the other side of the mountain, is a cave temple that extends over different levels. A legend says that about 50 years ago the patroness of the pagoda was confronted in the upper cave by two snakes, a white one and a green one. By meditating, she tamed the dangerous snakes and they did not harm anyone. The snakes disappeared after her death.

At Chau Doc, ferries cross over the Hau Giang to the Cham communities in **Cham Chau Giang**. They support themselves by weaving, and have retained their language and traditions; although Muslims, they call their mosque a *chua*. From the Cham settlements, you can also return to Long Xuan along the left river bank. On the way you pass **Phu Tan**, the birthplace of Huynh Phu Son, the founder of the Hoa Hao sect. The adherents of this once-militant sect now live secluded in the surrounding villages. Many of the men wear their hair in a knot, and long beards, to show that they belong to this sect. The Hoa Hao temples are similar to those of the Cao Dai, except that there's no Cao Dai, the eye in a triangle, over the entrances.

DONG NAI PROVINCE
Accommodations
BIEN HOA: Dong Nai Hotel, Bien Hoa, 57, Highway 15, tel. 22 67; **Vinh An Hotel**, Bien Hoa, 10, Highway 1. *Coastal spa of Long Hai:* **Palace Hotel**, 4, Le Loi St., tel. 1 01.
Tourist Information
Dong Nai-Tourist, 105, Highway 1, tel. 23 68.

CITY-STATE
HO CHI MINH CITY
Accommodations (area code: 848)
LUXURY: **Century Hotel**, 68 A, Nguyen Hue Blvd., tel. 23 18 18; **Continental Hotel**, 132, Dong Khoi St., tel. 29 92 01; **The First Hotel**, 201/3 Hoang Van Thu St., Tan Binh Dist., tel. 44 11 75; **Norfolk Hotel**, 117, Le Thanh Ton St., tel. 22 38 23; **Saigon Floating Hotel**, 1 A, Me Linh Platz, tel. 290783; **Saigon Star Hotel**, 204, Nguyen Thi Minh Khai St., tel. 23 02 60. *MODERATE:* **International Hotel**, 19, Vo Van Tan St., 3. Dist., tel. 29 00 09; **Airport Hotel**, Tan Son Nhat Airport Area, tel. 44 57 61; **Caravelle Hotel**, 19-23, Lam Son Platz, tel. 29 37 04; **Chains First Hotel**, 18, Hoang Viet St., Tan Binh Dist., tel. 44 11 99; **The Embassy Hotel**, 35, Nguyen Trung Trac St., tel. 23 19 81; **Palace Hotel**, 56-64, Nguyen Hue Blvd., tel. 29 28 60; *BUDGET:* **Bong Hong Hotel**, 123, Dong Khoi St., tel. 290613; **Champagne Hotel**, 129-133, Ham Nghi Blvd., tel. 22 49 22; **Festival Hotel**, 31, Cao Thang St., 3. Dist., tel. 39 07 08-9;
Getting There/Transportation
Tan Son Nhat **Airport**, 4 miles / 7 km northwest of the city center (city bus).

Train station: entrance on Nguyen Thong St., ticket sales daily 7 - 11 am, 1 - 3 pm. Tickets also sold at 136, Ham Nghi St., reservations required! **Airline offices**: *Vietnam Airlines* (international), 116, Nguyen Hue, tel. 292118, Mon - Sat 7:30 am - 4 pm, Sun 8:30 am - 1 pm; *Vietnam Airlines* (national), 27 B, Nguyen Dinh Chieu, tel. 299910; *Thai Airways*, tel. 446235, represented by Vietnam Airlines, 116, Nguyen Hue; *Lufthansa*, c/o Saigon Floating Hotel, 1 A, Me Linh Platz, tel. 29 07 83 and Tan Son Nhat-Airport, tel. 4 44 01 01; *Air France*, 130, Dong Khoi (in the Caravelle Hotel), tel. 29 09 82, Mon - Fri 8 am - noon, 2 - 5 pm, Sat 8 am - noon.

The largest **bus stations**: Ben Xe Mien Dong on Xo Viet Nghe Tinh St. (buses to the north and northeast); Ben Xe Tay Ninh, Le Dai Han St. (to the west and northwest); Ben Xe Van Thanh, Dien Bien Phu St. (to the north and east); Ben Xe Cho Lon at the bus station in Cholon (to the south and southwest). There are **minibuses** to the delta, which leave regularly from Dien Bien Phu.

City buses stop on the large square in front of the market Ben Than at the end of Loi St. **Boats** to the delta leave from the pier in the Saigon River.

Further Information

Banks: You can change money in the larger hotels. Trade bank, 29, Ben Chuong Duong St. (travelers' checks and most currencies), Visa and Mastercard, 7:30 am - noon, 1 - 4:30 pm except Sun and Sat afternoons.

Main Post Office Dong Khoi St. (near the cathedral), 6:30 am - 7 pm, international service 7 am - 9 pm, tel. 9 65 55.

Museums: *National Museum* (Bao Tang Lich Su) in the Zoological Gardens, 7:30 - 11:30 am and 1 - 4:30 pm; *Museum of Fine Arts* (painting, art of the Fu Nan, etc.) 218, Nguyen Thi Minh Khai, 7:30 - 4:30 pm except Mon.; *Ho Chi Minh Museum* im Nha Rong (Dragon House) on the Saigon River, 1, Nguyen Tat Thanh St., 8 - 11:30 am, 2 - 6 pm except Mon and Fri; *Museum of the Revolution*, Gia Long Palace, 25, Ly Tu Trung St., 8:30 - 11:30 am, 1:30 - 4 pm. **Opera house** at the end of Le Loi St., theater and music performances.

Open-air Stage, 126, Cach Mang Thang Tan St., Rock and Pop music on weekends; **Water puppet shows** in the zoological gardens daily 8 am - 2 pm.

Ky Hoa Amusement Park, 3, Thang 2 St., open daily 7 am - 9:30 pm.

Cathedral Notre Dame, Dong Khoi St.

Markets: *Fish market* on the bridge of Ong Lanh at the end of Nguyen Thai Hoc St./Cholon; *bird market* Thu An Kieu St./ Cholon;

Hospitals: Cho Ray Hospital, 20 B, Nguyen Chi Thanh St./Cholon with a department for foreigners, tel. 5 51 37/38.

Pharmacy: 201, Dong Khoi St.

Restaurants

All hotels have restaurants, often quite well-known ones. There are a number of restaurants on Nguyen Hue St. and on Dong Khoi St., which runs parallel to it. Restaurant ships: Cosevina I and Cosevina II, tel. 29 15 06, My Canh and Ben Nghe sailboats.

Cafés/Discos/Bars

There are cafés and garden cafés on Dong Khoi St. (Brodard Nr. 131) and Le Loi Boulevard (Givard Nr. 169). Bars and discos with dancing in all the major hotels, especially on weekends.

Tourist Information

Saigon-Tourist, 49, Le Than Ton St., tel. 29 89 14; **Vinatour**, 128 A, Pasteur St., tel. 29 98 68;

Vietnam-Tourist, 71, Nguyen Hue St., tel. 29 07 72.

ZONE BA RIA - VUNG TAU
Accommodations (area code: 84 64)

LUXURY-MODERATE: **The Canadian Hotel**, 48, Quang Trung St., tel. 5 93 21; **Grand Hotel**, 26, Quang Rung St., tel. 5 24 69; **Hai Au Hotel**, 100, Ha Long St., tel. 52278; **Pacific Hotel**, 4, Le Loi St., tel. 52311; **Rex Hotel**, 1. Duy Tan St., tel. 52135.

Tourist Information

Ba Ria - Vung Tau-Tourist, 18, Thuy Van St., tel. 5 21 38; **OSC-Tourist**, 2, Le Loi St., tel. 5 24 05.

TAY NINH PROVINCE
Accommodations (area code: 84 66)

TAY NINH: Hoa Binh Hotel, 1 A, 30.4. St., tel. 2 23 76.

Tourist Information

Tay Ninh Tourist, 1 A, 30.4. St. tel. 22376.

LONG AN PROVINCE
Accommodations (area code: 84 72)

TAN AN: Huong Tram Hotel, 6, Nguyen Trung Trac St., tel. 2 63 88;

Tourist Information

Long An-Tourist, 62, Nguyen Trung Trac, tel. 2 63 88.

TIEN GIANG PROVINCE
Accommodations (area code: 84 73)

MY THO: Cuu Long Hotel (Song Hien), 101, Trung Trac St., tel. 7 21 05.

Tourist Information

Tien Giang-Tourist, 63 Trung Trac St., tel. 7 21 05.

BEN TRE PROVINCE
Accommodations (area code: 84 75)

BEN TRE: Dong Khoi Hotel, 16 A, Hai Ba Trung St., tel. 2 22 40.

Tourist Information

Ben Tre-Tourist, 65, Dai Lo Dinh Khoi St., tel. 2 21 97.

VINH LONG PROVINCE
Accommodations (area code: 84 74)

VINH LONG: Cuu Long Hotel, 1, 01.05. St., tel. 23357; **Truong An Hotel**, tel. 22382.

Further Information

Bus station 2 miles / 3 km west of the city center; **local buses** stop at the post office. There are pedestrian ferries across the Tien Giang to the southern bank; point of departure for boat trips to the island of An Binh; Museum in the former French town hall.

Tourist Information
Vinh Long-Tourist, 1, 01.05. Str, tel. 22494.

DONG THAP PROVINCE
Accommodations (area code: 84 67)
SA DEC: Sat Dec Hotel, 108/5 A, Hung Von St., tel. 56 14 30; **Cao Lanh Hotel,** Binh Kieu St., tel. 31 96.

Tourist Information
Dong Thap-Tourist, 108/5A, Hung Vuon St., tel. 56 14 30.

CAN THO PROVINCE
Accommodations (area code: 84 71)
CAN THO: Hau Giang Hotel, 34, Nam Ky Khoi Nghia St., tel. 2 18 06; **Hoa Binh Hotel,** 5, Hoa Binh St., tel. 2 05 36; **Quoc Te Hotel** (International), 12, Hai Ba Trung St., tel. 22079.

Further Information
Bus station 2 km outside of town on Nguyen Trai St.; **Bank** (cash only), 2, Ngo Gia Tu St.; Post office, Hoa Binh St.; **Military museum,** 2, Hoa Binh St.

Tourist Information
Can Tho-Tourist, 27, Chau Van Liem, tel. 2 18 53/4; **Hau Giang-Tourist,** 34, Nam Ky Khoi Nghia St., tel. 2 18 06.

SOC TRANG PROVINCE
Accommodations (area code: 84 71)
SOC TRANG: Phong Lan Hotel, 124, Dong Khoi St.; **Tay Nam Hotel,** Nguyen Chi Tan St.

Further Information
On the 14th day of the 10th lunar month, the Pagoda Festival is celebrated with boat races and Khmer dances.

Tourist Information
Soc Tran-Tourist, 12, Nguyen Van Troi St.

KIEN GIANG PROVINCE
Accommodations (area code: 84 77)
RACH GIA: To Chau Hotel, 6 B, Le Loi Str.; **Binh Minh Hotel,** 1, Ham Nghi St.

Further Information
Museum with excavations from Oc Eo (Fu Nan), 21, Nguyen Van Troi St., 7:30-10:30 am, 1:30-4:30 pm except Mon.
Bus station 4 miles / 7 km south of town; boats at the south end of Bach Dang St. to Long Xuyen, Ha Tien (twelve hours) and Chau Doc (twelve hours).

HA TIEN: *BUDGET:* **Dong Ho Hotel, To**

Chau Hotel and **Ha Tien Hotel,** all on Ben Tran Hau St.

Further Information
Border with Cambodia is 4 miles / 6 km away; there are no border crossings.
Bus station on the To Chau River;
Ferries leave opposite the To Chau Hotel to Rach Gia (18 hours) and Chau Doc.

Tourist Information
Kien Giang-Tourist, 12, Ly Tu Trong St., tel. 6 20 81;

MINH HAI PROVINCE
Accommodations (area code: 84 78)
CA MAU: Minh Hai Hotel, 14, Hoang Van Thu St., tel. 3 16 21; **Ca Mau,** 20, Phan Ngoc Hien, tel. 31.
Vietnam's most southerly province with Ca Mau Peninsula consists of floodlands crisscrossed with rivers and canals. The salty earth is covered in mangrove forests. From Ca Mau there's access to bird sanctuaries and national parks; arrange visits through the local tourist office.

Tourist Information
Minh Hai-Tourist, 14, Hoang Van Thu St., tel. 3 14 68.

AN GIANG PROVINCE
Accommodations (area code: 84 76)
LONG XUYEN: Cuu Long Hotel (Mekong), 21, Nguyen Van Cung St., tel. 52365;
Long Xuyen Hotel, 17, Nguyen Van Cung St., tel. 5 21 84; **Song Hau Hotel,** Hai Ba Trung St., tel. 5 23 08; **Than Binh Hotel,** 12, Nguyen Hue St., tel. 5 21 84.

Further Information
Bus station 1 mile / 1.5 km south of town on Tran Hung Dao St.; **Ships:** Quay on the Long Xuyen Canal.
Ferries to Can Tho and Chau Doc as well as Rach Gia.

CHAU DOC: Chau Doc Hotel, 17, Doc Phu Thu St., Tel 8 34 86; **Thai Binh Hotel,** 37, Bao Ho Thoai St.

Further Information
The market is on the river bank; the **bus station** is 1 mile / 2 km further south, also on the river bank.
Ferries to the Cham settlement with its large mosque on the opposite bank of the river; pilgrimage center of Nuy Sam, 3 miles / 5 km away on the Cambodian border.

Tourist Information
An Giang-Tourist, 83-85, Nguyen Hue St., tel. 5 26 35.

LANGUAGE, WRITING, AND LITERATURE

Like the Chinese, Japanese, and Korean languages, as well as those of the Muong and Thai ethnic minorities, the Vietnamese language consists of one-syllable words which, when spoken at different pitches, can have completely different meanings. The Vietnamese vocabulary has distinct similarities with these minorities, as well as with the linguistic family of the Mon-Khmer. The language has also taken over words from Han Chinese; today, furthermore, words have been adopted from European languages, particularly technical or scientific terms.

The Vietnamese, like the Japanese and Koreans, have adopted the Chinese characters for the written reproduction of their language. All three of these nations,

Preceding pages: Having your picture taken is fun! School in a Northern Vietnamese village. Above: The Vietnamese like to read. Right: The printed word has authority.

however, have found that certain feelings and ways of thinking peculiar to their own languages can't adequately be conveyed with the Chinese symbols, and have therefore developed additional symbols or modified the Chinese ones.

In independent Dai Viet, *nom* writing developed. A layman can hardly distinguish between these forms of writing; yet *nom* was to play a key role in the development of Vietnamese literature.

Until 1945, both written and spoken Chinese remained the official language of the country, and that used by its educated classes. However, emperors, poets, and generals all also wrote in Vietnamese in *nom* characters. Only the mandarins, schooled in Confucianism, insisted on maintaining the Chinese language, which commoners couldn't understand, in order to underline their prestige.

After the 17th century, missionaries tried to develop ways of writing the Vietnamese language in the Roman alphabet. Phonetics, however, proved a stumbling-block; it seemed impossible accurately to reproduce the sounds of Vietnamese in this manner. The French Jesuit Alexandre de Rhodes immersed himself in the Vietnamese language and way of thinking, and ultimately managed to solve the problem. At first, he tried to use a form of musical notation, unsuccessfully. Then he hit upon the idea of using three Greek signs to help indicate the proper tone:

high tone = ahut (á)
low tone = gravis (à)
falling tone = kumflex (â)

He transcribed the heavily falling tone with the dot of the Greek iota (a), while a questioning or rising tone was written with half a question mark over the letter (å).

To give an example of how intonation can affect meaning, take the syllable ma:

high tone	má (mother)
low tone	mà (but)
falling tone	mâ (horse)
heavy tone	mạ (young rice-shoot)

| questioning tone | mả (grave) |
| without a sign | ma (evil spirit) |

Without these signs, Vietnamese transcribed into Roman characters is incomprehensible. At first, only Vietnam's Christians used this form of Latinate transcription, which allowed them access to Christian literature. During the colonial period, French became the official administrative language, but was also commonly used by the country's Francophile upper classes. Vietnam's Communist rulers, who sought to abolish illiteracy as quickly as possible, recognized that the Roman alphabet was easier to learn than the complicated characters of the Chinese or *nam* scripts. In 1945, *quc ngu* became the national form of writing; and the Vietnamese lost their means of access to centuries of written tradition at one fell swoop. Today, scholars again learn Chinese and *nom*, which allows them to access the huge collection of literary and scientific works preserved in the Han Nom Institute in Hanoi.

Vietnamese literature can be divided into three sections. The first, and largest group are works of history and geography, collections of customs and traditions commissioned by the various dynasties, each of which comprises from 20 to 100 volumes. Because of the custom of glossing references to previous works and commentaries, even the contents of some works which are lost have been more or less preserved. These works are written in Chinese. A second group includes lyrical poetry and rhythmic prose. Also a courtly form of literature, works in this style were written by emperors and aristocrats, poets and generals, and, since the 18th century, by educated women from the imperial court, as well as men. Women, however, were not allowed into the Confucian centers of learning, and thus could not attain the rank of a mandarin. This second literary genre generally deals with love of one's country and village, national pride or observations of nature. These works were written in Chinese, but also in *nom* characters.

In the second half of the 18th century, woman increasingly began to protest the fact that, in a Confucian society, they were only alloted the role of loyal wife sworn to faithfulness to her husband for a thousand years. Some poetesses were daring enough to bemoan the lot of an unwed mother and to point out the guilt of the immoral man responsible. Far ahead of its time was the verse novel *Kim Van Kieu* by the Hue court poet Nguyen Du, which portrayed a woman who dared to take charge of her own life.

The third group is popular and folk literature, including tales, sagas, stories of daily life, and, above all, innumerable legends. Many customs, such as paying a dowry in betel nuts, or various festival proceedings, customs, and traditions, derive from legends which document actual events from the country's earliest history.

Above: A dowry of betel nuts in a traditional wedding. Right: Many young couples today want a "European" wedding.

The deeds of the deified spirits and heroes, to whom the living have built temples and monuments, are also told in legends and cannot be understood without them. The Vietnamese know and love their legends. They are written in *nom*, in a humorous, sometimes earthy and sarcastic style, clearly enjoying making fun of themselves and other people. Roles are reduced to black and white: mandarins and land-owners are always greedy, possessive and hard-hearted despots. Rascals large and small get away with all kinds of things with these idiots. National heroes, on the other hand, show strength, superiority, readiness to help, and disproportionate courage.

Modern writing has, since the end of the 19th century, been strongly influenced by European, and especially French, literature. Only in the last few years have contemporary authors been able to free themselves from the restrictions of the Communist ideology, and poems and novels begun to stray from the routes established by convention.

NAMES

Tran Kim Hoang and Nguyen Xuan Hoa hand over their business cards. Later, the recipient remembers having met a man and a woman who seemed to be married. Certainly, this isn't evidenced by their names; both names could equally well belong to a man or a woman, and nothing shows that they're married. Once, women added *Thi* to their names, and men *Van*; today, this is old-fashioned. Women keep their names when they marry.

The first syllable is the family or the clan name, going back to the founder of a person's native village. There are a limited number of these names; most common are Nguyen, Tran, Le, Pham, Vu, Do, Hoang, Dang, Duong, and Dinh. Children receive their father's clan name.

The middle name is chosen by the parents, and usually goes back to a family tradition. The third name is the name you're generally called, used by friends and colleagues, bosses and employees,

friends and acquaintances. If you're speaking to an older person and want to show respect, you insert a *ba* before the name for a woman, *ong* for a man. Children don't call their parents by their first names: "Daddy" is *bo* in the north, *ba* in the south; mothers go by *me* and *ma*.

There's no limit to the selection of use-names: flowers, animals, objects, wishes, feelings, gods, heroes, or numbers all come into play. Young parents generally look for modern names, while grandparents favor traditional ones. The three names should harmonize together as well as possible. Superstitious parents choose ugly names to fool the spirits. Families with lots of children use Hai, Ba, Tu, Chinh, which mean Second, Third, Fourth, etc. When there get to be too many, the name Ut or Chot may appear, which means End. Sometimes you may meet a Ut Nhi or Ut Tu, a Second or a Fourth End. Only in the country are women addressed as "wife of..." Later on, a man and woman are known as "Mother and Father of" their oldest son.

THE DRUMS OF DONG SON CULTURE

Bronze drums of various shapes and sizes can be found all over Southeast Asia. In some areas, rain-drums are still in use during harvest ceremonies, and some tribes in the Vietnamese highlands bury their chieftains in bronze drums. Experts are still divided on the question of the drums' actual purpose; it's possible that they served a number of different functions. French scientists have found bronze drums at excavation sites in the village of Dong Son, in Thanh Hoa Province, as well as in the Red River Delta and at individual sites in Central Vietnam and the Mekong Delta. But such drums have also been found in southern China.

In 1902, the Austrian scientist F. Heger divided 165 drums into four groups.

Above: Bronze drum of the Dong Son culture. Right: Top of a bronze drum with star and concentric decorative rings.

After 1918, the French H. Parmentier counted as many as 350 drums. Type I are large, medium-sized or even small drums which come from the general area of Dong Son Culture. There's no bottom, or floor, to the main resonating body. A drum consists of three parts: a spherical base, a straight-sided or gently curved cylinder, and a pot-bellied section which is covered over with a top plate.

The drums are elaborately decorated: the middle section, in particular, is ornamented with horizontal and vertical bands, geometric forms and figures with stylized headgear. Furthermore, there are images of people in boats with prows resembling the heads of birds, and sterns ending in a bird's tail. A star in the middle of the top plate, also called a sun, is surrounded by a series of concentric circles with representations of birds, animals and people in houses. On this plate, there are also small sculpted frogs and horses, both with and without riders. The drums of this type have four sets of handles.

Type II drums consist of only two parts, a straight lower section extended outward to form a base, and a heavy upper section covered over with a plate, which extends out as far as about an inch and a half (3 cm) on either side. The decorative motifs are basically the same as those described above; the star generally has eight points, and there are four to six frogs sculpted on the top surface. The drums have two pairs of handles. Drums of this type have been found in central China and North Vietnam.

The drums of type III are not all that different. The body of the drum is concave, the top plate extends over the edges, and the star is usually twelve-pointed. The handles are very small. The frogs on top are arranged in groups of three on four sides. On some drums, these are joined by representations of elephants or snails. Types I-III are described as Indonesian drums.

Type IV, the so-called Chinese drums, are generally smaller, and the designs are often supplemented with Chinese characters. The star is, again, twelve-pointed, and the concentric circles contain the twelve animals of the Zodiac. This type of drum was common in central China and Yunnan. However, the drums found in Yunnan between 1955 and 1957, ascribed to the Dian Empire period, don't easily fit into any of the categories described here.

The animals on the upper surfaces of Group IV drums are extremely stylized. Most common are fish, foxes, various deer, pelicans, cranes, storks, and other birds in flight. A motif which recurs time and again is the bird's-eye, stylized as a circle with a dot in the middle.

The houses represented here resemble pile buildings of the Malay-Indonesian-Oceanic world, and were not known in China in the period of the drums' creation. Scientists, therefore, assume that the Dong Son artists and artisans learned their craft in China but must themselves

have come originally from regions influenced by Malay-Indonesian cultures. The outsized birds sitting on the house roofs may represent guardian spirits.

On the drums, humans are represented either lying, standing and performing various activities, or crouching. They thresh rice, letting the grains fall upon drums. This form of honoring the dead is also seen among primitive peoples in Borneo.

The most striking images are of people in boats, some of which are also bearing drums. Warriors, weapons and equipment bear feather ornaments corresponding to the height of the person or object. They may somehow relate to the bird cults of the South Sea Islands. The men's bearing is ceremoniously solemn; the boats, each rowed by a single man, move slowly. As no one person seems to have a leading role, they can't be depictions of martial actions. One infers, therefore, that they're representations of death rites, shamanistic cults, or initiation ceremonies.

FROM CONFUCIUS TO MARX

Well into the 20th century, knowledge and education in Vietnam were generally based on the Confucian system of teaching and testing. Cornerstones were the Five Classics and the Four Analects, which had been written well before the year 1. The first tests were held at the beginning of the Dai Viet Empire in 1072. At first, only sons of the royal families or the aristocracy could attend the educational facilities in the Temple of Confucius in Thang Long (Hanoi) or, after 1803, in Hue. From 1252 on, this institution was at least theoretically available to youths from every walk of life. Not until 1803, with the founding of regional educational institutions which could prepare and qualify students to take the tests in the capital, was education actually available to every man. After studying, a few of those alumni who didn't end up as civil servants went back to teach the children in their native villages. Women were never able to receive a Confucian education or the rank of a mandarin. The hierarchy of the mandarinate, with civilian and military mandarins, was created in the year 1089.

Although the *nom* script, derived from Chinese pictographs, had long been used, the mandarins were able to suppress it efficiently so that their own status was at no time threatened. There were four sections of the tests: 1. Writing from memory, without a single mistake, a text from the body of Confucian literature; 2. Oral translation from these writings, and composing a poem in rhythmic prose; 3. Drawing up an ordnance, an imperial proclamation and a report to the Emperor; 4. Composing a commentary. In 1646, the Nguyen lords in Hue expanded the tests, adding questions about the army and the system of weights and measures. In the 19th century, the elitist order was

Above: Some temples also serve as schools. Right: The Vietnamese are a young people; one-third of the population are students.

somewhat undermined by such abuses as selling of titles or inheritance of ranks.

The colonial government banned the tests in 1915 in Hanoi and in 1918 in Hue. European education, however, was only available to a few Vietnamese. The French were solely interested in training laborers; higher education was there only for Francophile city-dwellers. As a result, in 1945, at the end of the colonial period, more than 80% of the population was illiterate. Ho Chi Minh and his revolutionaries had realized that it would be quicker to teach the people to read, so as to be able to propagandize their ideas, using the transcriptions developed by the missionaries, based on the Roman alphabet, rather than trying to teach them the complicated Chinese or *nom* characters. They called this writing *quoc ngu*, national writing, and forbade Chinese language and writing in 1945. Education made great strides; illiteracy dropped. The wars of independence, however, created more educational gaps. At present, there are plenty of Vietnamese who graduated from schools and universities in the former East Bloc. While education for children is compulsory (though not mandatory), there's a severe lack of well-trained and adequately-paid teachers, curricula, teaching materials, schools, and students. Only a part of the population, which is 75% rural, sees any reason why their children should have a school education. The school system provides free elementary education, grades 1-5, but teaching materials do have to be paid for. Tuition must be paid, however, for the next four years of middle school, grades 6-9, with a diploma; and teaching materials have to be paid for, as well. The three-year high school also costs money. Graduating from one of these entitles you to enter college or university.

The Vietnamese are a "young people"; one-third of the population is in school. A large percentage of the students, however, leave elementary, middle, and high

schools before completing the course of study: statistically speaking, in 1992/93 it was 9.24% of the elementary-school students, 21.57% of the middle, and 27.4% of the high school ones. Still, there are only 2.3 million truly illiterate people out of a population of more than 72 million. At present, Vietnam has some 15,000 elementary and middle schools, 1080 high schools, and 102 universities. The state is responsible for training and paying teachers. Classes are large, often containing more than 40 students, so that teaching is done in shifts, in 28 hours on six weekdays. In the elementary schools, one teacher will cover every subject; high school teachers generally have 16 to 18 hours a week. Their training lasts only two to three years, although there are efforts to raise this to four years. Grading is from 1 to 10; 9 and 10 are extremely good. School begins in September; there are two weeks of vacation during the Tet festival. Summer vacation is in July and August; teachers have to use one month of this time for their own training.

THE WATER PUPPET PLAYS

Flags are waving over the lake by the village temple. A mood of expectant excitement has fallen over the spectators. Suddenly, the first firework goes off. Submarine "duck" firecrackers detonate below the lake surface. A duck appears, flaps its wings, submerges again, reappears. When the *hien teu*, a young farmer in a simple tunic, appears, the spell is broken and the spectators follow the play with laughter and catcalls.

The *hien teu* recounts that he was banished from heaven because he had stolen a heavenly peach; he has therefore been sent back to earth to try to untangle the mess of earthly affairs. His story is interrupted by a *phot*, a snob, but he chases him away. However, he keeps popping up again from the water and splashing the

Above: Water puppet plays, fascinating for young and old, exist only in Vietnam. Right: Every house has its Thanh Tet, New Year's pictures which bring luck for the year ahead.

audience. Then the sacred animals appear. The dragon spews flames; the phoenix, vain, flaps its wings; the unicorn strikes a martial pose; and the turtle swims contentedly across the lake. There follow scenes with historic tales from classical operas, wars of the national heroes, dances, and fights. As many as 30 scenes are shown in the course of one play.

The audience is well acquainted with what's going on, and knows all the characters and their roles. Puppet plays originated in the Indian regions. In Vietnamese villages at the end of the Tet festival, rotating lanterns are hung over the lake, reflecting in the water. This play of light has combined with the puppet plays to create the genre of water puppet plays. *Nua roi* were known as early as the 17th century, and reached their highest flowering in the 19th century. They are supposed to have originated in the Thay Pagoda; but they were also known early on at the Giong Pagoda in the village of Phu Dong, near Hanoi.

The players, who worked in guilds under a master, had their own guardian spirit, who was worshipped in the small *thuy dinh* temples on the water. From here, standing in the water, the players move the puppets, large and small, across the water's surface. The puppets were all carved by the same masters responsible for the woodcarvings and ornamentation of a given temple. Of some 200 original texts, 70 have survived.

Chinese and European travelers, as well as inscriptions on stone stelae, tell of the impressive plays at the Imperial Court in Thang Long. These were held near the old Bien Long Bridge, which enabled them to achieve truly fantastic effects.

Until a few years ago, the tradition seemed virtually to have died out; now, it's seeing a revival throughout the country.

TET NGUYEN DAM –
THE NEW YEAR'S FESTIVAL

Chuc Mong Nam Moi, Happy New Year – long before the event, you see this on greeting cards and banners, and even on the packaging of sweets and noodles. The year begins, according to the lunar calendar, with the first new moon of spring, which, according to our reckoning, falls between mid-January and mid-February. Preparations, however, begin several weeks in advance. Vietnamese from all over the world flock home to celebrate the holiday with their families; others travel abroad to visit their families there. Most of them have been saving for the holiday for a long time; some people even rack up considerable debts at the last minute.

On the 23rd day of the last lunar month, kitchen and house have to be spotlessly clean. This is the day on which the kitchen god goes to the gods' New Year's festival, and he shouldn't be able to have anything bad to report. A large

piece of pork also has to be purchased ahead of time; sometimes five or six families get together and slaughter an entire pig.

Then there are the rice cakes to make, without which Tet just wouldn't be Tet. Round *banh day*, Cakes of Heaven, and four-cornered *banh chung*, Cakes of the Earth, are made of glutinous rice which, in Vietnam, is seldom used for any other purpose. Added to this is a paste made of sweetened green beans. The mixture is steamed briefly and formed into round cakes to make *banh day*. *Banh chung* need a bit longer: a layer of bean paste is spread on a layer of rice and topped with pork and black pepper, then covered with another layer of bean paste and another of rice. The resulting square cakes are wrapped tightly in leaves of the *dong* bush and bound tightly with thin strips of bamboo. The *banh chung* then have to cook for 20 to 24 hours. There's a legend about their invention. The Hung emperor called his 22 sons to him and said that, as he was growing old, one of them should

take over for him. He would name as his successor the one who could present him with the best dish. The sons, accordingly, spread throughout the country. Only Linh Lang, the youngest, went to his mother for advice. She was a simple peasant woman whom the Emperor had briefly favored. When she heard of his wish, she got right to work. "The emperor's subjects," she said, "have to live from rice. Sometimes they eat beans with it, and only rarely do they get pork." Then she shaped square cakes for the earth and round ones for Heaven. The Emperor tasted all of the meals which his sons brought to him, as well as that of Linh Lang. He had never before tasted the food his subjects ate; and he liked it so much that he promptly made Linh Lang his successor.

Rice cakes also figure in a Buddhist New Year's legend. Buddha had dis-

covered that the restless souls, *ma* and *quy*, caused a lot of problems for the people on earth, and took away their rice. The spirits wanted to scare Buddha and asked what he was most afraid of. "I'm only afraid of rice and rice cakes," he replied. The spirits accordingly threw rice at him, and the people were able to eat their fill. When Buddha asked the spirits, in turn, what they most feared, they replied that they were afraid of the bows and arrows with which the living tried to drive them away. Buddha said that they should give the living a piece of land as large as a single garment, and then he would see to it that they left the spirits in peace. They agreed. But Buddha then made the garment grow until it covered the whole country, and gave it to the people. At the end of every year, the spirits try to get the country back. For this reason, people set up bamboo poles between the 23rd and 30th day of the last lunar month, and hang on it either a piece of clothing or a bow and arrows. These *cat neu* trees are to keep the spirits away.

Above: Setting off fireworks often results in injury. Right: New Year's festival in Dong Da village, Ha Bac province.

In these last days before the Tet holiday, the Vietnamese go to special markets to purchase budding apricot trees or twigs (*dao*) in dark or light pink, and little orange trees (*quat*). No house in Bac Bo is without its *dao* and *quat*, which bloom in time for the festival. In the south, the houses are decorated with yellow *mai* (forsythia). And people are very careful about selecting the proper New Year's pictures, *Thanh Tet*.

On the last evening of the old year, each family gathers around its ancestor altar, thanks the ancestors and asks for their protection in the new year ahead. A cooked chicken on the altar is furnished as a special meal for the dead. Then everyone eats and drinks until the explosions of fireworks announce the stroke of midnight. There may have been some scattered bangs here and there over the last few days, but midnight ushers in a veritable inferno. The earth seems to shake for minutes, and the smell of powder lingers for a long time in the warm, damp air. *Hai pho* is the term for the chains of firecrackers, each of which ignites the next one, which culminate with a cannon-like boom calculated to drive away all the evil spirits.

Whatever happens in the first few hours of the new year will continue to have effect for the next twelve months. The Vietnamese try to influence their luck a bit, ordering, for example, strapping young men to come and stand in front of their doors on New Year's morning. At this time, it would be extremely bad luck to meet an old man or a pregnant woman.

The festival extends over three days, with visits to parents and relations, neighbors and friends. On the third day, you have to visit your boss or your teacher, and present gifts. Children also receive small gifts, often crisp new bills. Markets are held in the temples and pagodas, where buffalo and cock fighting, wrestling and other games take place. Children swing between high bamboo poles, while men are absorbed in chess or *to tom*, a card game with 120 cards.

THE VIETNAMESE VILLAGE

A blanket of gray clouds lies heavily over the rice fields. Stooped under a steady mist of fine, penetrating drizzle, the women moving across the fields sink up to their knees in the moist earth; undeterred, they set out the young rice shoots in arrow-straight rows. Their heads and faces are hidden by their broad, conical hats made of braided straw. The temperature is around 45 or 50°F (8-10°C). Their clothes are drenched with moisture, but this fine February rain is ideal for the rice.

A bamboo fence surrounds a village in the Red River Delta. Within the fence, there was originally a defensive wall which could only be traversed by means of its four gates. One of these gates still survives. Behind it starts the broad street, paved with stones. At the edge of the village is the *chua*, or Buddhist temple, inhabited anew by monks for the last few years. The Vietnamese like to tell you that the monks and nuns retire to the monasteries because of love woes. Right next to the *chua* is the temple for the mother goddess, the *tu phu*. Only a few statues are left here. An old man says that when their cult was officially forbidden, the statues were brought to the neighboring village, where they still sit locked up today; now, a quarrel has started with the neighboring village, because they won't give the statues back.

At either end of the village is a large well surrounded by a stone wall. On the broad, open square, all that remains of the *dinh* complex is the central building. The high, sweeping roof towers over all the other buildings. Today, the square in front of the *dinh* is used as a marketplace. Markets are a woman's business. They buy and sell, and the money they earn

Right: Flocks of ducks are taken to the fields with the farmers in the morning, there to disport themselves on the irrigation ditches.

from the produce of their gardens and chicken coops stays in their own pockets. They carry their wares on bamboo poles across their shoulders with a basket hanging from either end.

On the main street is the little tea house, its roof supported by wooden poles, its walls made of bast matting. Men light their water-pipes at the oil lamp's flickering flame, and discuss the news of the day. There are children everywhere. The old man in a long black coat, with a thin beard and high cheekbones, is highly regarded throughout the village. He may once have been a mandarin or a Taoist scholar.

To the right and left of the village street, the farms lie behind walls and closed gates. Ranging from simple portals to elaborate stone gateways guarded by sculpted sentry figures, the doors indicate the family's wealth. You can't see the houses from the gate; the path leading up to them makes a couple of sharp turns to prevent the access of evil spirits, who can only move in straight lines.

The buildings themselves stand on a large patch of cleared, packed earth, where rice and fruits are dried and stored. The door in the middle of the main house is open, and you can see through it to the ancestor altar in the opposite wall. In front of this is a large flat couch, where the man of the house sits and drinks tea with a couple of other locals. Originally, Vietnamese peasants had only simple floor mats on which they ate and slept. Today, many farmhouses have low, woven beds as well as tables and chairs; wealthy homes even boast cupboards and chests with wood or enamel inlays. On both sides of the main room are the side rooms, divided by thin walls; these are the women's sleeping quarters, council rooms, or storage for valuable objects. The kitchen and animal stalls are in separate buildings.

In very small establishments, the water

buffalo may live under the same roof as the family. He is treated as a member of the family, and if he has to be slaughtered, he's generally sold. He's one of the Vietnamese farmer's most valuable possessions. These powerful animals let themselves be led, and even ridden, by children. In the Red River Delta, where every available corner of land is used for the cultivation of rice or vegetables, farmers can only keep one buffalo, because it's hard to feed them. In Central Vietnam and the Mekong Delta, however, where there's plenty of feed available, a yoke of two buffalo are hitched to the farmer's plow to break the heavy ground for the next harvest.

A well-to-do farmer will have supply houses and storerooms, a house for friends, relations and guests, and other, additional houses. Within the walls of his complex, there may also be vegetable gardens or orchards, and even a spring or pond which cools the place off in summer. Trees may also grow around the house; they can be used for their wood.

The bamboo that grows around the villages in Northern Vietnam provides the farmers with bamboo shoots to eat and in fact accompanies them from birth to the grave, furnishing material for cradles and coffins, beds and tools, building and jewelry.

In central and southern Vietnam, the villages are shaded by coconut palms, which play much the same role here as bamboos do in the north.

The rice-paddies are surrounded by an extensive network of canals and narrow irrigation ditches, where men, women and children catch fish and shellfish. Those who can't afford fish eat their rice with the fish sauce *nuoc mam*. This is made according to family recipes, but it's also produced by large companies, where huge amounts of fish and shellfish are salted down and fermented.

Hundreds of ducks swim on the canals. The farmers take them with them to the fields in the morning, and drive them back home along the village street every night.

 **... get you going.**

AVAILABLE TITLES

Australia
Bali / Lombok
Berlin and Potsdam
Brittany
California
  Las Vegas, Reno, Baja California
Cambodia / Laos
Canada
  Ontario, Québec, Atlantic Provinces
Caribbean
  The Greater Antilles,
  Bermuda, Bahamas
Caribbean - *The Lesser Antilles*
China
Crete
Cyprus
Egypt
Florida
Greece - *The Mainland*
Hawaii
Hungary
India
  Northern, Northeastern
  and Central-India
India - *Southern India*
Indonesia
  Sumatra, Java, Bali,
  Lombok, Sulawesi
Ireland
Kenya
Malaysia
Mexico
Morocco
Moscow / St Petersburg
Munich
  Excursions to Castels,
  Lakes & Mountains
Nepal
New York - *City and State*
New Zealand
Paris
Philippines
Prague / Czech Republic
Provence
Rome
Spain *(North)*
Spain
  Mediterranean Coast,
  Southern Spain, Balearic Islands

Thailand
Turkey
Tuscany
Vietnam

FORTHCOMING

Burma
Canada *(West)*
Corsica
Dominican Republic
Israel
London / England and Wales
Portugal
Scotland
South Africa
Sri Lanka
U.S.A. - *The East, Midwest and South*
U.S.A. - *The West, Rockies and Texas*

TABLE OF CONTENTS

PREPARING FOR YOUR TRIP

For additional information, contact the Embassy of the Socialist Republic of Vietnam (see the section on "Diplomatic Representatives") or a travel agent.

Climate - When to go

The best seasons in Vietnam are the winter months. The descriptions which follow are meant as an aid to orientation. Vietnam lies in the path of monsoons, trade winds and typhoons. This conjunction of influences can lead to unusual extremes of weather.

January: The coldest month, throughout the country. In Bac Bo (northern part of the country), the northeast monsoon arrives; temperatures may fall to 50°F (10°C) for a few days, and don't usually get above 64°F (18°C). There's steady drizzle, and a blanket of low-hanging gray clouds. This is the start of the rice-planting season.

In the Southern Highlands and Nam Bo (the southern part of the country), however, skies are clear, and there's no rain.

February: Last month of winter. In Bac Bo, and sometimes to Hue, the northeast monsoon continues with its drizzle. Temperatures rise. In Trung Bo (central Vietnam), the dry season may already be starting, especially south of Cloud Pass.

In Nam Bo, February is the driest month, with clear skies.

March: Spring begins. Bac Bo's temperatures are around 68°F (20°C). Only scattered drizzle. The wind stays from the northeast. In the mountainous northwest, the hot season begins; the dry season starts in Trung Bo. In Nam Bo, there are occasional showers.

April: End of the northeast monsoon, and the winds gradually shift to the southwest. In Bac Bo, there may be occasional showers, but generally the dry season is beginning. In the northwest and in Trung Bo, up to the Vinh area, there are hot winds from the mountains of Laos. In Nam Bo, the hot season is starting, also with southwesterly winds.

May: Summer is starting – and the rainy season, all over the country. In Bac Bo, it may cool off to 68-77°F (20 - 25°C). In Trung Bo, the hot winds from Laos continue. In the southern highlands and Nam Bo, there may be some southwesterly storms coming from the Gulf of Bengal.

June: Southwesterly winds from the Gulf of Bengal, trade winds from the western Pacific. In Bac Bo, the humid heat of summer sets in, with heavy rain showers interspersed with hot periods. In Nam Bo and the southern highlands, it's cloudy, with thunderstorms.

July/August: The height of summer's heat and humidity. In Bac Bo, there are frequent storms and rain. In Trung Bo, the Laos winds abate, and the rainy season begins. In Nam Bo, the rain lessens in August.

September: In the north, the temperatures drop slightly. In Trung Bo (Hue), wind and rainshowers. Most typhoons happen in September.

October: In Bac Bo, temperatures decrease to 68°F (20°C). In Trung Bo, heavy rainfall continues.

November: In Bac Bo, the dry season begins, with clear skies and pleasant temperatures. In Trung Bo, there's still a lot of rain; the rainy season ends in Nam Bo.

December: Dry season throughout the country, with a decrease in temperature. In Bac Bo, December is the first month of winter, with temperatures between 64-68°F (18 - 20°C) and clear skies.

Visa

If you're travelling on a group tour, the organizer will arrange for your visa. Individuals can also arrange for visas through a travel agency if they book their flights there. There's a charge for visas, and it may take up to three weeks for a visa to come through. Individuals who aren't reserving in advance should apply directly to the Vietnamese embassy for visas.

Whatever the case, a traveler has to fill out two visa applications and enclose two passport photos (4 x 6 cm), and send these documents, together with his/her passport, to the travel agency. Applications directly to the embassy must include a check for the visa processing fee and a stamped, self-addressed envelope (registered mail).

Visas are issued for up to six weeks; if necessary, they can be extended once you're in Vietnam.

Inoculations

At the moment, inoculations are only required if you're traveling into the country from a region where there's yellow fever. It's wise, however, to take precautions in advance against malaria, hepatitis and typhus, as well as polio and tetanus. Ask your doctor, the health authorities, or a hospital specializing in tropical diseases; and be especially careful if you're traveling with children.

Clothing

The clothes you bring along should be light, made of cotton or linen, and easy to wash. Every hotel offers a laundry service, generally round the clock. In the North and in the mountains between October and February, you'll need wool garments or warmer clothing for the evening. Long pants and thermal underwear will do the trick and don't take up too much room in your suitcase. Rain gear is useful year round, and essential in summer. And a sturdy pair of shoes are also important; you need them not only for hiking, but because many of the roads and paths you'll be using are in less than ideal condition.

Hotel rooms and airplanes are often over-cooled by air conditioning; take a jacket or sweater to keep from catching a cold.

Don't forget to bring a bathing suit! Beachwear is not acceptable in hotels or on the streets; this doesn't mean, however, that you won't see young Vietnamese girls in miniskirts and bikinis. Dirty clothes or a sloppy appearance are not appreciated; and many individual tourists may have encountered difficulties purely as a result of their external appearance.

Money

Vietnamese currency (bills or coins) may not be brought in and out of the country (see "Currency").

GETTING THERE

By plane: Most travelers to Vietnam arrive and depart by plane.

The **Hanoi** airport, Noi Bai, is about 18 miles (30 km) from the city center; the shuttle bus to the city costs $ 1.50, a taxi about $ 25. It's serviced by *Air France, Air Laos, Aeroflot, Cathay Pacific, China Southern Airlines, Malaysian Airline System, Singapore Airlines, Thai Airways International,* and *Vietnam Airlines.*

Airport tax for international flights departing from Hanoi is 6 $ (cash).

The airport in **Ho Chi Minh City**, Than Son Nhat, is 4 miles (7 km) from the city center; shuttle bus; taxi costs about 10 $). It's serviced by *Air Cambodia, Air France, Air Laos, Aeroflot, Cathay Pacific, China Airlines, China Southern Airlines, EVA Air, Garuda Indonesia, KLM, Lufthansa, Malaysian Airline System, Pacific Airlines, Philippine Airlines, Quantas Airways, Singapore Airlines, Thai Airways International,* and *Vietnam Airlines.*

Airport tax for international flights departing from Ho Chi Minh City is 8 $ (cash).

By road: At the moment, the only road connection between Vietnam and Cambodia is Highway 22 from Ho Chi Minh City and Phnom Penh. The border crossing Moc Bai has to be entered in your visa.

At present, the border between Vietnam and Laos is not open to tourists. The border crossing at Dong Dang, Lang Son Province, between Vietnam and the People's Republic of China, is currently only open to organized groups on round-trip tours.

By train: Vietnam - China connections via the border station Dong Dang, in the province of Lang Son, are supposed to be reopened for tourists in the not-too-distant future.

By boat: Cruise ships can stop in the harbors of Haiphong, Hong Gai (Halong Bay), Da Nang and Ho Chi Minh City. Up to now, no foreign cruise ship of a major line goes to Vietnam. There are plans to create a line between Da Nang and the island of Hai Nan in southern China.

Border formalities

When entering the country, you have to fill out two entry forms and two customs declarations; you keep one copy of each. You have to save these documents and present them when you're leaving the country. The customs declarations have to list all the banks and exchange offices where you've changed money (see "Customs").

TRAVELLING IN VIETNAM

By plane:

You can reserve international flights in Hanoi, at 60, Nguyen Du; domestic flights at 1, Quang Trung, tel: 5 55 83, or at travel agencies. Make sure to book in advance.

For about ten days before and after the Tet festival, all flights, domestic and international, will be completely booked out long in advance by the Vietnamese. Within Vietnam, you're allowed 44 pounds (20 kg) of luggage.

Since 1989, Hang Khong Vietnam

(Vietnam Airlines) has been able to increase its passenger capacity by buying a number of Soviet airplanes as well as airbuses. At present, there's regular service along the following domestic routes:

from Hanoi: Hanoi (HAN) - Ho Chi Minh City (SGN); Hanoi - Buon Ma Thuot (BMV); Hanoi - Da Nang (DAD); Hanoi - Hue (HUI); Hanoi - Nha Trang (NHA); Hanoi - Play Cu (PXU); Hanoi - Dien Bien Phu.

Reservations: Ho Chi Minh City, District 1, Nguyen Dinh Chieu 27 B, tel: 29 99 80.

from Ho Chi Minh City: Ho Chi Minh City (SGN) - Hanoi (HAN); HCM - Buon Ma Thuot (BMV); HCM - Can Tho (VCA); HCM - Da Lat (DLI); HCM - Da Nang (DAD); HCM - Haiphong (HPH); HCM - Hue (HUI); HCM - Nha Trang (NHA); HCM - Play Cu (PXU); HCM - Quy Nhon (UIH)

from Da Nang: Da Nang (DAD) - Ho Chi Minh City (SGN); Da Nang - Hanoi (HAN); Da Nang - Buon Ma Thuot (BMV); Da Nang - Nha Trang (NHA); Da Nang - Play Cu (PXU); Da Nang - Quy Nhon (UIH);

from Hue: Hue (HUI) - Ho Chi Minh City (SGN); Hue - Hanoi (HAN); Hue - Da Lat (DLI)

There's daily service along the Hanoi - Da Nang - HCM routes; other routes are flown 2 to 5 times a week.

Airline Offices in Vietnam

Air France
Hanoi, 1, Ba Trieu, tel: 4 25 34 84
Ho Chi Minh City, 130, Dong Khoi, tel: 29 09 81 / 2
KLM
Ho Chi Minh City, 244, Rue Pasteur, tel: 2319 90 / 1
Lufthansa
Ho Chi Minh City, 132 - 134, Dong Khoi, tel: 29 85 29 / 29 85 49
Hang Khong Vietnam (domestic)
Hanoi, 60, Nguyen Du, tel: 5 55 83

Ho Chi Minh City, 27 B, Nguyen Dinh Chieu, tel: 29 99 80

By train:

The following train connections are available:

Hanoi - Ho Chi Minh City via Hue, Da Nang - Nha Trang. Regular trains, TN 1, run daily and stop in all the larger towns. The express, TBN 9, runs Tue, Thu, Fri, Sat, Sun. On Mon. and Wed., the special express CM7 stops only in Vinh, Hue, Da Nang, Nha Trang. A couchette costs about 120 $, and the trip lasts about two days.

Hanoi - Haiphong. Two express trains a day; tickets: 3 $; trip lasts three hours.

Hanoi - Lao Cai (Sa Pa) via Viet Tri, Yen Bai. One express train a day along a 12-hour route.

Hanoi - Lang via über Bac Giang, Kep. Two trains a day. The express takes about seven hours and costs 3 $.

Hanoi - Thai Nguyen - Hong Gai (Halong Bay) via Kep, Uong Bi.

By boat:

Coastal ships run along the following routes:

Haiphong - Da Nang - Ho Chi Minh City - Vung Tau.

Haiphong - Halong Bay - Hong Gai.

Travel agencies in Vietnam

In Ho Chi Minh City there are presently some 300 travel agencies; in Hanoi more than 100. The following list includes only the major state agencies.

Vinatour, Hanoi, 54, Nguyen Du, tel: 25 29 86

Vinatour, Ho Chi Minh City, 128 A, Rue Pasteur, tel: 29 98 68,

Khanh Hoa Tourist, Nha Trang, 1, Tran Hung Dao , tel: 2 27 53

Khanh Hoa Tourist, Ho Chi Minh City, 138, Nguyen Trai, tel: 33 40 47

Saigontourist Travel Service Center, Ho Chi Minh City, 49, Le Thanh Ton, tel: 23 01 02, 29 81 29,

Hanoi office, Hanoi, Thang Loi Hotel - Yen Phu, tel: 26 82 21

Hanoi Tourist Sevice Center, Hanoi, 25, Tran Hung Dao, tel: 25 60 36

Transportation

Bicycle rickshaws (*xich lo,* French cyclo) are the main means of transportation for people and objects. For Western visitors, they're also extremely affordable; a city trip costs about 3,000 dong, even for two people with luggage. The driver, of course, hopes that he'll be able to get more money from a foreign visitor, and you shouldn't begrudge him this. Just make sure that you clearly announce your destination and agree on a price before you get in the rickshaw, to avoid any difficulties or misunderstandings with a non-English speaking driver at the end of the ride.

Bicycles (*xe dap*): Most Vietnamese still commute to work by bicycle, and also use it to transport groceries and other loads.

In most cities, you can rent bicycles for 1 - 2 $ a day, depending on the model. Most bicycles lack lights and a bell, and the brakes don't always work, either. Setting up your air pump at the side of the sidewalk is a recognized sign that you need help. Bicycles can only be parked in parking lots, which are guarded, for a fee of about 300 dong.

Motorcycles (*xe dap Honda*): It's almost impossible to rent a motorcycle. You need a Vietnamese driver's license, and the problems of insurance are only starting to be solved.

Taxi: You can take a taxi for city or cross-country trips in every major city, paying either by distance travelled or agreeing on a fixed price. Only Hanoi and HCM have taxi stands; it's best to call for a taxi from a hotel or travel agency.

Vietnamese travel agencies furnish **rental cars** either on a per-mile, per-day, or per-excursion basis. The price includes gas and driver, although the latter generally doesn't speak any foreign languages. Cars usually cost between 25 and 50 cents a kilometer, and around 30 $ a day (100 km), depending on the model, options (air conditioning), etc. Rarely, you'll get a Russian Wolga, usually a Japanese car with air conditioning. Guides are also available through the travel agencies, and cost 15 - 25 $, including accommodation and board, depending on how many foreign languages they can speak, but irrespective of the number of persons in a party. Groups of around ten people can rend Japanese mini-buses.

On Vietnamese roads, speed is determined by the state of the roads, the number of cars, construction work and bridges. You shouldn't plan to go more than about 20 miles/30 km in an hour, including time for stop-offs for photos or tea.

Bus (*xe do*): Buses traverse the entire country. They're cheap and fast, provided that you're willing to zoom past all the scenic beauties and sights along the way. Often, passengers are squeezed in so tightly that they can't see out the windows. Most buses have low seats which are so close together that you can't stretch out your legs. The only stops are at small cookshacks on the roadside.

City buses (*xe buyt*): In Hanoi, the colonial-era streetcar had to be closed in 1989 because it had simply gotten too old. From Saigon to Cholon and other neighborhoods, however, there are quite good buses.

Local buses (*xe buyt*): These buses run from the major cities to towns within a vicinity of up to 60 miles/100 km, and are primarily used by commuters.

Long-distance buses (*xe do*) traverse the whole country, are very cheap, and stop in every small town.

Express buses (*xe do toc hanh*) depart from major cities in the very early morning and stop only in other major cities. You have to reserve your seat at least a day in advance.

Minibuses are a bit more expensive, and more comfortable for foreign tourists. They, too, run from city to city. They don't have a fixed schedule, and don't leave from public bus stations; you have to ask where they stop, and when.

Bus stations (*ben xe*) for express buses (*ben xe toc hanh*) are located in every major city; there are often two or more, for local and long-distance buses. You can reserve tickets (*ve xe*) at the station or at official sales outlets.

PRACTICAL TIPS

Bugs

In the tropics, cockroaches are unavoidable house pets, purchased with lettuce, vegetables or other foodstuffs. As roommates, they're unpleasant but fortunately completely harmless. Mothballs placed by the sink can be an effective repellent because of their strong smell. Unpackaged foodstuffs, fruit, or dirty dishes in your room won't only attract cockroaches. Insects don't like air conditioning. After nightfall, mosquitos will enter any lit room as soon as you open the windows.

Camping

There are, as yet, no camping sites, with the exception of Da Lat.

Children / Beggars

Particularly in out-of-the-way areas, children, who regard the "long noses" as objects of infinite curiosity, can become a real annoyance. The best strategy is to make contact with one or two out of the crowd. Hands and eyes are the best ways to communicate with children; if you deal with them, rather than ignoring them, you'll get free more quickly. Giving out candy can lead to squabbling, and the next traveler will be all the more annoyed at the requests for candy or pens and pencils. For a while, all foreigners were hailed with the rhythmic call of *lien-xo*, or Russian; but you don't often hear that any more.

And a word about beggars: Apart from the professionals at the temples and tourist spots, there are also those who are quietly and truly poor, particularly veterans crippled in the war. If they don't have a family to care for them, they're in very bad shape, and could really use a little help.

Currency

1 $ is worth about 11,000 dong (1995). The exchange rate is no longer calculated every day, but remains constant for long periods. Experience shows that the official rate of exchange is subject to some variation within the country, tending to be higher in HCM than in Hanoi, and worse in smaller towns. The rate is not such as to tempt one to exchange on the black market, which is seen as an economic crime.

You can exchange money at hotel reception desks or the Bank for Foreign Trade, which has branches in the major cities. In Hanoi and HCM, you can exchange cash (U.S. dollars, pounds sterling, deutschmarks, French and Swiss francs, yen, Hongkong and Singapore dollars, and bath) and travellers' checks. You can pay in cash, and exchange cash, anywhere; but travellers' checks are only accepted in Hanoi, HCM, Da Nang and Nha Trang.

You can pay for almost everything in dollars, providing you have enough small bills (1 $, 5 $). If you go out, you can try to change money with the hotel staff, in restaurants or shops. But it's good to have dong on hand, as well, for such things as museum admission, single stamps, or any sum under one dollar. On the other hand, some services can only be paid for in dollars, such as doctor or hospital fees, flights, airport tax, some hotel bills, and the like.

You can only exchange dong back into dollars or deutschmarks upon leaving the country, in the airport, and then only into the currency which your customs certificate shows you to have brought into the country, and upon calculation of the exchanges and purchases recorded upon that document.

Credit cards: Visa and Master Card are the most useful. The larger hotels and banks in Hanoi and Ho Chi Minh City will also accept Eurocards, Eripluscards, and Diner's Club. Easiest of all is just to pay with dollars, in cash.

Customs

You have to fill out two customs declarations upon entering the country. One copy stays at the customs office; you have to take the other one with you and give it back when you leave. You have to enter every money exchange transaction on this document. Taking Vietnamese currency (even coins) in and out of the country is prohibited.

You can bring as much foreign currency or precious metals into the country as you like; they don't have to be declared if the total value is under 5,000 $, but anything over this sum must be declared.

You can bring into the country, duty-free, all appliances and objects for personal use during the journey; presents, in reasonable amounts; one camera and one video camera, with equipment; a typewriter; a tape recorder or other electrical/electronic appliances for personal use during the trip; 200 cigarettes; 1 liter of alcohol; and a reasonable amount of perfume. Bringing in weapons, explosives, ammunition, flammable articles, or drugs is forbidden.

You can bring out souvenirs, as long as they're not worth more than the sums of money that you've exchanged and entered on your customs declaration. Save all receipts from purchases; you may have to show them when you leave the country.

Taking antiques or old books out of the country is prohibited (see "Shopping"). For video and audio cassettes, you need a special permit, which is issued at the travel agencies.

Electricity

There are both 110-volt currencies 50 HZ and 220-volt 50 HZ. Bring an adapter with a flat plug. There are often power surges which might damage sensitive appliances (such as computers). Hotels are generally equipped with generators in case the power goes out temporarily. It's a good idea to have a flashlight with you. It's not difficult to buy batteries. Plugs and switches are often damaged; use with caution.

Emergency

In an emergency, go to your guide, the hotel staff, or the reception.

Festivals and holidays

Legal holidays, according to the Gregorian calendar:

January 1: New Year's
February 3: Founding of the Communist party
April 30 (1975): Day of the liberation of Saigon
May 1: May Day (Labor Day)
May 19: Ho Chi Minh's birthday
September 2: National holiday, declaration of the Republic in 1945

Ancestor and temple festivals

These are based on the lunar calendar (see "Calendar – Lunar Calendar").

day / lunar month

04 / 01: fireworks festival in the village of Dong Ky, Ha Bac Province.
05 / 01: On Dong Da hill (Hanoi), 1779 victory of Nguyen Hue (Emperor Quang Trung) over the Chinese.
06 / 01: In Co Loa (Hanoi), festival for Emperor An Duong, 3rd century BC.
06 / 02: Memorial day for the Trung sisters, national heroines, 40-43 AD.
15 / 03: Den Hung, Vinh Phu Province, a festival held for the legendary Hung Emperors.
15 / 03: In Hoa Lu, Ninh Binh Province, festival for the *dinh* and Early Le Dynasty.
16 / 08: On Con Son mountain, festival of the Hun Pagoda and the Den Kiep Bac.

Many of these, as well as other regional and local festivals, are described in individual chapters in the body of this book.

Flight confirmation

All flights have to be confirmed ahead of time at airline offices or through a travel agency.

Food and drink

At first sight, Vietnamese food resembles Chinese; but anyone with a discriminating palate will soon recognize the differences. Vietnamese food tends to be spiced with more finesse, and made tastier through the use of fresh vegetables and herbs. The green part of the coriander plant is also known as Vietnamese parsley.

Lobster, crabs, shrimps, and other crustaceans, seen as expensive delicacies in Europe, are common and quite cheap in Vietnam. *Nuoc mam*, fish sauce, may seem unusual to a European palate, but is included in every Vietnamese meal, replacing the soy sauce which you find in other Asian countries.

Even in simple restaurants, meals are prepared with imagination and attractively presented; cooks give thought to the coordination of colors as well as the harmony of flavors. Although hotels often have good restaurants, it's in the small places and family eateries that you'll generally find the best Vietnamese specialties, as well as a wide range of Chinese and French food. Every meal is freshly prepared for each individual guest.

A Vietnamese meal consists of several courses which are served at the same time: meat or fish, rice, noodles, egg dishes, vegetables, salads, and soups,

Calendar - Lunar Calendar

The lunar calendar was created by an Imperial minister in China in the year 2637 BC. The lunar year consists of 12 months; each month has 30 days, and each day 2 x 12 hours. The lunar calendar is 10 days and 21 hours shorter than the solar calendar. The lunar calendar is divided into ten *can* (tribes) and 12 *chi* (branches), each assigned to a sign of the zodiac. Tribes and branches are either masculine (+) or feminine (-). Down to the present day, East Asian astrologers continue to calculate lucky and unlucky days according to this calendar. Each year stands under one element and one animal of the zodiac. Because there are ten elements and twelve animals in the zodiac, each year has its own combination over a 60-year cycle; the combinations only repeat when this cycle is completed. At the age of 60, youth ends, and a new, no less happy stage is ushered in: age.

1995 is a Year of the Pig.

10 *can* (tribes)	12 *chi* (branches)	Zodiac sign	Year
+ giap	+ ty	Rat	1996
- at	- suu	Buffalo	1997
+ binh	+ dan	Tiger	1998
- dinh	- mao	Cat	1999
+ mau	+ thin	Dragon	2000
- ky	-ty	Snake	2001
+ canh	+ ngo	Horse	2002
- tan	- mui	Goat	2003
+ nham	+ than	Monkey	2004
- quy	- dau	Rooster	2005
+ (giap)	+ tuat	Dog	2006
- (at)	- hoi	Pig	2007

which are not eaten before a meal but rather during it or even afterwards. Particularly excellent are the small, spicy spring rolls, which have only the name in common with the Chinese variety. Beef, goat's meat, pork or chicken are used for meat dishes. Other delicious specialties are fish or eel soup, as well as all manner of deep-sea and freshwater fish.

The day begins with a bowl of soup (*pho*) in the morning; but this can also be eaten for lunch and dinner. *Pho bac,* Soup of the North, is a noodle soup with meat and vegetables; "Saigon Breakfast" is a soup with shrimp. These soups are a great start to a long, eventful day; don't knock it 'til you've tried it.

Green tea is served at every possible opportunity: greeting or taking leave of a guest, at private and official functions, in offices and temples, after a meal, even after coffee and ice cream. It's refreshing and good for the system.

Hotel rooms always have pots of hot water, which has been boiled, and green tea so that guests can prepare their own. The ice water which you'll find in a pot or carafe in your room has also been boiled.

Don't drink any tap water, and only drink beverages from sealed bottles – beer is only safe when it's foaming. Vietnamese beers (*bia*) are tasty and much cheaper than imported brands. Try Saigon 333; just ask for *ba ba ba.*

Only drink fruit juice if it's freshly

squeezed, and without ice cubes. Be careful about overdoing on alcoholic beverages in this hot climate.

Coffee is grown in the country, roasted very dark, and served like espresso, often extremely sweet.

Hotels

Currently, Vietnam is witnessing the construction of a number of international-standard hotels, financed with foreign capital, as well as private mini-hotels in converted villas from the French colonial days and new one-family houses for the Vietnamese, where you can often rent out a room or two. In Hanoi, there are supposed to be more than 500 such mini-hotels; in Ho Chi Minh City there are probably more. In smaller towns, as well, state and party organizations are making hotels and guesthouses available to foreign tourists, and constructing new facilities.

It's too early to say much about the quality and standards of the new buildings, particularly as houses are extremely susceptible to damage in this hot, humid climate if proper attention is not paid to cleanliness.

Accommodations are scarce around the Tet holiday, when many Vietnamese living abroad return to visit their families and often stay in hotels due to lack of space in private homes.

Hotels are divided into four categories; prices are rising.

Luxury: Renovated old French luxury hotels or new buildings financed from abroad, which meet international standards. Rooms 100 $ and up.

Category 1: Usually meet international standards; rooms between 60 - 100 $.

Tourist hotels: In large cities and also in the provinces; rooms 30 - 60 $.

Simple hotels, in some cases mini-hotels: Prices range from 6 and 20 $.

In another category are the truly cheap hotels, where you pay around 2 $ per night.

Even simple hotels try to furnish such comforts as televisions, refrigerators, air conditioning, telephone, running water, and thermoses with hot water and ice water. Mosquito nets are almost a matter of course, as are bath or shower, even if they're basic, and a toilet in every room. The linen is clean, even if the detergent often lacks bleach.

Many hotels also have discos or dance events with a considerable decibel level. Noise stops at 10 pm, or 11 pm in Hanoi and Ho Chi Minh City.

Hours of business

The opening hours of stores are flexible. Most shops are open from 8 am until at least 7 pm. By 9 pm, however, the streets are completely quiet. Offices, banks, and other agencies are open from 8-11 am, and sometimes from 2-4 pm.

The Vietnamese get up early; they usually have a long way to go to get to work, and the roads get crowded quite early. Those who can afford it take a midday break, especially in the hot seasons. For the Vietnamese, who have often suffered from food shortages, the noon meal is a veritably ceremonious affair, when they don't want to be disturbed.

Landmark protection

Since 1989, the landmark protection agency has started more conservation and restoration projects than in the 45 previous years. In Vietnam, distinctions are made between *trung tu* or *tu tao*, restoration true to the original, with no alteration in style, and *dai tu* or *khi tao*, expansions, additions or new building in the style of the original period.

Buildings under landmark protection bear a plaque with the inscription *Di tich lich su da xep hang cam khong duoc vi pham.*

Language and writing

A small glossary, as you often find in travel guides, isn't much help in Vietnam, since a word spoken with the wrong intonation is incomprehensible to a Vietnamese person, and anyone not familiar with the language can't hope to produce the intonation correctly without previous training.

Media

International newspapers are sold in major hotels. A few Vietnamese papers appear in English and French.

Most rooms contain television sets which broadcast national programs or even videos.

Since 1975, the Voice of Vietnam has been broadcasting in eleven languages.

Medications and doctors

Bring with you adequate supplies of any medications you may need. The Western medications that are sold here are often leftovers from other tourists, often poorly stored and well past their expiration date.

It's quite important to carry a small medical kit with you, including bandages and first-aid cream, an ace bandage, diarrhea and constipation remedies, and pills for colds, infections and fever. Insect bite medications are useful; but an even better idea is to take vitamin B complex as a preventative measure. Perspiration usually works to prevent insect bites. Bring a thermometer and disposable syringes in case you need an injection.

The prime causes of stomach and intestinal disorders are lettuce, fruit salad, ice, tap water, or an excess of unaccustomed dishes and iced drinks. The most effective way to prevent or cure diarrhea is to stick to a diet of rice and tea, and drink as much as you can. If you nee a doctor, ask the hotel reception, your guide, or a tourist organization.

It's often difficult to communicate with doctors and nurses; you'll usually need a translator.

Hospitals are listed in the "Guidepost" section after each chapter of this book. If you fall seriously ill, try to get home or fly to Bangkok or Singapore.

Medications are sold at doctors' offices, hospitals and pharmacies. You have to pay for medical treatment immediately, in cash, in U.S. dollars. Take along a bill and translate it to present to your health or travel insurance company when you get home.

Since 1991, more and more cases of AIDS have been reported. The World Health Organization expects that by the year 2000 there will be some 30,000 cases of AIDS in Vietnam.

Menu (thuc don)

boiled rice	com
fried rice (north)	com rang
fried rice (south)	com phan
noodles	mi
noodles (rice flour)	bim
glass noodles	mien
meat	thit
beef	bo
pork	heo
goat	de
veal	be
offal	tim
chicken	ga
duck	vit
fish	ca
squid (calamari)	muc
mussels	So
snake	ran
shrimp	ton
eel	luon
frog's legs	ech
soup	pho
beef soup	pho bo
chicken soup	pho ga
boiled	nau
grilled	muong
sweet and sour	chua ngot
steamed	hap
roast, on a spit	vy
pancakes stuffed with meat	banh xao
pineapple	dua or thom
banana	chuoi
coconut	dua
mango	xoai

beer	bi
green tea	tia
ice	da
mineral water	nuoc suoi
lemon juice	nuoc chanh
orange juice	nuoc cam
coconut milk	nuoc dua
coffee	ca phe
black coffee	ca phe den
coffee with milk	ca ph sua
sugar	duong
without ice	khong co da
glass	mot ly
bottle	mot ca
alcohol	ri ou

Night Life - Entertainment

In addition to hotel bars, there are a great many discos or dance events. Sometimes, traditional or modern music is presented, or theater performances. Cinemas often present foreign films, both Asian and European.

Massage parlors do offer other services, although not in every case. The general trend, however, is to go in the direction of Bangkok. Official figures estimate the number of prostitutes in the country at around 200,000. The actual number, through all classes of society, is considerably higher.

Photography

Photographing out of an airplane window, or photographing military and traffic installations, is not allowed. Don't photograph people without asking their permission. Part of Vietnamese life takes place on the streets in front of people's houses; this is still counted a private area. No one likes to be photographed working hard or wearing dirty work clothes. Photographers should ask themselves whether they'd like to be photographed by a stranger if they were in the same situation.

You can buy film in Vietnam, but it's often old or has been poorly stored. It's a good idea to bring film, batteries and other photographic equipment with you from home.

At large airports, the x-rays on the safety inspection machines are now film-safe. In smaller, provincial airports, however, this is far from certain, and it's best to carry your film through the safety check by hand.

Post office - telephone

You can recognize post offices by the sign *Buu Dien*. You can only send international mail from a post office or a hotel reception desk; it's quickest if you sent it from Ho Chi Minh City or Hanoi. Don't post it into sidewalk mailboxes! Postcards and letters take from six days to three weeks to reach Europe or the United States.

There's a wide variety of colorful, imaginative Vietnamese commemorative stamps; you can get them at any post office. State souvenir shops sell collector's albums, arranged by year.

To send a post card air mail to Europe costs less than 1 $; a letter somewhat more than 1 $ (depending on the exchange rate). You can pay for stamps in dong. Both stamps and envelopes tend to be badly gummed, or not at all; there are glue-pots in post offices and at hotel reception desks.

Telephone: From Hanoi and Ho Chi Minh City, and soon also from other big cities, telephone calls, telexes and faxes can be direct-dialed and are transmitted by satellite. There are no telephone booths with direct dialling.

Telex: at the post office.

Fax: at the post office, very expensive!

Hotels charge various rates for these services. In general, the lines at the post office are quite short. Don't forget to take the time difference into account when calling or faxing abroad.

Provinces

The provinces are administrative entities with a great deal of autonomy.

Some of them were combined after 1945; but these combinations don't seem to have worked very well, and many of them have separated again since 1989. It's often important to know the name of a province, because there are many towns with the same name in different parts of the country.

Currently, the capital of Vietnam is Thu Do Hanoi; there are two city-states, Thanh Pho Ho Chi Minh and Thanh Pho Haiphong, and 50 provinces (*Thinh*), each with its own provincial capital (*Thanh Do*).

Province	Capital

The North - Bac Bo

Ha Giang	Ha Giang
Tuyen Quang	Tuyen Quang
Cao Bang	Cao Bang
Lang Son	Lang Son
Lai Chau	Lai Chau
Lao Cai	Lao Cai
Yen Bai	Yen Bai
Bac Thai	Thai Nguyen
Son La	Son La
Vinh Phu	Viet Tri
Ha Bac	Bac Giang
Quang Ninh	Hong Gai
Ha Tay	Ha Dong
Hoa Binh	Hoa Binh
Hai Hung	Hai Duong
Thay Binh	Thay Binh
Nam Ha	Nam Dinh
Ninh Binh	Ninh Binh

Central Vietnam - Trung Bo

Thanh Hoa	Thanh Hoa
Nghe An	Vinh
Ha Tinh	Ha Tinh
Quang Binh	Dong Hoi
Quang Tri	Dong Ha
Thua Thien-Hue	Hue
Quang Nam-Da Nang	Da Nang
Quang Ngai	Quang Ngai
Binh Dinh	Quy Nhon
Phu Yen	Tuy Hoa
Khanh Hoa	Nha Trang

Ninh Thuan	Phan Rang
Binh Thuan	Phan Thiet
Kon Tum	Kon Tum
Gia Lai	Play Cu
Dac Lac	Buon Ma Thuot
Lam Dong	Da Lat

The South - Nam Bo

Song Be	Thu Dau Mot
Tay Ninh	Tay Ninh
Dong Nai	Bien Hoa
Long An	Tan An
Dong Thap	Cao Lanh
Tra Vinh	Tra Vinh
An Giang	Long Xuyen
Tien Giang	My Tho
Ben Tre	Ben Tre
Vinh Long	Vinh Long
Tra Vinh	Tra Vinh
Can Tho	Can Tho
Soc Trang	Soc Trang
Kien Giang	Rach Gia
Minh Hai	Ca Mau
Ba Ria Vung Tau	Vung Tau -
	(special zone)

Restaurants

Since 1989, countless private restaurants, cafes and cookshacks have sprung up in big cities, small towns, or even along the road. The Vietnamese appreciate good food, but don't care so much about a restaurant's interior decoration. Thus, many very simple restaurants often offer excellent food (see "Food and Drink").

Security

With the growing emphasis on property and higher living standards, petty crimes have risen considerably over the last few years, both in number and in lack of scruple. Particularly in crowded alleyways in old neighborhoods, shopping streets, at festivals and at train stations – anywhere you might normally expect to find a purse-snatcher or pickpocket – you should keep a close eye on your pocketbook, camera, and other personal objects. The Vietnamese can be extremely skilful, at picking pockets as at other occupations.

Lock your money and valuables in the hotel safe, and lock your suitcase when you leave a room; otherwise, your insurance won't compensate you for any losses you incur. Leave your valuable jewelry at home. If you have travellers' checks, don't forget to keep the numbers written down somewhere separate from the checks, so that you can issue a stop-payment on them if they're stolen. You should also pack a xerox of the first page of your passport, as well as your plane ticket; this considerably facilitates the process of reissuing them, should this be necessary.

Shopping

Both state-owned and private shops can offer a wide selection of enamel and lacquer work and inlays, silk paintings and embroidery. Ceramics, as well as objects made of rattan and bamboo, are also some typical Vietnamese products and nice souvenirs.

You can buy green tea, coffee and spices at the markets. The best place to buy black tea (export quality), however, is at duty-free shops in the international airports.

Taking antiques or old books out of the country is prohibited. There are exceptions, but you have to get a special export permission certificate. (More information is available from Vietnamese travel agencies.)

If you want to bring antiques or valuable souvenirs from a neighboring country into Vietnam, have this confirmed on your customs declaration when you enter the country, to avoid any difficulties when you leave.

Temples / Memorial sites

In Buddhist temples (*chua*), you only have to remove your shoes in front of the shrine. If there are non-Buddhist temples within a temple complex, it's important to honor Buddha before doing anything else.

Time difference

Vietnam is six hours ahead of Central European time, five hours in summer. It's seven hours ahead of Greenwich Mean Time (England), twelve hours ahead of Eastern Standard Time (New York), and sixteen hours ahead of Pacific Standard Time (Los Angeles).

Tipping

Tips of 10 % or 15 % are often included in the bill. If you'd like to tip for especially good service, however, it's always very much appreciated.

Tourism

Until 1989, there were considerable limitations on tourism (*Du Lich*) in Vietnam. The number of tourists from East Bloc countries was many times higher than that of tourists, generally on package tours, from the West; and there was no tourist infrastructure to speak of. Since then, however, the hotel and transportation networks are being built up and expanded; the driving force behind this change are foreign investments and private initiatives. The state is also promoting and financing tourism for its potential as an economic factor.

Since 1993, travellers have been able to move freely throughout the country with the exception of a few military sites or restricted areas near the border; and it's no longer necessary to get special permission to travel through many of the areas in which permits were once required.

Weights and Measures

Vietnam uses the metric system.

ADDRESSES
Embassies of the Socialist Republic of Vietnam

Austria: Anton-Langer-Gasse 26, A-1130 Wien, tel: 8043377, fax: 802 2223.
Belgium and EU: 130 Avenue de la

Floride, 1180 Bruxelles, tel: 3 74 91 33, fax: 3 74 93 76.
France: 62 rue de Boileau, 75016 Paris, tel: 5 24 50 63, fax: 5 24 39 48.
Germany: Konstantinstr. 37, 53179 Bonn, tel: (0228) 35 70 21/22, fax: (0228) 35 18 66.
Great Britain: 12-14 Victoria Rd., London W85RD, tel: 9378564, 9371912.
Italy: Piazza Barberini 12, 00187 Rome, tel: 4 75 52 86, 4 82 52 86.
Sweden: Örby Slottvag 26, 125 36 Alvjö.
Switzerland and the United Nations: 34, Chemin Francois-Lehmann, CH-1218 Grand-Saconnex-Genève, tel: 7982485 / 79 82 48 57.

Embassies in Vietnam

Australia: 66 Ly Thuong Kiet, tel: 252763
Belgium: 51, Nguyen Du, tel: 25 21 76
Cambodia: 71, Tran Hung Dao, corner of Quang Trung, tel: 25 37 89
Canada: 39 Nguyew Dinh Chieu, tel: 26 58 40
France: 49, Ba Trieu, tel: 25 43 67, 257654
Germany: (Dai Su Quan Nuoc Cong Hoa Lien Bang Duc), 29, Tran Phu,tel: 25 38 36, Hanoi-Quan Ba Dinh, tel: (42) 53663 or (42) 55402
Great Britain: 16, Ly Thuong Kiet, tel: 25 25 10
Italy: 9, Le Phung Hieu. tel: 26 62 46
Laos: 22-24, Tran Binh Trong, tel: 254576; the visa office is in the consulate at 40, Quang Trung
Myanmar (Burma): A3, Van Phuc, tel: 25 33 69
Netherlands: 53, Ly Thai To, tel: 257746
Poland: 3 Chua Mot Cot, tel: 25 20 27
Sweden: 358, Van Phuc, tel: 25 48 24
Switzerland: 77B, Kim Ma, tel: 23 20 19
Thailand: E1, Trung Tu, tel: 25 60 53

AUTHOR

Annaliese Wulf has gained profound knowledge and understanding of the history and culture of South, Southeast and East Asia on her numerous trips to the region. Since 1981, she's concentrated particularly on Vietnam, gaining the reputation of a Vietnam expert through many long trips throughout the country.

PHOTOGRAPHERS

AKG, Berlin 24, 27, 45
Beck, Josef cover, 66, 114, 144, 149, 150, 156, 163, 164, 167, 190, 200
Bock, Henning (Hundertprozent) 203
Goldstein, Charlotte 25, 229
Hahn, Wilfried 44
Höltkemeyer, Bettina 61
Janicke, Volkmar 22, 43, 128/129, 130, 133, 146, 148L, 182
Kaehler, Wolfgang 151, 189L, 189R
Keller, Hans-Jörg 1, 10/11, 14, 15, 18, 28, 29, 32, 39, 40, 52/53, 54/55, 64, 70, 74, 78, 79, 88, 95, 96, 97, 98, 99, 100, 108, 109, 111, 112, 113, 118, 119, 120, 121, 122, 123, 124, 125, 126, 138, 139, 143, 170, 174, 176, 184, 194, 202, 204, 207, 209, 213, 215, 235
Kemp, Hans 8/9, 12, 16, 33, 37, 38, 46, 47, 117, 135, 141, 147, 162, 172, 180, 192/193, 197, 206, 220/221
Rein, Udo 23, 30, 35, 71, 72, 75, 102, 115, 116, 148R, 168, 201, 205, 208, 224, 225, 230, 232L, 232R
Rex, Peter 2, 19, 34, 56, 134, 154, 158, 177, 188, 214, 219, 223
Riethmüller, Robert 36, 73, 85, 153
Saitner, Gerard 42, 50, 63, 76, 77, 81, 82, 92, 103, 104, 105, 107, 137, 160, 185, 222, 227, 233
Scheibner, Johann 159, 179, 186
Stankiewicz, Thomas 210, 211
Stowers, Chris 26
von Schaper, Hans 21, 60, 136, 228
Wulf, Annaliese 48, 49, 51, 84, 94, 161, 165, 166, 226, 231